Literacy and Power

D0207043

'This is a map of the field of critical literacy – drawn with precision and care. Our guide on the journey is a scholar and teacher, political activist and woman warrior of the greatest strength and wisdom.'
Alan Luke, Queensland University of Technology, Australia

'Hilary Janks argues that to critically change the educational system you need to understand the interrelationship between language and power. Her framework of dominance, diversity, access and design constitutes a complete theory of critical literacy, one that explains the successes and failures of past and current educational movements. Her thinking has helped me and the U.S. and Canadian teachers I work with outgrow our very selves as we plan new, more powerful, and more critical ways to change education.'
Jerome C. Harste, Indiana University, Bloomington, USA

'Unlike the biblical prophets, Janks is honoured in her own country, South Africa, for her enormous contribution to language and literacy education in complex linguistic and socio-cultural contexts. As a writer, her special gift is to make the complex accessible in ways that move readers to cry, to laugh, and most of all, to begin or to renew a commitment to critical literacy teaching and research.'
Yvonne Reed, University of the Witwatersrand, Johannesburg

'Readers who know Janks' ground-breaking work with critical language awareness with teachers and learners in South Africa have been waiting for this book. For those who don't, now at last there's an opportunity to learn how to make critical discourse analysis a central part of a pedagogical repertoire for critical literacy. Immediately helpful to teachers, teacher educators and researchers who are concerned with literacy and power, this fabulous book provides a review of key theory, original approaches to text analyses, and illuminating accounts from classrooms. It makes you want to teach. This will become the essential guidebook for language and literacy educators and researchers.'
Barbara Comber, University of South Australia

'Hilary Janks develops an innovative model of critical literacy which makes a major contribution to the field. You will look at texts in new ways after reading this book. It will transform your understanding of how language works, it will give you new insights into language and politics in South Africa, and it will provide a principled basis for rethinking the teaching of language and literacy in your own context.'
Roz Ivanič, Lancaster University, UK

'Admirers of Janks' scholarship will welcome *Literacy and Power* and recognise its qualities of lucidity, argumentative coherence, courage and compassion. With its organisation around four interdependent themes of domination, access, diversity and design, this book is the best introduction to critical literacies around.'
Terry Locke, University of Waikato, New Zealand

Hilary Janks is a professor in Applied English Language Studies at the University of Witwatersrand, Johannesburg, South Africa.

Language, Culture, and Teaching
Sonia Nieto, Series Editor

Visit **www.routledge.com/education** for additional information on titles in the Language, Culture, and Teaching series.

Literacy and Power

Hilary Janks

Routledge
Taylor & Francis Group

NEW YORK AND LONDON

First published 2010
by Routledge
270 Madison Ave, New York, NY 10016

Simultaneously published in the UK
by Routledge
2 Park Square, Milton Park, Abingdon, Oxon OX14 4RN

Routledge is an imprint of the Taylor & Francis Group, an informa business

© 2010 Taylor & Francis

Typeset in Minion by
RefineCatch Limited, Bungay, Suffolk
Printed and bound in the United States of America on acid-free paper by Edwards Brothers, Inc.

Library of Congress Cataloging-in-Publication Data
Janks, Hilary.
   Literacy and power / Hilary Janks.
      p. cm. — (Language, culture, and teaching)
   Includes bibliographical references and index.
   1. Literacy—Political aspects—South Africa.   2. Language and education—South Africa.
   3. Multilingualism—South Africa.   4. Language policy—South Africa.   I. Title.
   LC158.S6J36 2010
   302.2′2440968—dc22   2009017641

ISBN10: 0–8058–5577–7 (hbk)
ISBN10: 0–415–99963–4 (pbk)
ISBN10: 0–203–86995–8 (ebk)

ISBN13: 978–0–8058–5577–7 (hbk)
ISBN13: 978–0–415–99963–2 (pbk)
ISBN13: 978–0–203–86995–6 (ebk)

For John

who has been my partner in all things every step of the way

Contents

Foreword

With the profound simplicity of her compelling first sentence, author Hilary Janks introduces you to both the topic of this book, literacy, and the critical and eloquent way in which she addresses it. Through stories, analytical questions, engaging anecdotes, fascinating examples, and concrete activities, she defines what critical literacy means and, in the process, brings you on a journey of discovery and reflection that will help you view language and literacy in much more profound ways than is the case in most texts.

Literacy and Power is the perfect next addition to the Language, Culture, and Teaching Series (LCT), a series for pre-service and practicing teachers and teacher educators that encourages critical thought and thoughtful action in teaching and learning. If you are already teaching, no doubt many of you are working in diverse settings and searching for theories and strategies to help you connect with your students. If you are not yet teaching, most of you will probably find yourselves working in diverse communities with students whose identities – race/ethnicity, language, social class, and so on – differ from your own. The books in the LCT series ask you to recognize that there is no 'generic' student, but that instead all students come to school with their individual sociocultural realities and specific sociopolitical contexts. Hilary Janks' book, although geared particularly to English and language teachers, will help all teachers bridge the gap between their own reality and that of their students.

This book asks you to reflect on the role of critical literacy in education. While some may argue that matters such as power, privilege, identity and diversity are peripheral to the language arts (after all, what do they have to do with reading Shakespeare? or teaching phonics? or writing a five-paragraph essay?), Janks argues convincingly that without an awareness of these issues, teachers are doomed to approach their teaching, and their students, in simplistic and uncritical ways that will do little to prepare them for the complex and heterogeneous world in which we live. In fact, one could argue that it is impossible to be a teacher of language and literacy today without taking into account identity, power, privilege and access because these issues are at the very heart of language and literacy. All one has to do is think about the debates over whole language versus phonics, bilingual education versus English only, Ebonics vs. Standard English, and the many other controversies related to language and literacy that we have witnessed over the years. In reality, a close look at U.S. educational history makes it obvious that few controversies have been *unrelated* to language and literacy as understood in its broader context. All teachers – not just those who teach the language arts directly – need to be prepared to learn about, reflect on, and apply these concepts in their teaching. This book provides just the tools you will need to do these things.

As will be evident right away, Janks draws heavily, although certainly not exclusively, on her own considerable experience as a literacy educator in South Africa. As such, she uses examples – tragic or humorous but always enlightening – about the history of Apartheid and its implications for language and literacy. But she also uses examples from other countries and continents that, although grounded in a specific context, are also universal in nature. The *Chameleon Dance* in Chapter 2 although firmly grounded in South Africa has been used for courses in critical race theory in the US. The *Edge Razor* advert in the same chapter could have appeared in any number of places, but not for example in religious communities which require women's bodies to be covered. The story of *The Egg and Sperm Race* in Chapter 3, which comically but powerfully describes the manifestations of sexism, takes place in the United States but is not specific to one country. As such, whether you teach in a large urban area on the West Coast, a small suburban enclave in the Northeast, or anywhere else in the United States, or whether you teach in Soweto, South Wales, or London, the relevance of her examples for your own classroom will be clear.

For Janks, language and literacy are inherently political activities and teachers are inherently political agents, whether they see themselves in this way or not. This does not mean that the role of teachers is to brainwash students into believing particular truths. On the contrary, to be a political teacher means to help students uncover the multiple realities that they will face in their reading, writing and living. Janks makes this clear in her thoughtful definitions of 'big P' and 'little p' politics, emphasizing the point that 'little p' politics is about how we live our lives in community with others. Literacy is certainly part of how we do so. Beginning in the first chapter, she introduces you to various ways, or orientations, of understanding literacy. Subsequent chapters consider the questions of language and power, how to read, write, design and redesign texts critically, the meanings of diversity and inequality, the question of access, and the future of critical literacy. Throughout you will be entertained, enlightened and prepared to take your place among critical educators of language and literacy, regardless of where you may find yourself.

Literacy and Power, although a hopeful book, is not a pie-in-the-sky tale about change. Doing literacy in the way that Janks proposes in these pages is hard work, work that must be sustained over time and done in collaboration with others. Her stories of change in South African schools are cautionary tales that conclude with a sobering lesson on the stubborn nature of business as usual in literacy classrooms. Her statement at the end of Chapter 7 underscores why critical literacy is best done collaboratively: 'Perhaps,' she writes, 'redesigning ourselves and each other is too risky and dangerous to attempt alone.'

As you read this book, you may find yourself smiling, and even laughing out loud at some of the examples Janks provide, while at other times you will be moved, intrigued, or saddened. And throughout, you will find yourself rethinking, reprocessing and recreating some of your most cherished ideas or preconceived notions about language and literacy. It is my hope that this will be your experience because it is precisely the intention of this elegant book, as well as the goal of all the books in the Language, Culture, and Teaching Series.

Sonia Nieto
March 2009

Preface

Competing definitions of literacy and competing approaches to teaching it have divided the field of literacy, so much so, that they have been widely referred to as the 'literacy wars'. The theoretical disagreements centre on whether literacy is a cognitive skill or a social practice, either-or thinking that generates further binaries: phonics or whole language, bottom up or top down, back to basics or meaning making, popular culture or the literary canon, genre approaches to writing or progressive approaches and so on ad infinitum.

In my view literacy is both a set of cognitive skills and a set of practices. New brain imaging research shows conclusively that learning to read creates new pathways in the brain. Reading depends on the ability to recognise the visual shapes of letters and words, to understand letter sound relationships and the structure of words and sentences, as well as the ability to synthesise all of these processes in order to make meaning from print. Readers have to recognise words, memorise patterns, synthesise information, comprehend meaning, evaluate content, all cognitive abilities. But being able to read and write is not enough. Some teachers and parents *can* read and write, but they prefer not to. The social practices of reading a book for pleasure, of using writing to work out thoughts, of reading newspapers, of writing poetry, of reading non-fiction, of surfing the net, of making notes, of researching information are not part of everyone's daily lives. How I wonder do parents and teachers who are not readers and writers themselves convince their children and their students that literacy matters both in and out of school?

The sophistication of modern methods of communication requires us to be able to decode and analyse the information that bombards us, the advertisements that entice us, the political spin that deceives us. Messages are conveyed in words and pictures and moving images, with or without sound and colour and gesture, via media capable of delivering multiple messages simultaneously. 'Reading' and producing meaning are increasingly complex activities for which there is no one right teaching approach. As teachers and teacher educators, we need to work together, taking what we can from different approaches to accommodate the learning styles of different students.

This book works against the dividing practices in the field. I write from a social practices perspective because that is what I know well, not because I believe in either-or thinking. I attempt to effect a synthesis of the different socio-cultural orientations to literacy and I leave it to cognitive scientists, psychologists and psycho-linguists to draw together the threads of their different orientations to literacy.

I will show how literacy is tied to questions of power and that how we choose to teach literacy is political. I refer to the approach to teaching literacy that takes power seriously as 'critical literacy'. The purpose of this book is to develop and refine an interdependent model of critical literacy that is both accessible and useful to teachers and teacher educators working in a range of contexts.

Some of this material has been published before as journal articles that are not easily accessible to readers outside of South Africa. Here I have integrated them into the overall argument of the book, so that the book provides a coherent account of my thinking since the mid 1990s. It builds on the earlier work that was undertaken to develop the *Critical Language Awareness Series* which focused on critical deconstruction, but moves towards the theory and practice of critical literacy for reconstruction.

Chapter 1 explores and interrogates definitions of literacy. Chapter 2 looks at orientations to literacy and presents an interdependent model for critical literacy education. Chapters 3–8 expand the discussion of each of the key terms in this model – dominance/power, access, diversity and design – both in themselves and in their relation to the other terms. These chapters also explore the consequences of ignoring or back-grounding any of these terms. My aim is to develop a pedagogy in which these different orientations pull together, like guy ropes on a tent, to keep critical literacy work taut. Throughout the book, text in grey boxes illustrates the ideas so that readers can see what the theory looks like in practice.

Chapter 9 considers the impact of the non-rational unconscious on work in the area of critical literacy and flirts with ideas beyond the rational, trying to imagine the critical in relation to desire, identification and pleasure. Finally it looks at ways in which the model can and has been used and considers the limitations of critical literacy as well as its continuing importance.

Acknowledgments

I began working as a teacher educator with Jonathon Paton and Denise Newfield. I was extremely fortunate to start my academic career with colleagues who were serious about education but who laughed a lot; who were innovative and lively teachers; generous friends and who were committed to making English teaching count in the struggle against apartheid, despite the presence of police spies in our classes.

In the 1980s I realised that with degrees in literature, I was simply not properly qualified for my job. How could I prepare teachers to teach English to students whose home languages were Sesotho, Setswana, IsiZulu, IsiXhosa, Tshivenda or any of the other African languages spoken in South Africa without any knowledge of linguistics or pedagogies for teaching language in multilingual classrooms? In registering for a degree in Applied Linguistics in 1984, I began the journey that has culminated in this book. Many of my fellow students became my close friends and professional colleagues. I am indebted to Debra Aarons, Yvonne Reed and Pippa Stein who have shaped my thinking over two decades and to Jo Nowicki who gave me the book on language awareness that started me on my research trajectory. I am also indebted to Rosemary Wildsmith, Norman Blight and Ishbel Hingle, our teachers who went on to form the Department of Applied English Language Studies with us.

My degrees in Applied Linguistics took me to Lancaster University, to work with Norman Fairclough. It was 1989, the year in which *Language and Power* was first published. The title of this book, *Literacy and Power*, is a deliberate inter-textual reference to Norman's work, my way of acknowledging the intellectual debt that I owe to him. Ros Ivanič and Romy

Clark took me under their wing and looked after me from visit to visit. Ros co-authored the article we wrote for Norman's edited collection, insisted that I be the first author, and mentored me in the art of academic publishing. She was a giant in more ways than one. At Lancaster, I met Esther Ramani from India and in 1992 when we established the Department of Applied English Studies we persuaded her to join us and to take over the leadership of the new Department. She has stayed in South Africa and has been my friend ever since.

AELS has been my academic home since 1992. The many colleagues that I have worked with over the years have provided new directions for language and literacy education in South Africa and each has made an important contribution to my own thinking about multimodal and multilingual literacies, academic literacies, school literacies, spatiality, critical literacy and digital literacies. I thank Pippa Stein (now sorely missed), Yvonne Reed, Stella Granville, Susan van Zyl, Pinky Makoe, Carolyn McKinney, Kerryn Dixon, Ana Ferreira, Patricia Shariff, Chris Orsmonde, Ingrid Riener, Magauta Mphahlele, Leila Kajee, Nonhlanhla Dhlamini, Ben Afful and Vis Moodley for their shared sense of purpose, collective self-irony, inspiration and care.

The AELS project would not have been possible without our amazing students and I have been lucky to work with many graduate students who were also colleagues, as well as students from other parts of Africa. Their work has broadened my understanding beyond measure. Postgraduate research weekends have become a highlight of the AELS year. Working with postgraduate students in education, many of whom have years of experience in schools or universities, is a singular privilege. Their research across a range of sites and topics is the most exciting form of life-long education the academy has to offer its staff. The other opportunity for learning can be found in productive research partnerships, and I am deeply indebted to Paulina Sethole and the staff at her school for sharing their working lives and their classrooms with me. They taught me more than they will ever know.

More recently I have had the opportunity to put my theory of diversity as a productive resource to the test in my partnership with Mary Scholes in the Postgraduate Project Office. Mary is an environmental scientist, who together with her husband Bob, has introduced me to new ways of seeing and understanding the world. Hildegard Chapman, our project administrator needs a special vote of thanks for her work in constructing my endnote data base and tidying up my manuscript. In addition, I need to thank Jonathon Williams, who, as a student in publishing, did a sterling job of managing my permissions.

But this is not all. My second academic home has been the Centre for Studies in Literacy, Policy and Learning Cultures in the Hawke Research Institute at the University of South Australia. Barbara Comber, Phil Cormack and Helen Nixon, together with Jacky Cook, David Homer and Rob Hattam, have been my steadfast academic friends. Barbara, Helen and Phil have unselfishly introduced me to colleagues in other parts of Australia (Alan and Carmen Luke, Barbara Kamler, Annette Patterson, Bronwyn Mellor, Marnie O'Neill, Wayne Martino and Judith Rivalland) and given me the chance to work with awesome teachers (Helen Grant, Marg Wells and Ruth Trimble). As if that were not enough, they have in addition shared their international network of colleagues committed to literacy and social justice. They used their established positions to provide me with access, connecting me to colleagues in the US, the UK, Canada, providing the opportunity for me to work with Vivian Vasquez, Pat Thomson, Andy Manning and Jerome Harste. I was lucky enough to meet Bill Green, Jo-anne Reid, Alison Lee, Wendy Morgan, Ray Misson and Peter Freebody at conferences and each in their own way has contributed to my thinking. Bill Green has been my theory-beacon since I first met him in 1985. Terry Locke, from New Zealand, found me and that was my lucky day. Working with him and the other founding members of the journal *English Teaching Practice and Critique* has been both formative and pleasurable. Terry is a superb editor and he has taught me a great deal. Courtney Cazden has been my sounding board and friend in Boston.

Once one has a network, it snowballs and everyone you know leads to more other interesting people. Most importantly, my network led me to Naomi Silverman and Sonia Nieto. This book would never have happened without their encouragement, their joy in the project, their absolute commitment to my work and their unending patience, advice and constructive feedback. Naomi is a remarkable commissioning editor whose publishing list has made a significant political contribution to social justice in education. Her experience has provided the touchstone throughout this project. Sonia Nieto epitomises the kind of academic whose work Naomi is proud to publish. Widely recognised for her contribution to multicultural education, Sonia is an icon in the US. Her stature is belied by her modesty, her warmth, her down-to-earth values and her investment in others. Both Naomi and Sonia have been my trusted friends and guides throughout. Together with Meeta Pendharkar, they made a formidable publishing team.

I wish to express a particular word of appreciation to Jerry Harste, who not only gave me permission to use the visual images produced by his students, including the remarkable image on the cover, but also urged me to expand my model and thus provided the initial impetus for this book.

While my intellectual work has been fed by my colleagues and students and the work they have done, it has been sustained by my family and my friends. Eunice held the house together and Debra and Cally from afar, Natalie, Jill, Gerrit, the two Marys as well as, Len, Carrie and Renette contributed in different ways to keeping me together. My father, Gerald, taught me to love language and ideas; my mother, Sadie, taught me to care about people and to love books. My sons, Gregory and Daniel, and now their partners Sonia and Tiffany, more than my work, have given my life meaning and made everything worthwhile. I take pride in their expertise and real joy in learning from them. Greg, himself a writer, told me to find a great opening sentence from which the rest could flow. I took his advice. Daniel took the photographs and provided ongoing computer support.

Watching my granddaughter, Sadie Elaine, discover her world renews my faith in children's determination to learn; to do what it takes; and to move on to the next challenge. She reminds me that as teachers we have simply to create the conditions of possibility for students to learn, we have to give them recognition for their efforts, praise for their triumphs and we have to be ready to catch them when they fall. We have simply to be there, every step of the way.

I have dedicated this book to my husband, John, who has always been there for me – my personal cheering team and safety net. I appreciate his careful proof reading, his wonderful meals and his unstinting generosity. His principles serve as my moral compass; his dry wit keeps me both sane and honest; and his love is the ground on which I stand. I thank him for making everything possible.

We are grateful to the following publishers for permitting work from previously published journal articles and book chapters to be reprinted in this book.

Janks, H. (1997). Critical Discourse Analysis as a research tool. *Discourse: Studies in the Cultural Politics of Education*, 18(3), 329–342 (page 66). http://www.informaworld.com

Janks, H. (1998). Reading *Womanpower*. *Pretexts*, 7(2), 195–212 (page 37). http://www.informaworld.com

Janks, H. (2000). Domination, access, diversity and design: A synthesis model for critical literacy education. *Educational Review*, 52(2), 175–186 (page 26). http://www.informaworld.com

Janks, H. (2001). We rewrote the book: Constructions of literacy in South Africa. In R. de Cilla, H.-J. Krumm, & R. Wodak (Eds.) *Loss of communication in the Information Age*. Wien: Verlag der Österreichischen Akademie des Wissenschaften (page 5).

Janks, H. (2002). Critical literacy: Beyond reason. *Australian Educational Researcher*, 29(1), 7–27 (page 213).

Janks, H. (2003). Seeding change in South Africa: New literacies, new subjectivities, new futures. In B. Doecke, D. Homer, & H. Nixon (Eds.) *English teachers at work*. South Australia: Wakefield Press and the Australian Association for the Teaching of English (page 192).

Janks, H. (2004). The access paradox. *English in Australia*, AATE joint IFTE Issue, 139, 33–42 (page 127).

Janks, H. (2005). Deconstruction and reconstruction: Diversity as a productive resource. *Discourse: Studies in the Cultural Politics of Education*, 26(1), 31–44 (page 104). http://www.informaworld.com

Janks, H. (2006). The interplay of grammar, meaning and identity. In K. Cadman, & K. O'Regan (Eds.) *Tales out of school*, special edition of *TESOL in Context*, Journal of the Australian Council of TESOL Associations. Series 'S', 49–69 (page 280).

Janks, H. (2006). Games go abroad. *English Studies in Africa*, 49(1), 115–138 (page 206).

Janks, H. (2008). Critical literacy: Methods, models and motivations. In K. Cooper & E. White (Eds.) *Social perspectives and teaching practices*. Rotterdam: Sense Publishers (page 159).

Janks, H. (2009). Writing: A critical literacy perspective. In R. Beard, D. Myhill, M. Nystrand, & J. Riley (Eds.) *The SAGE handbook of writing development*. London: Sage (page 155).

Ferreira, A., Janks, H., Barnsley, I., Marriott, C., Rudman, M., Ludlow, H., & Nussey, R. (forthcoming). *Reconciliation pedagogy in South African classrooms: From the personal to the political*. London and New York: Routledge (page 171).

CHAPTER 1

Turning to Literacy

Introduction

Many languages do not have a word for *literacy*. This first came to my notice when reading about work done on the literacy practices of taxi drivers in South Africa. The Social Uses of Literacy researchers claimed that

> In the discourse of most of the drivers and owners we spoke to . . ., the word 'literacy' did not feature. This was partly because the two African languages encountered in this research – Xhosa and Sotho – do not contain words for 'literacy' and 'illiteracy'.
> (Breir, Matsepela & Sait, 1996: 230)

Having checked this with a colleague in the Department of African Languages, I felt confident to use this information in a paper that I was presenting at a trilingual conference in Vienna on literacy in the information age. The conference offered simultaneous translation across German, French and English. Here I discovered that French and German also have no word for *literacy*, ironic really at a conference on literacy. The interpreters translated 'literacy' as either communicative competence[1] or alphabetic ability,[2] neither of which do the concept of literacy justice.

What then is the usefulness of the word *literacy*? Why do we need it? Does it enable or constrain our thinking? In common usage, literacy is

---

[1] '*Kommunicationsfähigkeit* in German; *capacité de communication* in French.
[2] *Analphabetismus* in German; and *analphabétisme*, in French.

understood to be the ability to read and write and was 'formed as an antithesis to *illiteracy*' in 1883 (OED department, 1980). More recently, literacy has been defined as a social practice. The notion of a literacy practice implies patterned and conventional ways of using written language that are defined by culture and regulated by social institutions. Different communities do literacy differently.

But none of this is simple. What exactly does the ability to read, for example, entail? Readers of this book will have no difficulty reading aloud the following quotation from Michael Halliday.

> The concept of grammatical metaphor, itself perhaps a metaphorical extension of the term from its rhetorical sense as a figure of speech, enables us to bring together a number of features of discourse which at first sight look rather different from each other. But when we recognize the different kinds of meaning that come together in the lexico-grammar, and especially the basic distinction between idea-tional and interpersonal meaning, we can see that what look like two different sets of phenomena are really instances of the same phenomenon arising in these two different contexts.
>
> (Halliday, 1985: 345)

I imagine that most of you recognise and understand the individual words used in this text, and that where you do not, you can make educated guesses as to their meaning. However, I suspect that the meaning of the paragraph as a whole escapes all but a few who understand Halliday's Systemic Functional Grammar and are members of a systemics 'community of practice' (Wenger, 1998). What creates difficulty in understanding this text are words that have specific meanings in this specialist discourse such as 'ideational' and 'interpersonal', the linking of common words such as 'grammatical' and 'metaphor' to mean something more than a simple combination of the meanings embedded in each, the fact that the text is taken out of context, and the fact that as readers we may not have enough background knowledge to bring to bear on the text. If we can read the text aloud, that is decode the symbols on the page and produce them as sound, aloud or silently in our heads, are we literate? Or does literacy imply an ability to derive meaning from text? If it does, then are people who cannot read Halliday's text illiterate? If they are illiterate, then how are they reading this book? How much literacy makes one literate? How many communities of practice do we need to belong to in order to do literacy across a range of practices?

The binary opposition between literacy and illiteracy is therefore not as clear cut as may at first appear. Moreover, this binary produces further oppressive binaries. In languages which do not have a word for literacy,

literacy is often translated as 'educated' or 'schooled', with notions of refined, learned, well-bred, civilised, cultivated, cultured, genteel, lying just beneath the surface.[3] Literacy came to be seen as the mark of a 'liberally educated or learned person', as early as 1550 (OED department, 1980), at a time when few people had access to this technology. Subsequently, literacy was harnessed to support the now refuted 'great-divide' theory of social anthropologists which divided primitive ('savage') and modern ('civilised') people according to their mental abilities, pre-logical/logical, concrete/abstract, pre-literate/literate (Gee, 1990: 24; Street, 1984: 53). According to both Street and Gee, there is in fact no evidence that people who come from predominantly oral cultures are cognitively or intellectually inferior to their literate counterparts. Scribner and Cole (1981) conducted research on the Vai in Liberia in which they were unable to show that literacy produced cognitive gains. All they could show was that each form of literacy produced specific skills related to that particular literacy. More recent research in neuro-science that uses brain imaging has been able to show reading produces pathways in the brain that do not exist prior to the development of literacy (Wolf, 2007).

Heath's (1983) seminal ethnographic study of three communities in South Carolina demonstrates that children who grow up in communities with different oral and literate practices develop different facilities with language which, although equally powerful resources for making meaning, are not equally valued by the school system which children from these communities enter. Children's different 'ways with words' (Heath, 1983), what Scribner and Cole (1981) would see as skills specific to particular literacies, are not used as potential resources for all. Where some ways are privileged over others, the system sets up distinctions (Bourdieu, 1984, 1991) that advantage some children at the expense of others. It should be no surprise that these schools privileged middle class literacy norms over sophisticated forms of orality. Moreover, the kind of literacy that is favoured bears little relation to literacy practices rooted in children's lives and their communities. Rather, school literacy is seen as a neutral technology and a decontextualised set of skills; what Street calls the 'autonomous' model of literacy (Street, 1984).

That ordinary people should learn to read and write only became imaginable after the invention of the alphabetic system and the invention of the printing press. One has to hold on to the picture of monks poring

---

[3] Afrikaans, a language derived in South Africa from Dutch, is one of South Africa's 11 official languages. All the meanings given here for 'literate' can be found in the word '*beskaaf*', offered as one of the dictionary definitions of literacy (*Groot Woordeboek*, 1963). Many of these meanings are also captured in the German translation of literacy as *bildungsgrad*.

over the production of illuminated manuscripts and wise rabbis copying the torah on parchment scrolls. Writing was once the work of specialist scribes, with reading entrusted to priests and sages. Literacy has always been dictated by the developments of technology: papyrus, parchment, quills, pencils, paper, pens, typewriters, computers.

Possible research project for students

Find out about the origins of modern writing implements and the different effects these different technologies had on writing. See, for example, the history of the pen (at e.g. http://inventors.about.com/library/weekly/aa100197.htm or http://www.rickconner.net/penspotters/history.htm).

In our own age new digital technologies have effected a communication revolution, enabling permanent records of embodied oral texts, instant reproduction and transmission of both verbal and visual texts and the production of multimodal texts which make meaning by combining a number of modes of communication: verbal, visual, aural, spatial, gestural. If we take seriously the different

F   A

C

es

of writing, then we have to recognise the importance of the visual in modern forms of communication. Not only are photographs, emoticons (☺), pictures and drawings able to carry the message of texts along with the verbal, but the choice of fonts, columns, layout (the overall design of a page), shape the meanings conveyed; one has only to think of full-page colour advertisements in magazines, for example.

Moreover, in post-industrial knowledge economies, work is increasingly polarised into symbolic analytic work and service work. Symbolic analytic work, which requires problem solving and innovation, is dependent on elite literacies. More routine service work which relies on a reduced functional literacy is less valued and is poorly paid. In the information age, the literacy stakes are therefore higher and, as always, there is differential access to the newer literacy technologies, the latest means of production and the elite literacies that they enable (Alba, Gonzalez-Gaudiano, Lankshear, & Peters, 2000; Gee, Hull, & Lankshear, 1996).

It should already be clear that it is not possible to separate literacy from questions of power. So far, we have seen:

- how the binary literacy/illiteracy offers only negative subject positions for people who are not literate;
- how what counts as valued 'ways with words' is defined by institutions that favour the practices of middle class communities over those of working class communities (Heath, 1983);
- that literacy is privileged over orality;
- that who gets access to communication technologies is socially stratified. Individuals are socially located across different structures of privilege: gender, race, class, geography, religion, ethnicity, nationality, language – the more privileged one is, the greater one's chances are of becoming literate across a range of media and modalities.

It is also important to remember that literacy is just one among many social 'goods' that are distributed. Where we sit in the social hierarchy also affects our ability to access resources such as housing, land, health care, clean water, food and transport. Each of these in their turn impacts on the kind of educational opportunities we are afforded and our ability to make the most of them. It is simply harder for hungry children who have to walk long distances to schools where there are few books to become literate in a school language, which is not the language they speak at home. While world literacy statistics are always open to interpretation, it is clear that literacy levels in wealthy developed countries, the political north, are much higher than those of poor, underdeveloped countries in the political south (UNESCO, 2000).

Refusing the Binary

What one might ask does it feel like to be illiterate? This is how Lilly-Rose Hlakanyane, a student at the University of the Witwatersrand, in South Africa writes about it.[4] Lilly-Rose Hlakanyane is a mature, African woman in her late thirties whose main language is IsiXhosa and who teaches English at a secondary school in a rural town in the Eastern Cape. At the time Lilly-Rose, who had a Bachelor of Education degree, was registered for our Further Diploma in English, an in-service, flexible delivery, part distance-mode, course for teachers. The following extracts are taken from a personal literacy history that she wrote for Yvonne Reed, who teaches the course.[5]

---

[4] This discussion of Hlakanyane's literacy history first appeared in *Loss of Communication in the Information Age*, edited by R. de Cilla, H.-J. Krumm and R. Wodak (Janks, 2001).

[5] I am grateful to Yvonne Reed and to Lilly-Rose Hlakanyane for permission to use this work.

Extract One

One day I went to town with my mother when I was doing Standard 1 (Grade 3). On our way back in a bus I saw a young man who was sitting next to me on a three seater. His perusal of a newspaper interested me. I watched him closer trying to know why he was so fast. What I saw was that heads of pictures were facing downwards. At first I couldn't believe what I saw. I looked at him, trying to get whether he was aware of this, only to find that he was so absorbed in his reading that he was even moving his lips. I was more puzzled. How could he read with words like this? He continued from one page to the next and I started to realise that this one cannot read and write, because I was doing Standard 1 and I knew how to hold a book. It was somebody from our location working in the mines in Johannesburg. I smiled alone because I couldn't dare say anything or show it to my mother because it would mean that I have no respect for adults. At home I told my brother who told me that he is a mineworker and illiterate. He was disguising because he knew that not everybody in the bus knew him well, who could wonder why he was reading a newspaper.

Here the young Lilly-Rose witnesses an adult man pretending to be literate. In only her third year of school, she experiences herself as knowledgeable about print-based literacy and she 'smiled alone' in amusement at the pretentious man. Only cultural norms of respect for elders in the community prevent her from sharing the joke with her mother.

In her second extract, the adult Hlakanyane experiences herself as 'illiterate' when she finds herself in a context where print-based literacy is no longer sufficient for her needs.

Extract Two: Computer Literacy

This was a disgrace and embarrassing experience for me and my friend at this university. It was our first day in the Library to go there for reading material. We were supposed to look for reading material from the computer. We whispered to each other when noticing that everybody was helping himself or herself here assisted by the computer. We approached a lady who was working on the counter. She referred us to a table where there was nobody. We toiled around there until a certain lady came to help us although that was not her desk. She gave us library booklets and told us to occupy any computer in there. I thought maybe my friend is better than myself because she is a college lecturer. We went to one computer thinking that we were going to help one another. When we were sitting in front of the computer we couldn't move fast. We noticed that this was a waste of time and time was against us for a lecture. I said to my friend I cannot start operating a computer within these few minutes we have. Let's ask anyone to help us. If no-one can, let's leave for the lecture. This time we got someone who sat down with us who did everything for us while teaching us. Unfortunately the books were not available. We never thought of going in there again. We asked the co-ordinator if there is another place where we can get reading material other than in the library. The resource centre was a solution for us to avoid the computer.[6]

In this extract Hlakanyane reveals her sense of shame and humiliation by words such as 'disgrace', 'embarrassing experience', and 'whispered to each other'. She also conveys how difficult it was for her and her friend by saying 'we toiled' and 'we couldn't move fast'. Finally her sense of disempowerment is captured when towards the end of the paragraph she says 'someone did everything for us' and 'we never thought of going in there again'.

In her final extract Hlakanyane brings these two experiences together and reflects on them.

Extract Three: The Events of the Young Man in the Bus and of the Computer

From the day I was feeling embarrassed in the library, I was just like the young man who was hiding from other people that he was illiterate. When you are illiterate you think of people around you. What are they going to say about me when they discover this about me? You feel ashamed of yourself among literate people. What I experienced about a computer makes me know exactly how that man was feeling when he noticed that people are literate now. He pretended to be like them. I got into his boots. I know exactly what it means. At the moment I have no time to start computer lessons but what I experienced motivated me to do something. We were illiterates among literates. When we were outside we both agreed that a computer is a need these days.

Finally, her own experience of not having digital literacy enables her to understand how the man on the bus was feeling. She recognises the shame that produced his literacy disguise and no longer finds his behaviour amusing. What Hlakanyane understands is that her literacy needs have outstripped her literacy abilities and that she will have to do something about it. In this she offers us an important way of thinking about literacy development as ongoing. All of us face new literacy challenges every day whether we are a child making scribbles to 'label' a drawing, an academic writing a

---

[6] The Liberty Life Resource Centre was established in the Division of Applied English Language Studies at the University of the Witwatersrand to provide students not used to libraries with more user-friendly access to print and non-print material. Donor money was raised to achieve this.

first book, a media student learning how to deconstruct an advertisement, a school principal learning how to use a computer to write letters, a taxi-driver mastering a new route with the help of a road map, or readers of this book who are still trying to work out what on earth Halliday was saying.

At my age most people forget how to count. I'm just learning.

For years all that Jimmy Khobella could count, were his blessings. Thanks to his friends' kindness, he somehow managed to get by without being able to read or write. Although he is grateful to them, he sometimes feels he was a burden.

Maybe that's why he doesn't take his new found skills for granted. To us he may look 73 years old, but inside he's more like a six year old with a whole new world to discover.

More and more people like Jimmy are attending the courses being run by the Institute of Natural Resources to learn their three R's. It's just one of the many projects that Standard Bank is proudly sponsoring, with the aim of helping people to work out a better life for themselves.

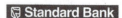 **Standard Bank**

With us you can go so much further.

http://www.standardbank.co.za

Figure 1.1 An Advertisement for Standard Bank, published in *The Teacher*, October 1997. Source: *The Teacher*, October 1997. Standard Bank advertisement. Used with permission.

In case I have given the impression that feelings of inadequacy in relation to illiteracy are individual and psychological, it is important to show how these attitudes are socially and textually produced. Figure 1.1 (opposite) is an advertisement for Standard Bank, which was published in *The Teacher*, October 1997. The advertisement is designed to enhance the image of the bank, which promotes itself by publicising its involvement in Adult Literacy Programmes. In the process, it infantilises one of the learners on the programme within a deficit construction of illiteracy.

> It is worth stopping to consider how both the visual and the verbal choices work to position Mr Khobella and effectively negate whatever he has learnt from a lifetime of experience. Which words, which visual signifiers, which aspects of the layout do this work?

> If one begins to collect everyday texts to do with literacy, such as the text in Figure 1.1, they can be used as resources for classroom discussions. Questions such as the following may begin to help students think about how photographs, advertisements, newspaper articles, cartoons or poems portray literacy.
>
> 1. How is literacy represented? As something positive or something negative? As a problem or as a solution?
> 2. What claims are made for literacy?
> 3. Who is shown reading or writing? Who is not shown? Are they enjoying themselves or not? Who is shown as unable to read or write?
> 4. Because all written language is situated in time and place, it is important to understand where and when the literacy event shown in the text is taking place.
> 5. What counts as literacy in the text? Is it only reading and writing? Does text-messaging or drawing money from an ATM or searching the internet count as literacy?
>
> Students can also produce images of literacy by taking photographs of literacy in context (billboards, shop signs, graffiti, T-shirts) and literacy events (hiring a video, getting a receipt, making cards or posters) in their own homes and neighbourhoods, for discussion in class.

Becoming a Teacher of Literacy

I never used to think of myself as a literacy teacher. I began my professional life in the early 1970s as a high school English teacher, trained to teach literature. The high school syllabus was dominated by literature and my passion was teaching students to appreciate, understand and enjoy the English canon. I also became interested in young adult fiction and worked hard at getting my students 'hooked on books' (Fader, 1976). Although the 'language' curriculum at the time placed a great deal of emphasis on reading and comprehension and the writing curriculum included both 'creative' and 'factual' writing genres, I did not conceptualise my work as teaching literacy.

In the 1980s, now as a teacher educator, I discovered the work of Barnes, Britton and Rosen (1969), Britton (1970) and Barnes (1976), and became increasingly interested in the relationship between language and learning, and more broadly, in socio-cultural approaches to language. Although the London Institute of Education, where Britton and Rosen were based, together with the London Association of Teachers of English, offered important new pedagogies for multicultural, multilingual classrooms, they were still working predominantly with an English first language curriculum, as was I. At this stage I saw myself as a teacher of both English literature and English language to native speakers of English.

The 1976 Soweto uprising in South Africa, sparked by primary school students protesting about the medium of instruction in African education, helped me to take seriously questions about language and education. At the same time as I began to work politically for the desegregation of schooling, I began to prepare myself for teaching English as a second language. As a teacher educator and activist, I was no longer willing to focus exclusively on English mother tongue education. I re-qualified as an applied linguist and began to see myself more and more as an English language educator with an ability to work across English as a first language and English as an additional language in multilingual classrooms. Since then in my practice as an English teacher educator I have worked to ensure that English teachers are competent to teach both literature and language.

South Africa, the context in which I work, has profoundly shaped my thinking about what it means to teach a dominant world language such as English. English, a colonial language in this context, is spoken as a first language by only 8.2% of the population (Statistics South Africa). In real numbers, this means that only three and a half million people speak English as their main language in a population of 45 million people. South Africa, having been colonised first by the Dutch then by the British, has a history of two colonial languages. Afrikaans, an indigenous South African language spoken by 13.3% of the population, is derived from Dutch. From

1925 until the advent of democracy in 1994, English and Afrikaans were the official languages of the country. After the Nationalist Party came to power in 1948, Afrikaans came to be seen as the language of apartheid and oppression. English was preferred as a lingua franca and the right to choose English rather than Afrikaans as the medium of instruction in schools became part of the freedom struggle.

The new constitution of South Africa recognises 11 official languages: Afrikaans, English, IsiNdebele, IsiXhosa, IsiZulu, Sepedi, Sesotho, Setswana, SiSwati, Tshivenda, Xitsonga.[7] Many black South Africans speak more than one African language, especially in the urban areas. Yet, because English is seen as the language of power and access, there is a danger that this 11-language policy could lead to the de facto dominance of English. Sachs, a constitutional court judge, therefore maintains that in South Africa 'all language rights are rights against English' (1994: 1). Access to English in South Africa has to be tempered by respect for, and maintenance of, students' African languages. Multilingual policies in education are necessary in order to balance the force of English. How should one teach English in contexts of diversity? What is a responsible approach to teaching an omnivorous language such as English?

In South Africa where the struggle for language rights was intrinsically bound up with the struggle for human rights, I could not but be aware that language is fundamentally tied to questions of power. In schools where African children were forced to learn half their subjects through the medium of Afrikaans and half their subjects through the medium of English, languages in which neither they nor their teachers were adequately fluent, the fundamental connection between language and learning was clear. Even today, African children's learning and their sense of identity are compromised when they have to learn through the medium of English. But South Africa is not the only place where children bring many languages to the classroom. Nor is it the only place where children learn through a foreign medium. Nor is it the only place where English poses a threat to other languages (Phillipson, 1992). Ethnic, cultural and linguistic diversity are now the norm in communities and classrooms across the world and the issues that teachers of English in South Africa have to confront, are issues for all teachers who teach through the medium of English. Teachers of English have an additional responsibility. Bourdieu (1991) draws our attention to the fact that while the education system generally fails to provide students from subordinated groups in society with *knowledge of* and *access to* the legitimate language, it succeeds in

---

[7] The naming and spelling of these languages is contested. I have elected to use the forms that appear in the Constitution of South Africa.

teaching them *recognition of* (misrecognition of) its legitimacy (1991: 62). What is needed is language education that reverses this – that gives mastery of English, together with a critical view of its status as a global language (Granville *et al.*, 1998). In addition, as English teachers we need to produce students who understand why linguistic diversity is a resource for creativity and cognition, who value all the languages that they speak, and who recognise the paucity of English only (Janks, 2004). Linguistic access is the focus of Chapter 6.

So issues of access and diversity are tied to issues of power; to questions of domination and subordination; to processes of legitimation and negation, of inclusion and exclusion. Increasingly my involvement with language education was helping me to understand the multiple threads tying language to power. In particular, at that time, I became interested in the ways in which language was being used by the Apartheid State to maintain and reproduce a system of white privilege and racial domination. I thought it important to increase students' awareness of the way language was being used to oppress the black majority, to win elections, to deny education, to construct others, to position readers, to hide the truth and to legitimate oppression. I began to work on Critical Language Awareness (CLA) materials, for use in South African schools. I still saw myself as a language teacher but now I had found a way of bringing this together with a social justice agenda for education.

At the time, there was no shortage of theory to draw on in my own disciplines of linguistics and education: critical linguistics (Fowler, Hodge, Kress, & Trew, 1979; Fowler & Kress, 1979); critical discourse analysis (Fairclough, 1989); feminist linguistics (Cameron, 1985, 1990, 1995; Spender, 1980; Threadgold, 1997; Weedon, 1987); Marxist linguistics (Volosinov, 1986); and critical pedagogy (Apple, 1979; Giroux, 1981; Shor, 1980; Simon, 1992). In addition, a great deal of relevant work was being published in social theory. Much of this work was opaque and needed to be mediated before it could be used in schools. Critical Language Awareness, developed at Lancaster University (Fairclough, 1992), was the classroom application of this theory. My own research, based at Lancaster, was to explore the feasibility of translating this complex theory into viable classroom activities. It culminated in the publication of the *Critical Language Awareness Series*, a set of six workbooks designed to teach students about the relationship between language and power (Janks, 1993).

The word *critical* enters this discourse to mean something different from what we normally understand by 'critical thinking'. It no longer only means reasoned analysis based on an examination of evidence and argument. Here it is used to signal analysis that seeks to uncover the social interests at work, to ascertain what is at stake in textual and social practices. Who benefits? Who is disadvantaged? In short, it signals a focus on power, on the ways in which meanings are 'mobilised in the defence of domination' (Thompson, 1984: 35) in what is sometimes called ideology critique. Throughout the book I shall continue to use the word 'critical' to signal a focus on power. I might have called this book *Critical Literacy* instead of *Literacy and Power*, if the word 'critical' were not so ambiguous.

I was introduced to critical literacy in the 1990s when I saw how English educators in Australia were building on the work of Paulo Freire. Putting 'critical' in front of the word 'literacy' serves the same function as it does in front of the words 'psychology' (Rose, 1989), 'geography' (Soja, 1996) or 'multiculturalism' (May, 1999). It signals a move to question the naturalised assumptions of the discipline, its truths, its discourses and its attendant practices. In the early 1970s, Paulo Freire wrote

> If learning to read and write is to constitute an act of knowing, the learners must assume from the beginning the role of creative subjects. It is not a matter of memorizing and repeating given syllables and phrases, but rather of reflecting critically on the process of reading and writing itself, and on the profound significance of language.
>
> Insofar as language is impossible without thought, and language and thought are impossible without the world to which they refer, the human word is more than mere vocabulary – it is word-and-action. The cognitive dimensions of the literacy process must include the relationships of men [sic] with their world.
>
> (Freire, 1972a)

Freire was the first to challenge our assumptions about literacy as simply teaching students the skills necessary for reading and writing and in insisting that we 'reflect critically on the process of reading and writing itself'. He helps us to understand that reading the word cannot be separated from reading the world. Street (1984) develops this further when he distinguishes between the autonomous and ideological models of literacy.

Freire's two seminal books, *Cultural Action for Freedom* (1972a) and *Pedagogy of the Oppressed* (1972b), show how in the process of learning how to read both the *word* and the *world* critically, adult literacy learners regain their sense of themselves as agents who can act to transform the social situations in which they find themselves. He used literacy as a means of breaking the 'culture of silence' of the poor and dispossessed. For Freire,

> Liberation is a praxis: the action and reflection of men upon their world in order to transform it.
>
> (1972b: 52)

Both reflection and action require words.

> To exist, humanly, is to *name* the world, to change it. Once named, the world in its turn reappears to its namers as a problem and requires of them a new *naming*. Men are not built in silence, but in word, in work, in action-reflection. . . . It is in speaking their word that men transform the world by naming it, dialogue imposes itself as the way in which men achieve significance as men.
>
> (1972b: 61)

Problem posing is the first step in action for freedom. The effectiveness of this approach to teaching literacy is exemplified by Brian Morgan's work with Chinese immigrant adults in Canada (1998) and by Vivian Vasquez's work with young children in Canada and the USA (Vasquez, 2001, 2004). The power to name one's world breaks the silence and builds people. This critical perspective on literacy effects a profound change of our understanding about the 'truth' of what literacy is, what it does and how we should do it.

For Foucault,

> '[t]ruth' is to be understood as a system of ordered procedures for the production, regulation, distribution, circulation and operation of statements. [It] is linked in a circular relation with systems of power which produce and sustain it, and to effects of power which it induces and which extend it. A 'regime' of truth. . . . The political question . . . is not error, illusion, alienated consciousness or ideology; it is truth itself.
>
> (1980: 133)

Foucault's work forces us to think about how all discourses, not just discourses of literacy, produce truth, how they are produced by power and how they produce effects of power. These ideas will be developed in Chapter 2.

In Australia, Luke (1992) focused on the ways in which literacy practices in schools disciplined children's bodies; how they had to sit still, face the front, not talk, keep their eyes on the teacher, and follow in the book. Gilbert's work (1989) explored the relationship between language, gender and the classroom; Davies studied children's reactions to feminist stories (1989) and the ways in which femininities and masculinities are constructed in classrooms (1993); and Kamler and her colleagues (1994) looked at the constructions of gender in young children's writing. Comber and O'Brien (1994) also worked with young primary school children to deconstruct everyday texts such as Mother's Day cards and toy catalogues (which they call 'junk-mail'), and Comber and Simpson examined cereal boxes (1995). In Western Australia, Chalkface Press had been established and was publishing critical materials for use in high school English classrooms. The early workbooks used post-structuralist theory to deconstruct literary texts (Mellor, Patterson, & O'Neill, 1987, 1991; Moon, 1992). A decade later, Fremantle Press published workbooks using post-colonial theory to help students rethink texts to do with ethnicity, gender and aboriginality, and to understand the positioning of texts dealing with the 'invasion' and settlement of Australia (Kenworthy & Kenworthy, 1997; Martino, 1997). Ray Misson and Wendy Morgan were also working with high school English students. They worked with both literary and non-literary, popular culture texts. Their ideas for working critically with the aesthetic, developed since the 1990s, appeared as a book in 2006 (Misson & Morgan, 2006). Morgan's classroom work on textual representations of Ned Kelly, an Australian folk hero (1992, 1994) is a superb exemplar of the kind of work being done with non-literary texts. The multiplicity of accounts was designed to destabilise all the accounts and to show that all textualisations are representations of the truth. The richness of all this classroom-based research combined with materials that made these new pedagogies available to both primary and high school teachers coincided with strong equity policies in Australian education at the time. More than anywhere else, these new ideas took root in classrooms, such that by the end of the 1990s critical literacy was firmly established in the English curriculum in Australia.

Critical Language Awareness (CLA), which offers linguistic tools for the critical analysis of texts, fits easily under the broader umbrella of critical literacy. What critical literacy offered me, as opposed to CLA, was a way to bring my interests together. It included primary school teachers and high school English teachers, literature teachers, CLA text analysts working with non-literary texts such as newspaper articles, maps, pictures, advertisements, junk mail. And that is not all. As early as 1993, Green and Bigum began theorising the impact of new technologies on literacy and literacy practices. As a result, critical literacy practitioners began working with computer and information literacy and with media literacy, the latter interfacing with the fields of cultural studies, including popular culture, and media studies (Buckingham, 2003; Buckingham & Sefton-Green, 1994; Hall, 1997; Nixon, 1999, 2003). Dyson (1997, 2003) has shown how characters, images and ideas from popular culture loom large in children's imaginations and permeate their textual productions. In addition, Gee, Hull and Lankshear (1996) and Lankshear (1997) looked at the impact on literacy of the new work order in post-industrial economies.

Wallace (2007), Brian Morgan (1998), Norton (2000), and Pennycook (1999, 2001) have been developing the theory and practice of what they are calling Critical ESL or critical approaches to TESOL (Teaching English to Speakers of Other Languages). ESL is an abbreviation for 'English as a second language', a naming practice that has been challenged for a number of reasons. In South Africa where many children grow up in multilingual communities, they dismiss the notion of mother tongue as a 'Western' concept invented in monolingual contexts. Also, under apartheid, second language had overtones of second class. It worried us that our own students, only half-jokingly, expanded the acronym ESL to 'English for slow learners'. South African language and education policy, which is based on the principle of additive multilingualism, now names any language that is not one's first language an 'additional' language, rather than a 'second' language. In a critique of TESOL, Pennycook (2001) suggests that we should think of these languages as other*ed*, rather than as other. 'Other' constructs English as the superior norm from which different languages deviate and belongs 'to a long history of colonial othering'. Other*ed* reminds us of the actions by which different languages are constructed as other, marginal and inferior by the centre (Pennycook, 1998). The *Critical Language Awareness Series* (Janks, 1993), in South Africa, was deliberately written for *all* South African students to refuse the first language/second language divide that was fundamental to segregated education under apartheid (Janks, 1995). The materials had to be linguistically accessible to all secondary school students learning through the medium of English.

Kress's contribution has been particularly important. His work (Kress, 2003) has drawn our attention to the ways in which our models of literacy continue to privilege the word. Together with van Leeuwen, he has helped us to see that texts are increasingly visual and that we have to take seriously the relationship between words, images and the overall design of print texts which are becoming increasingly multimodal (Kress & van Leeuwen, 1990, 2001).

The following is an illustration of how visual literacy as a situated practice enabled an old Zulu man with extensive knowledge of the bush to act as a guide on a bird walk in one of South Africa's national game parks, although none of us could speak his language, IsiZulu, and he could not speak English. Unable to read words, this *umfundisi*[8] knew Newman's *Birds of Southern Africa*, the standard field guide, better than the keen bird watchers in our party: he could find any bird in the book instantly. He used his knowledge of the birds to read the bird illustrations and he used the field guide to mediate this knowledge. He had all the literacy he

---

[8] *Umfundisi* means 'instructor' in IsiZulu and is a title of respect.

needed for the job; moreover he had taught himself. Like Jimmy Khobella, our guide was not literate according to limited conventional definitions of literacy and, as with Jimmy Khobella, it would be shameful to infantilise him.

Kress and van Leeuwen's work is fundamental to the multiliteracies project of the New London Group (2000). Because texts are increasingly multimodal – a text on the internet, for example, may include written words, pictures, moving images, colour, fonts of different sizes, sound, speech, with the different message streams working simultaneously – it becomes difficult to separate oracy from literacy. I nevertheless try where possible to distinguish between making meaning with and from written and visual texts on the one hand and spoken texts on the other. Moreover, maintaining a distinction between speaking, writing and designing (with words and visuals) is important because of the different affordances (Kress, 2003) of these signifying systems.

Literacy teachers can now capitalise on students' interest in and fluency with new technologies to develop their multi-modal literacies, across a range of media (newspapers, television, internet, radio, magazines) and modes (visual, spoken, written, gestural). The following questions offer one approach to how one might get students to think about their new literacies.

1. How many students in the class have mobile phones? Why is mobility important?
2. What languages do their phones offer?
3. How many students use a short text messaging service on their phones (known in South Africa as SMS text messaging)?
4. How many students use instant messaging on their phones?
5. How many students use email on their phones?
6. What sounds do mobile phones use to convey different meanings?
7. What visual messaging is possible on students' phones? Are their phones able to take photographs or videos?
8. What music do they have on their phones?
9. What languages and literacies do students need to use their phones?
   - What languages do students use with their phones? What communicative competence is needed for talking on a phone?
   - What kinds of things do mobile phone users have to read? Here are some examples: words, indicator symbols, keys, time, manuals, accounts.

- What writing competence do students need to send text messages? Do they use predictive text messaging? Why or why not? What special SMS language do they use? Why has this specialised language evolved? Is SMS changing written language?
- What computer literacies do they need? What do they have to know about menus, PINs, SIM cards, bluetooth, folders, computer games?
- What screen literacies do they need? What do they need to know about how space is organised, how scrolling is different from turning a page?
- What visual literacy do they need for the different phone functions? For example, what is needed to play a game on the phone or to use the calendar?

Where early work in critical literacy focused on critical reading, people like Clark and Ivanic (1997), Ivanic (1998) and Kamler (2001) have concentrated on critical writing. This is an important move because it enables us to think about where we might go after we have arrived at a critical reading of a text. Because texts are constructed word by word, image by image, they can be deconstructed – unpicked, unmade, the positions produced for the reader laid bare. But then what? A critical approach to writing helps us to think about how texts may be re-written and how multimodal texts can be redesigned. It enables us to transform texts, to remake the word. If repositioning texts is tied to an ethic of social justice then redesign can contribute to the kind of identity and social transformation that Freire's work advocates.

The word 'reading' although initially tied to reading verbal texts has been applied metaphorically to other modes of encoding meaning. So one can 'read' film, clothing, gestures, pictures, photographs, bodies and so on. The word 'writing' is not as expansive in its use. We do not talk about writing photographs, drawings or bodies. The word 'design', unlike the word 'write', does work across multiple modalities, multiple forms of meaning making or semiosis – you can design a text, a style of dress, a page, a poster, furniture, a room. De*sign* is a useful word to talk about the production of texts that use multiple *sign* systems. Rede*sign* necessitates re-*sign*-ing. Semiotics is the study of sign systems and semiosis is the use of signs to make meaning. The following task is an example of a redesign activity that readers might like to try with their students.

Redesign the Standard Bank advertisement in Figure 1.1. Feel free to use different verbal and visual signs, different layout and organisation of the text. What matters is that the design uses more respectful ways of representing Jimmy Khobella and literacy.

The notion of redesign was first introduced in 'a pedagogy of multiliteracies' (New London Group, 2000). In my own work, this is what I refer to as a 'pedagogy of reconstruction' (Janks, 2003: 183, 2005). I chose the word *reconstruction* for two reasons. First, because it offers a corrective balance to earlier work in critical literacy, including my own, that focused largely on *deconstruction*; second because it creates an intertextual reference to the Mandela government's 'reconstruction and development programme' (African National Congress, 1994) that guided the social and economic transformation of South Africa after the first democratic elections in 1994. Since 1994, my work has been directed towards understanding what critical literacy for reconstruction might look like. This work forms the basis of Chapter 8.

From the story that I have told of my own journey towards becoming a critical literacy teacher, I think it is possible to think of a *literacy* teacher as someone who works with others to make meaning with or from texts. A *critical literacy* teacher is, in addition, interested in what all kinds of texts (written, visual and oral) do to readers, viewers and listeners and whose interests are served by what these texts do. They also help students to rewrite themselves and their local situations by helping them to pose problems and to act, often in small ways, to make the world a fairer place. Different orientations to working with critical literacy help them to do so.

CHAPTER 2

Orientations to Literacy

How literacy is constructed is contested; it spans a wide range of meanings from basic or functional literacy to the advanced ability to manipulate symbols and abstractions. The processes involved in making meaning with and from texts, using a range of semiotic resources across different modalities and technologies, are complex. The need for sophisticated levels of literacy skills in the knowledge economy has led to what Green refers to as the 'literacy turn' or the 'triumph of literacy' (2002).

Models that seek to integrate different orientations to literacy, like those of Green[1] (2002) and Freebody and Luke (1990) are more helpful than those that insist on one or other approach. Essentially what both of these models argue is that readers need to:

- decode the text. They have to make sense of the written code in order to work out what the text is saying. This necessitates competence in the language;
- make meaning from the text by engaging with the writer's meanings. Reading is an active process of bringing one's own knowledge of culture, content, context, text-use and text-structure into an encounter with those of the writer, in an active process of meaning making;
- interrogate the text to examine its assumptions, its values and its

---

[1] Green's 3D model is discussed in some depth in Alba, González-Gaudino, Lankshear and Peters (2000, pp. 218–219). In calling this the '3D' model, Green metaphorically captures the notion of a three-dimensional way of seeing a text that gives depth rather than flatness.

positions. Readers need to understand what the text is doing to them and whose interests are served by the positions that are on offer. They have to imagine how the text could be otherwise, in order to produce resistant readings that can form the basis for redesign.

In the literature, decoding is often equated with *reading* and is associated with functional or basic literacy. Meaning making, *reading with the text*, is associated with the higher order cognitive skills that are necessary for the comprehension, analysis and evaluation of texts in context. The interrogation of texts, *reading against the text*, is tied to critical literacy and implies that readers recognise texts as selective versions of the world; they are not subjected to them and they can imagine how texts can be transformed to represent a different set of interests. Green refers to these as operational, cultural and critical literacies which are interlocked bringing the dimensions of language, meaning and power together (2002). Certainly critical literacy is dependent on an ability to decode text and to engage with its meanings. Gee (1990) maintains that critical reading is only possible if one is able to stand outside the codes of the text – the print code, the semantic and structuring codes, and the pragmatic code (Luke & Freebody, 1997). This can only be achieved if one has more than one discourse, more than one combination of 'saying (writing)-doing-being-valuing-believing' (Gee, 1990: 142), more than one way of thinking the world. Because texts are instantiations or realisations of discourses, it is easier to see them otherwise from the standpoint of a different discourse.[2]

Orientations to Critical Literacy

It should by now be clear that critical literacy works at the interface of language, literacy and power. We have already seen the slightly different orientations to literacy and power taken by critical linguists, adult literacy educators and high school literature teachers. What is common is their shared understanding that education broadly, and literacy education more specifically, is not a neutral activity. 'Curriculum is to be understood as constituting a particular, unavoidably partial "selection" from the culture' (Green, 2002: 9). These selections are positioned and positioning: the language that is chosen as the medium of instruction, the literary texts that

---

[2] Gee distinguishes discourse with a little 'd', which he uses for 'connected stretches of language that make sense, like conversations, stories, reports, arguments, essays' and Discourse with a capital 'D' which are socially embedded 'saying (writing)-doing-being-valuing-believing combinations' (Gee, 1990, p. 142). My use of the word discourse with a lower-case 'd' is the same as Gee's capital 'D' Discourse.

are prescribed, the particular selections of popular culture for inclusion (or exclusion) are some examples. All of these choices are fundamentally political along with the questions of: Who decides? Is the curriculum imposed from above by government? Do teachers decide? How much say do students have?

This book is concerned with approaches to language and literacy that take power seriously. It is not so much concerned with the specifics of curriculum content but with developing in students a critical stance in relation to content. Such a stance is predicated on students' gaining access to and facility with the language and literacy tools they need to be both critical and creative, problem posers and problem solvers, social analysts and social agents.

In my synthesis for critical literacy education (Janks, 2000),[3] I argued that different realisations of critical literacy operate with different conceptualisations of the relationship between language and power by foregrounding one or other of domination, access, diversity or design. What makes this more than just a synthesis, however, is my argument that these orientations are crucially interdependent. After a brief look at each of the key terms and the pedagogies they give rise to, I will explain how I theorised their interdependence.

Domination

Theorists working with this view of power see language, other symbolic forms, and discourse more broadly, as a powerful means of maintaining and reproducing relations of domination. According to Eagleton (1991: 11), 'men and women fight out their social and political battles at the level of signs, meanings and representations'. Critical discourse analysis is used to understand how language works to position readers in the interests of power. It assumes a critical theory of ideology (Thompson, 1990) which sees power as negative and productive of inequitable social relations. The pedagogy associated with it, called Critical Language Awareness (CLA), originated in Lancaster and is primarily associated with the work of Clark *et al.* (1987) and Fairclough (1989, 1992, 1995).

> Critical Language Awareness emphasises the fact that texts are constructed. Anything that has been constructed can be de-constructed. This unmaking or unpicking of the text increases our awareness of the choices[4] that the writer or speaker has made. Every choice

---

[3] This discussion first appeared in *Educational Review*, 52(2), 175–186 (Janks, 2000).

[4] 'Choice' here does not mean free choice. As members of a society we are constituted in and by the available discourses that speak through us, constraining what we are able to say and the ways in which we can say it.

foregrounds what was selected and hides, silences or backgrounds what was not selected. Awareness of this prepares the reader to ask critical questions: why did the writer or speaker make these choices? Whose interests do they serve? Who is empowered or disempowered by the language used?

(Janks, 1993: iii)

Access

Dominance and access come together in a different question that confronts teachers of language and literacy. How does one provide access to dominant forms, while at the same time valuing and promoting the diverse languages and literacies of our students and in the broader society? If we provide students with access to dominant forms, this contributes to maintaining the dominance of these forms. If, on the other hand, we deny students access, we perpetuate their marginalisation in a society that continues to recognise the value and importance of these forms. This is what Lodge (1997) and Janks (2004) refer to as the 'access paradox'. These dominant forms include dominant languages, dominant varieties, dominant discourses (Gee, 1990),[5] dominant literacies and knowledges, dominant genres, dominant modes of visual representation and a range of cultural practices related to social interaction.

The genre theorists (Cope & Kalantzis, 1993; Derwianka, 1990; Kress, 1999; Martin, Christie, & Rothery, 1987) have done important work in describing the features of six dominant school genres (recounts, instructions, narratives, reports, explanations and arguments), many of which, prior to their work, we somehow assumed students could see and do. Genre pedagogy has asked us to think about how and whether to make generic features visible in order to give students from marginalised discourses greater access to them.

Explicit pedagogy (Bernstein, 1996; Delpit, 1988) and access are among the key issues that confront educationists working in the area of Academic Development in institutions with increasingly diverse student populations, in South Africa and elsewhere (Benesch, 2001; de Groot, Dison, & Rule, 1996; Lillis, 2001; Lodge, 1997; Partridge & Starfield, 2007; Starfield, 2000).

Diversity

Different ways of reading and writing the world in a range of modalities[6] are a central resource for changing consciousness. Because discourses are

---

[5] See footnote 1.

[6] Here, I am using *reading* and *writing* in the broadest sense to include reading and producing signs that use a wide range of semiotic systems.

linked to a wide range of social identities and are embedded in diverse social institutions, they provide the need and the means for reflecting on our own taken-for-granted ways of saying (writing), doing, thinking and valuing (Gee, 1990: 142). The differences between discourses is productive. As individual human subjects enter into new discourses they acquire alternative and additional ways of being in the world – that is, new social identities. Kress (1995: 6) says that diversity in schools could be an important means for making students

> feel at ease with continuous, intense change; comfortable with sharp differences of culture and social values met every day; [so that they] treat them as normal, as unremarkable and natural; and above all, as an essential productive resource for innovation rather than as a cause for anxiety and anger.

However, difference tends to be organised according to relations of power, into hierarchies, and it can lead as easily to domination and conflict as to change and innovation. The New Literacy Studies (Breir & Prinsloo, 1996; Gee, 1994; Street, 1984, 1996) and work on multilingual education in South Africa (Heugh, Siegruhn, & Pluddemann, 1995; Welch, 1996) show the necessity for education to be more inclusive of students' diverse languages and literacies. In the interests of equity, inclusivity ensures that students' different 'ways with words' (Heath, 1983) have a place in the classroom. In addition, Kostogriz (2002) sees cultural collisions as a driving force that enables us to re-mediate and re-present the world and that produces the creative energy necessary for transformation and change.

Design

Design encompasses the idea of productive power – the ability to harness the multiplicity of semiotic systems across diverse cultural locations to challenge and change existing discourses. It recognises the importance of human creativity and students' ability to generate an infinite number of new meanings. The New London Group's (2000) work in multiliteracies stresses that students have to be taught how to use and select from all the available semiotic resources for representation in order to make meaning, while at the same time combining and recombining these resources so as to create possibilities for transformation and reconstruction (Cope & Kalantzis, 1997). This is what the New London Group calls 'design'. The multiliteracies project is influenced by developments in media education, cultural studies, new technologies and information literacy in a context of globalisation, all of which together are revolutionising students' literacy practices and the nature of work. While critical literacy that focused on domination tended to emphasise critical 'reading' and deconstruction across a range of modalities, the work on design emphasises multi-modal production and reconstruction using a range of media and technologies.

The Interdependence of Different Orientations to Critical Literacy

In order to show that these different orientations to literacy education are equally important and, moreover, that *they are crucially interdependent*, I took each of the key ideas and looked at the effects if the ideas embedded in the other orientations are ignored. This is summarised in Table 2.1.

Table 2.1 The Synthesis Model of Critical Literacy

Domination without access	This maintains the exclusionary force of dominant discourses.
Domination without diversity	Domination without difference and diversity loses the ruptures that produce contestation and change.
Domination without design	The deconstruction of dominance, without reconstruction or design, removes human agency.
Access without domination	Access without a theory of domination leads to the naturalisation of powerful discourses without an understanding of how these powerful forms came to be powerful.
Access without diversity	This fails to recognise that difference fundamentally affects pathways to access and involves issues of history, identity and value.
Access without design	This maintains and reifies dominant forms without considering how they can be transformed.
Diversity without domination	This leads to a celebration of diversity without any recognition that difference is structured in dominance and that not all discourses/genres/languages/literacies are equally powerful.
Diversity without access	Diversity without access to powerful forms of language ghettoises students.
Diversity without design	Diversity provides the means, the ideas, the alternative perspectives for reconstruction and transformation. Without design, the potential that diversity offers is not realised.
Design without domination	Design, without an understanding of how dominant discourses/practices perpetuate themselves, runs the risk of an unconscious reproduction of these forms.
Design without access	This runs the risk of whatever is designed remaining on the margins.
Design without diversity	This privileges dominant forms and fails to use the design resources provided by difference.

Janks, H. First published in *Educational Review* http://www.tandf.co.uk/journals

What this analysis shows is that critical literacy has to take seriously the ways in which meaning systems are implicated in reproducing domination and it has to provide access to dominant languages, literacies and genres while simultaneously using diversity as a productive resource for redesigning social futures and for changing the horizon of possibility (Simon, 1992). This includes both changing dominant discourses as well as changing which discourses are dominant.

Any one of domination, diversity, access or design without the others creates a problematic imbalance. Genre theory without creativity runs the risk of reifying existing genres; deconstruction without reconstruction or design reduces human agency; diversity without access ghettoises students. Domination without difference and diversity loses the ruptures that produce contestation and change. Reconstruction needs deconstruction in order to understand 'the manifold relationships of force that take shape and come into play in the machinery of production' (Foucault, 1978: 94). We need to find ways of holding all of these elements in productive tension to achieve what is a shared goal of all critical literacy work: equity and social justice. We need to weave them together in complex moves from deconstruction to reconstruction to deconstruction, from access to deconstruction to redesign, from diversity to deconstruction to new forms of access. These different moves need to control and balance one another.

The Integration of Domination, Diversity, Access and Design in Practice

Integrating these concepts does not prevent us from working on only one orientation with our students at a time. Provided such work is counterbalanced by later activities that bring the other orientations into play, it is possible to move in and out of the different orientations to critical literacy encapsulated by each of the concepts. What matters is that all of these concepts are given equal weight in the design of the curriculum. The two examples that follow show the interplay of these concepts in a one-day Institute and in a whole course.

The first example is from an Institute that I ran, together with an Australian colleague, Pat Thomson, at a conference for Australian educators, and the second is from my own teaching in South Africa.

Institute for Australian Teachers

Pat Thomson and I offered a pre-conference Institute at the joint national conference of the Australian Association for the Teaching of English, the Australian Federation of Modern Languages Teachers and the Australian

---

Permission to use the actual advertisement was refused. The name of the product has been changed but a description of the original advertisement is included here.

The Edge razor for women advertisement is 17 cms across and 22cms down. It consists of four rows of pictures of a woman supposedly shaving. Each picture is enclosed within a separate rectangular frame, eight in the first row, four in the second row, six in the third row and thirteen in the fourth row. The first two rows are four cms down, the third is six cms and the fourth is 3cms. The width is adjusted according to the number of picture in each row, but in many of the rectangles the woman appears squashed into the frame. The woman is particularly cramped in the second row, where, in addition, each image is depicted within a picture frame.

The woman is tall, thin, blonde, young and pretty. She is wearing a sleeveless body-fitting, straight-cut dress with a mini skirt that is well above the knee and white wedge-heeled sandals. Without a razor in her hand she mimes the act of shaving, under her arms, behind her ankle, under her leg, between her legs. She is shown standing, sitting, lying on her back, standing on one leg shaving the other leg which is raised, bending over forward, backwards and sideways. In the thirty-one pictures of this woman, each position is more awkward and off-balance than the next. Designed to suggest the silliness of shaving, it simply makes the woman look ridiculous.

Below these images is a separate box slightly narrower than the rows of women and centred. A photograph of the Edge razor is placed here together with the slogan. Whereas the pictures of the women are in shades of grey, this box is in pastel lilac. The words in this box say that women have to shave in 'tricky places', as illustrated in the images, but claims that the Edge razor will protect them in the 'places where they may need to shave. In the shower, on the way to the beach and behind the knee'. The humour pertaining to the silliness of shaving is continued in the pun on the word 'places'.

Figure 2.1 An Advertisement for 'Edge Razors', Targeted at Women.

Literacy Educators in 1999. For readers not familiar with these associations, their membership is drawn from Australian secondary school English teachers, Australian teachers who teach languages other than English, and Australian primary school teachers respectively. It was this mix that resulted in our attracting a highly diverse group of people to our critical literacy Institute. In this account I will focus on how we were able to use the concepts of domination, diversity, access and design for structuring the work that we did.[7]

In the first session we asked participants to introduce themselves by

---

[7] This is not a full account of the Institute but is merely an outline of the programme to show how the synthesising model of critical literacy can be realised in practice. It shows how we were able to use the organising concepts to structure different activities. I am grateful to Pat Thomson for permission to use our work.

telling the group what narratives, knowledges and literacies they brought with them. This took an hour and a half and showed how extensive the resources of the group were in terms of languages, lived first-hand experience and knowledge of different countries, religions, communities, cultural practices and different social locations in terms of class, gender, and an urban/rural consciousness.

We then asked participants to critically analyse an advertisement for Edge Razors[8] (Figure 2.1).

We deliberately chose this advertisement because of the multiple modalities of representation – visual, verbal, gestural, postural, clothing. All the groups produced readings which demonstrated the negative and sexist construction of women in this advertisement. Not one of the groups used the diversity of knowledge in the group. When asked to reread the advertisement using these knowledges as lenses, the group was able to see how the advertisement could also be read as immodest, Western, middle-class and ethnocentric, with little understanding of different values attached to body hair, clothing and privacy in different cultures. There was an interesting discussion on countries in which participants had worked where an advertisement like this could *not* be published. Participants knew how to read against the grain of a text, but they had not learnt how to use the full range of discourses that they had access to. Methods of critical discourse analysis had taught them to look for racism and sexism. In the workshop we called these 'dominant deconstructions'.

Having had a chance to critique a different Edge advertisement, this one addressed to a male market, participants were asked to design their own razor advertisement. Pat Thomson initiated this task by showing the group her redesign. Her advertisement showed pictures of Sinead O'Connor, Andre Agassi and the Dalai Lama, all with shaved heads. I have produced a different version of Thomson's design in Figure 2.2.

Her slogan was: 'Edge goes to your head'. She then subjected this advertisement to further critical analysis as she considered other people with shaved heads (people living with AIDS and cancer) whom she had chosen to exclude from her gender-neutral and culturally inclusive advertisement. The aim here was to show that each new design is also a construction that privileges some interests at the expense of others. Participants constructed and deconstructed their own group advertisements, now with a much greater awareness of the relationship between domination, diversity and design.

Access was not a concept we worked with overtly; rather, it informed

---

[8] This advertisement was first drawn to my attention by Ana Ferreira, Nadine O'Connell and Frank Rumboll.

Figure 2.2 Advertisement: 'Edge Goes to Your Head'.
Photograph by Daniel Janks

our pedagogy. We demonstrated its importance by endeavouring to give participants from different language teaching backgrounds and contexts, multiple ways into the ideas and practices that underpinned the workshop activities. We enabled their access by using the range of knowledges and literacies that the participants brought to the workshop and by allowing them to use both verbal and visual modalities.

Access to Academic Literacy

This example is taken from my own teaching at the University of the Witwatersrand in South Africa and concerns two highly intelligent post-graduate students, Wayne Schell and Nomowabo Mntambo.[9] They came to my Master's level critical literacy class with very different histories. Each of them found access to academic discourse an ongoing struggle.

Wayne was a closet dyslexic. He says:

> Part of what made life difficult for me at University was because I would not tell anyone that there was a problem. I thought I could make it through University and no one would know that I was dyslexic. This was mainly because the majority of people with whom they came into contact would class people who have learning

---

[9] Both of these students wish to be identified.

disabilities as mentally deficient. I could not let people think of me that way so I kept the secret quiet.

(Schell, Journal, 19 October 1998)

He is highly articulate but he finds writing slow and difficult:

> The real problem I have is that I cannot organise what it is I write. It starts with the small stuff . . . like sentences. They are great when I say them in my head, somehow when they get onto the paper they sort of change and become something that does not seem good. I manage to get the syntax all wrong and they do not say on the paper what they say in my head . . . Now the fun begins. When I put a group of these 'syntactically challenged' sentences together, it is as if one and one makes three, I magically create a 'logically challenged' paragraph.

(Schell, Journal, 19 October 1998)

Nomowabo is a mature black woman from the rural Eastern Cape. Her primary language is IsiXhosa and although she speaks completely fluent English, she finds reading academic English demanding:

> When I first got to the University I had to start at a slight disadvantage because I had so much catching up to do . . . all the discourses were new to me. I have never felt so stupid in my life. I had all this reading to do and much of it made no sense to me . . . I began to wonder if I had ever understood English.

(Mntambo, Interview, 1998)

Like Wayne, and Lilly-Rose (Chapter 1), she feels the need to hide her 'inabilities':

> For a long time I could not even write the two-page responses that she [the lecturer] required us to do because I felt all my stupidity would be there for all to see. At least if I did not respond to questions in class nobody would know how 'dumb' I felt.

(Mntambo, Interview, 1998)

Both of these students, mature professionals in their own right, found this struggle painful because of how it made them feel about themselves and their abilities. They experienced their *diversity* as giving them identities which were outside the mainstream; they recognised the *dominant* institutional genres and discourses as both hegemonic and desirable; they feared that they might never gain full *access* to them and they could not see that they had any resources for changing either the discourses or themselves. Moreover, each read the other as already through the 'discourse gates'. Nomowabo saw Wayne as an privileged white male, and Wayne, a Master's student, saw Nomowabo as my more advanced doctoral student.

I think the turning point for both of them came with the reading of Gee's *Social Linguistics and Literacies* (1990).[10] On the first page of his introduction Gee says:

> You learn the Discourse by becoming a member of the group: you start as a 'beginner', watch what's done, go along with the group *as if you know what you are doing when you don't*, and eventually you can do it on your own. [my italics]

This is what Gee calls 'mushfaking' (1990: 159). Suddenly Wayne and Nomowabo realised that they were not alone. Not only were *both of them* trying to walk the walk and talk the talk, but that this is how any one gains access to a secondary Discourse. What they also realised is that entering a new discourse did not necessitate their rejecting the discourses they already had. They began to revalue and reclaim their primary discourses as well as the other discourses they inhabited. Nomowabo, it should be noted, speaks four languages, is currently learning Sesotho, and is in addition a successful teacher educator. Wayne in the concluding entry to his academic log explains it thus:

> As I look back along this academic journey I have certainly learnt a lot. Perhaps the most important thing that I have learnt is that I am dyslexic. When I say that this is important it is because I have learnt that it is a characteristic of a Wayne and not the defining aspect of a Wayne. As I have learnt that this is just a part of a multifaceted person who is not one stable body but is made up of different parts in different discourses.
>
> (Schell, Interview, 16 November 1998)

This example shows how the issue of access is linked to the diverse subjectivities that students bring with them to the learning situation; how powerful discourses are simultaneously both a threat and the object of desire; how secondary discourses provide us with other ways of knowing the world, that is, with the productive diversity necessary for reconstruction and redesign. In reconstructing themselves, these students found positions from which to speak. Their stories reveal a synthesis of access, diversity, dominance and design.

---

[10] Because of his dyslexia, Wayne had to work long hours to manage the writing and reading assignments for the course. His particular struggle was with writing. Nomowabo, on the other hand, found that the linguistic demands of English at this level (and the demands of mastering a new secondary Discourse) made reading particularly difficult.

Looking Forward

This purpose of this book is to develop and refine this interdependent model of critical literacy. The next two chapters consider dominance/power. The next chapter looks at different theories of power and the relationship between language, power and identity. Chapter 4 provides approaches to analysing texts in order to understand how they work to position their readers and whose interests are served by this positioning.

CHAPTER **3**

Language and Power

The first dimension in my critical literacy synthesis model is domination. At the time that I produced this model, I was working with a neo-Marxist theory of power, which saw power as being in the hands of dominant groups in society who have power over subordinate groups. Classical Marxism focuses on class relations and the oppression of the working class. Subsequently Marxist theory expanded to include other forms of domination and subordination based on social formations such as gender, race, ethnicity, sexuality. Closely tied to this theory of power are theories of ideology, and the word 'critical' came to signal work that unmasked the ideological underpinning of texts and discourses. More recently, I have come to understand that Foucault's theory of power is as important for critical literacy. In *Discipline and Punish*, Foucault traces the historical movement from sovereign power, power *over*, to disciplinary power in which discourses produce truth and technologies of the self which constitute individuals as embodied social subjects (Foucault, 1975). In this chapter, I will explain both these theories of power and I will argue that both are important for understanding literacy. In order to include both in my own revised model of critical literacy, I need to replace the word 'domination' with the more inclusive word, 'power'.

Neo-Marxist Theories of Power

'Critical' as used in post-structuralist, neo-Marxist discourses requires that analysis is put to work to reveal the hidden ideologies of texts. Here the aim of critical deconstruction is to reveal how power works, to see the play of interests in the textual instantiations of discourses. Who benefits from these textual constructions? Who is disadvantaged? Power is seen as oppressive: social relations invest members of dominant groups with power over others whom they subordinate, constructing a world of 'top dogs' and 'underdogs' (1993). According to Marxist theorists such as Althusser (1971) and Gramsci (1971), subordinate groups can be persuaded, often below the level of consciousness, to consent to these relations or, where this fails, they can be coerced. The more people consent to the conditions of their existence, the less they have to be coerced. Consent is produced in institutions such as the family, the school, the media, and the church, which Althusser regards as ideological apparatuses. Part of the work of critical literacy is to make these workings of power visible, to denaturalise 'common sense' assumptions (Gramsci, 1971) and to reveal them as constructed representations of the social order, serving the interests of some at the expense of others. Critical literacy within this discourse is seen as an emancipatory project in which subordinated groups are rescued from 'false consciousness' (Eagleton, 1991: 89–90) in the interests of social justice; it relies on uncovering the ideological meanings in texts and practices. It assumes an ideologically free space from which to speak the truth, if not a more 'scientific' truth, then at least, in relation to social equity, a more ethical one.

Thompson (1990) gives a detailed account of the history of and struggle over the concept 'ideology', as does Eagleton (1991). For Thompson,

> The analysis of ideology . . . is primarily concerned with the ways in which symbolic forms intersect with relations of power. It is concerned with the ways in which meaning is mobilized in the social world and serves thereby to bolster up individuals or groups who occupy positions of power.
>
> (Thompson, 1990: 56)

Thompson calls his conception of ideology a 'critical conception of ideology' because he wants to reserve ideology for those meanings 'which serve to establish and sustain relations of domination' (1990: 56). According to Eagleton a number of theorists view ideology as

> the medium in which men and women fight out their social and political battles at the level of signs, meanings and representations.
>
> (1991: 11)

For him, ideology is concerned less with signification, than with 'conflicts within the field of signification' (p. 11). In terms of this view, it is possible to see the positions of both dominant and oppositional groups as ideological. For Thompson this does not constitute a critical conception of ideology. The strength of Thompson's theory of ideology is that it provides us with powerful machinery for understanding the relationship between language, power and domination. Its weakness is that it does not provide ways of analysing how subordinated groups harness language to contest or transform dominant practices, essential to the notion of design and reconstruction.

Thompson's Modes of Operation of Ideology [1]

One way of understanding ideology is to see how it works. In *Studies in the Theory of Ideology* (1984) and *Ideology and Modern Culture* (1990), Thompson distinguishes five general modes through which ideology can operate: legitimation, dissimulation, unification, fragmentation, reification. His theory is particularly useful because it offers a way of thinking about how ideology is realised in texts by identifying the linguistic and non-linguistic symbols which are regularly used to obtain particular ideological effects. He is careful to limit his claims: these symbols are not only or always used for these purposes, nor are these modes of ideology only realised in these ways; nevertheless he gives us a useful way of thinking the relation between symbolic forms and social effect.

Legitimation is the process by which relations of domination may be established and maintained 'by being presented as legitimate, that is, just and worthy of support' (1990: 61). According to Thompson this is usually achieved by three discursive strategies – rationalisation, universalisation and narrativisation. In rationalisation an argument is mounted to justify something. Rationalisation usually depends on a chain of reasoning. In universalisation a set of institutional arrangements which privilege certain groups only, are presented as serving the interests of all. In narrativisation stories are used to naturalise socially interested constructions of the world. Stories are presented as embodying universal timeless truths and are often used as a reference point for whole communities. Thompson includes histories, films, novels and jokes as examples of the power of narrative to construct realities which represent the apparent order of things.

Dissimulation is the process by which relations of domination are concealed or obscured. Euphemism is an obvious means of disguising unpleasant actions, events or social relations and of redescribing them positively. Displacement and trope are two other means of dissimulating. Displacement is where a term usually used to refer to one thing is used to

---

[1] This explanation of Thompson's modes of operation of ideology was first published in *Pretexts: Studies in Writing and Culture*, 7(2), 195–212, under the title 'Reading Womanpower'.

refer to another in order to transfer either positive or negative values from the one to the other. The Union Buildings in Pretoria, the seat of the apartheid administration for 47 years, was also the site of Mandela's inauguration ceremony. At the time the Pretoria City Council was running an advertising campaign to construct a new and positive image for the city. The word 'union', originally symbolising the State of Union achieved after the Anglo-Boer wars, was displaced in the advertisements so that 'union' came to stand for the union of all the people of South Africa in the new democracy. For Thompson, trope or the use of figurative language, which enables parts to stand for wholes and wholes to stand for parts as well as the non-literal and metaphorical use of language, is the third powerful means of obfuscation.

Unification and fragmentation are related processes in that they work in opposite directions – the one seeks to unite and join people for ideological purposes and the other seeks to split people off from one another. Unification establishes a collective identity which unites individuals despite their differences. Fragmentation is a process of splitting people off from one another despite their similarities in order to divide and rule. Unity is the means of establishing an 'us'; fragmentation is tied to this process of unification, as a collective identity is partly forged by the construction of an Other or Others, a 'them' who are different from 'us'. The relation between unification and fragmentation is captured well in the irony inherent in the motto on the South African coat of arms being 'Unity is Strength', while apartheid, which epitomises difference, division and fragmentation, was its reigning political ideology.

Thompson offers standardisation and symbolisation of unity as ways in which unification may be effected. Language standardisation is a good example of a social process used to naturalise the construction of a national language and a collective identity. The variety of the language which is codified as the standard is invariably the variety approved of or spoken by the dominant members of the society. Not all members of society have equal access to this variety so this unificatory move simultaneously dissimulates inequality. Symbols of unity can also be constructed to forge a collective identity. Non-linguistic examples include flags, uniforms, corporate logos, emblems. Linguistic examples include school songs, national anthems, slogans.

Reification is the last of Thompson's modes of operation of ideology. To reify is to turn a process into a thing or an event. Processes are encoded using verbs which have actors and which take place in time and space. Reified things just are – their socio-historical origins are concealed.

Reification: relations of domination and subordination may be established and sustained by representing a transitory, historical state of affairs as if it were permanent, natural, outside of time.

(Thompson, 1990: 65)

Reification is realised in symbolic forms by naturalisation, externalisation, passivisation and nominalisation. Nominalisation is the linguistic process of turning a verb into a nominal (i.e. a noun). Here an action is turned into a thing or a state. Passivisation, also a linguistic process, is used to convert active voice to passive voice. Both these processes delete actors and agency and change what is thematised (fronted) in the clause. Naturalisation is the means by which socially constructed realities are presented as natural and inevitable. This is what Barthes (1972: 143) calls 'myth' – the process of turning history into nature. Externalisation is a process whereby social rituals, customs, traditions and institutions become fixed and immutable, external to the socio-historical conditions of their production.

I have tabulated Thompson's ideas in order to create a useful rubric for analysing texts (Table 3.1). In thinking about texts, it is useful to see which modes of ideology are operative and how they are realised.

It is worth noticing that not all modes operate for every text. In the Khobella text, Standard Bank's social responsibility projects are used to legitimate the bank in post-apartheid South Africa, while dissimulating that it is a profit-making institution. As already discussed, the bank works with a literacy/illiteracy binary that constructs Khobella as dependent and a 'burden' to others. Literacy, used here as the standard for differentiation, is equated with 'a better life' despite research evidence which shows this to be a myth (Graff, 1978; Stuckey, 1991). South African research (Breir & Prinsloo, 1996) demonstrates a wide range of adult literacies that enable people without dominant print literacy to do much more than just 'get by'. By ignoring the social and historical conditions that produce illiteracy in South Africa, Khobella's inability to read, write or count is naturalised, it just is. Interventions then address the needs of individuals without leading to systemic change. The individualisation of the problem is emphasised by the photograph of Jimmy Khobella. (That we read this as Khobella is an effect of juxtaposition; it is much more likely to be a photograph of an actor or model.)

The first Edge advertisement (Figure 2.1) can also be used to illustrate Thompson's modes of operation of ideology. The photographs in the Edge text show women as clumsy, off-balance and ridiculous. Not only is the woman fully dressed but in the second row she is literally boxed-in, trapped. Humour dissimulates this demeaning representation and euphemism, 'all the tricky places', is used to obfuscate where exactly women shave. Shaving,

Table 3.1 Thompson's Modes of Operation of Ideology[2]

Representation of something as legitimate, worthy of support	LEGITIMATION	**RATIONALISATION** – construction of a chain of reasoning (based on the legality of rules, sanctity of traditions) to defend or justify a set of social rules. **UNIVERSALISATION** – institutional arrangements which serve individual interests represented as serving the interests of all. **NARRATIVISATION** – claims in stories which recount the past and treat the present as part of a timeless and cherished tradition, invention of traditions.	
Relations of domination concealed, denied, obscured	DISSIMULATION	**DISPLACEMENT** – one symbol displaced to symbol associated with it. **EUPHEMISM** – re-description for positive evaluation, naming slippage – shifting of sense. **TROPE** – the use of figurative language *Synecdoche:* whole for part or part for whole. *Metonymy:* attribute or related characteristic of something taken for the thing itself. *Metaphor:* application of term to an object to which it is not literally applicable.	
Unifies people – creates an 'us'	UNIFICATION	**STANDARDISATION** – symbolic form adapted to standard framework. **SYMBOLISATION OF UNITY** – collective identity which overrides differences and divisions.	
Divide and rule – 'us' and 'them'	FRAGMENTATION	**DIFFERENTIATION** – emphasising differences – fragmenting gaps that might unite and mount a challenge. **EXPURGATION OF THE OTHER** – construction of an enemy within or without which is evil, harmful or threatening, which individuals need collectively to expel or expurgate.	
Transitory states presented as permanent, natural outside of time	REIFICATION	**NATURALISATION – REIFICATION** – social historical state of affairs presented as natural. **EXTERNALISATION** – social historical phenomena portrayed as permanent and unchanging, ever-recurring customs, traditions, institutions. **NOMINALISATION/PASSIVISATION** – focus on particular 'themes' (fronting) at the expense of others, delete actors and agency, processes as things or events, elide references to time and space (tenseless).	

Permission to use the men's advertisement for the Edge razor was refused. The name of the product has been changed but a description of the original advertisement is included here.

The men's advertisement for the Edge razor is similar to the women's advertisement. It is the same size and has the same overall design. It is 16 cms across and 21 cms down. It consists of four rows of pictures of a man supposedly playing table-tennis. Instead of a razor, he has a table-tennis bat in his hand. Each picture is enclosed within a separate rectangular frame, eight in the first row, four in the second row, five in the third row and thirteen in the fourth row. The length of the first row is 3 cms down, the second is 4 cms, the third is 6 cms and the fourth is 2.5 cms. The width across is adjusted according to the number of picture in each row and in no frame is the man seen to be touching the edge of the frame or crammed into the space.

The man is tall, athletic, dark-haired, young and good-looking. He is wearing a sleeveless dark top, long track pants and trainers. In each image he is show standing, with both feet firmly on the ground, balanced and poised ready to hit the ball. He is in perfect control of his body. His body is shown facing the camera, turned to hit the ball with a forehand shot. Instead of mimicking the act of shaving, his body mimics the actions of the razor itself.

Below these images is a separate box slightly narrower than the rows of men and centred. A photograph of the men's Edge razor is placed here together with the slogan. The bright red razor stands out agains the shades of black, white and grey used elsewhere. The words refer to the razor, which 'rotates', 'swivels', 'pivots' and 'protects'. Its 'smart design' gives a 'quicker, closer, safer shave'. A very small font is used for this reference to shaving.

Figure 3.1 An Advertisement for 'Edge Razors', Targeted at Men.

a culture-specific practice, is reified and the Edge razor is legitimised by claims that it is 'faster' and 'safer' with a 'unique wire-guard system'. The use of pastel mauve for the razor and as the background colour for the print text, suggests that women who shave are feminine, as opposed to those who do not. The softness of the colour is echoed by the name of the razor, 'Silk Effects'.

That there is 'fragmentation' in relation to a gender binary can be seen by comparing this Edge advertisement with that for men (Figure 3.1).

Here red, a primary colour, which is much bolder than mauve, is used. The man is not shown shaving but in action. The movements of his body

Note to Table 3.1

[2] The final column is left blank as a space in which to insert one's analysis of specific texts. This creates a template for text analysis using Thompson's categories.

are a visual metaphor for the way the razor 'rotates', 'swivels' and 'pivots'. In every picture he is balanced, with both feet firmly on the ground. Metaphorically the man becomes the razor – he is the Edge and he has the edge. Saussure's structuralist proposition that one can often see what something is by seeing what it is not, holds true here (de Saussure, 1972/ 1990: 162). The differences between these advertisements show them to be socially constructed representations of gender, thus denaturalising them. Whose interests are served when men are shown to be more in control than women, is obvious. These texts were designed by the same advertising agency and published at the same time, June 1999. They appeared in different magazines, *Cosmopolitan* and *Men's Health*, and were probably not designed to be read against each other.

At the Institute run with Pat Thomson in Australia, the workshop participants were asked to put their own bodies into some of the positions used to represent men in the advertisement, then to put themselves into some of the positions used to represent women shaving. This was designed to let them experience how the male body positions give them a sense of being balanced and in control and the women's positions produce the opposite effect.

Thompson's modes of operation of ideology can also be used to design critical literacy activities for students. Figure 3.2, 'Common Identity, Different Identities' is an activity based on unification and fragmentation and the use of symbols to forge group identity. Figure 3.3, 'Leaving a Group', shows how apartheid produced fragmentation. If racial classification were biological rather than social, then it would not be possible for people to be re-classified. Figures 3.4a and 3.4b, 'Unequal Naming: The Gulf War' and 'Mad Dogs and Englishmen', shows the use of us/them language and how euphemisms are used to ameliorate *our* actions. The activity in Figure 3.4a is based on an adaptation of an article which appeared in the *Guardian Weekly*, 3 February 1991, which is reproduced unabridged in Figure 3.4b.

What is clear is that to be a member of a community, you need to understand the community's 'rules', including its rules for speaking. These rules help to create **a common identity** for members of the community. How far you have to follow the rules and how far you are allowed to break the rules differs in different communities.

There are also groups within communities – and the different groups all have **different identities** with more or less different rules.

COMMON IDENTITY

In groups or pairs, think about your own school. Look at its traditions, and motto. Also look at the words of your school's songs and warcries. How does your school create an identity for itself compared to other schools? Does your school try to make its students proud to belong to it? How?

DIFFERENT IDENTITIES

Think about the students in your school. How have they divided themselves into different social groups? Can you identify them by the things they do? By the way they dress? By the language they use? How else can you identify them? How easy is it to get into one of these groups? What do you have to do to get into a group?

For discussion

Why do most people need to be members of a group?
What kinds of groups do the people you know belong to?
What can happen when somebody decides not to belong to a group?

Figure 3.2 Common Identity, Different Identities.
© 1993 H. Janks. Source: *Language Identity and Power*. Johannesburg, Wits University Press and Hodder and Stoughton.

Read the passage first, then answer the questions.

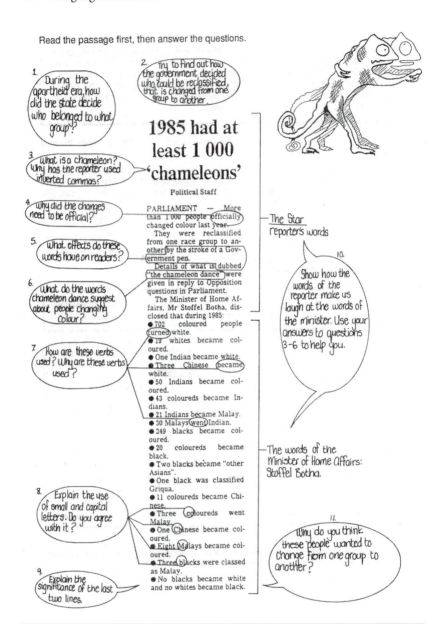

1. During the apartheid era, how did the state decide who belonged to what group?

2. Try to find out how the government decided who could be reclassified, that is changed from one group to another.

3. What is a chameleon? Why has the reporter used inverted commas?

4. Why did the changes need to be official?

5. What effects do these words have on readers?

6. What do the words chameleon dance suggest about people changing colour?

7. How are these verbs used? Why are these verbs used?

8. Explain the use of small and capital letters. Do you agree with it?

9. Explain the significance of the last two lines.

10. Show how the words of the reporter make us laugh at the words of the minister. Use your answers to questions 3-6 to help you.

11. Why do you think these people wanted to change from one group to another?

1985 had at least 1 000 'chameleons'

Political Staff

PARLIAMENT — More than 1 000 people officially changed colour last year.

They were reclassified from one race group to another by the stroke of a Government pen.

Details of what is dubbed "the chameleon dance" were given in reply to Opposition questions in Parliament.

The Minister of Home Affairs, Mr Stoffel Botha, disclosed that during 1985:

● 702 coloured people turned white.
● 19 whites became coloured.
● One Indian became white.
● Three Chinese became white.
● 50 Indians became coloured.
● 43 coloureds became Indians.
● 21 Indians became Malay.
● 30 Malays went Indian.
● 249 blacks became coloured.
● 20 coloureds became black.
● Two blacks became "other Asians".
● One black was classified Griqua.
● 11 coloureds became Chinese.
● Three coloureds went Malay.
● One Chinese became coloured.
● Eight Malays became coloured.
● Three blacks were classed as Malay.
● No blacks became white and no whites became black.

The Star reporter's words

The words of the Minister of Home Affairs: Stoffel Botha.

Figure 3.3 Leaving a Group.
© 1993 H. Janks. Source: *Language Identity and Power*. Johannesburg, Wits University Press and Hodder and Stoughton.

UNEQUAL NAMING: THE GULF WAR 1991

Find out what you can about the Gulf War. Who was fighting whom? Why? Who were their allies?

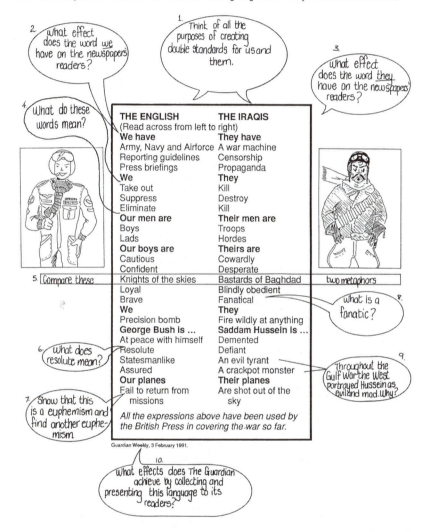

Figure 3.4a Unequal Naming: The Gulf War.
Source: *Language Identity and Power*. Johannesburg, Wits University Press and Hodder and Stoughton. © Guardian Newspapers. Used with permission.

Mad dogs and Englishmen

We have	They have
Army, Navy and Air Force	A war machine
Reporting guidelines	Censorship
Press briefings	Propaganda

We	They
Take out	Destroy
Suppress	Destroy
Eliminate	Kill
Neutralise or decapitate	Kill
Decapitate	Kill
Dig in	Cower in their foxholes

We launch	They launch
First strikes	Sneak missile attacks
Pre-emptively	Without provocation

Our men are . . .	Their men are . . .
Boys	Troops
Lads	Hordes

Our boys are . . .	Theirs are . . .
Professional	Brainwashed
Lion-hearts	Paper tigers
Cautious	Cowardly
Confident	Desperate
Heroes	Cornered
Dare-devils	Cannon fodder
Young knights of the skies	Bastards of Baghdad
Loyal	Blindly obedient
Desert rats	Mad dogs
Resolute	Ruthless
Brave	Fanatical

Our boys are motivated by	Their boys are motivated by
An old fashioned sense of duty	Fear of Saddam

Our boys	Their boys
Fly into the jaws of hell	Cower in concrete bunkers

Our ships are . . .	Iraq ships are . . .
An armada	A navy

Israeli non-retaliation is	Iraqi non-retaliation is
An act of great statesmanship	Blundering/Cowardly

The Belgians are . . .	The Belgians are also . . .
Yellow	Two-faced

Our missiles are . . .	Their missiles are . . .
Like Luke Skywalker zapping Darth Vader	Ageing duds (*rhymes with Scuds*)

Our missiles cause . . .	Their missiles cause . . .
Collateral damage	Civilian casualties

We . . .	They . . .
Precision bomb	Fire wildly at anything in the skies

Our PoWs are . . .	Their PoWs are . . .
Gallant boys	Overgrown schoolchildren

George Bush is . . .	Saddam Hussein is . . .
At peace with himself	Demented
Resolute	Defiant
Statesmanlike	An evil tyrant
Assured	A crackpot monster

Our planes . . .	Their planes . . .
Suffer a high rate of attrition	Are shot out of the sky
Fail to return from missions	Are Zapped

● *All the expressions above have been used by the British press in covering the war so far.*

Figure 3.4b Mad Dogs and Englishmen.
© Guardian Newspapers.

The activity in Figure 3.5, 'Top Dogs and Underdogs', is designed to make students think about dominant and subordinate groups in society. The activity, which I developed in 1993, was designed to show children that individuals are differently empowered in their different identities. Nevertheless it reproduces a binary logic based on dominant and dominated social positions.

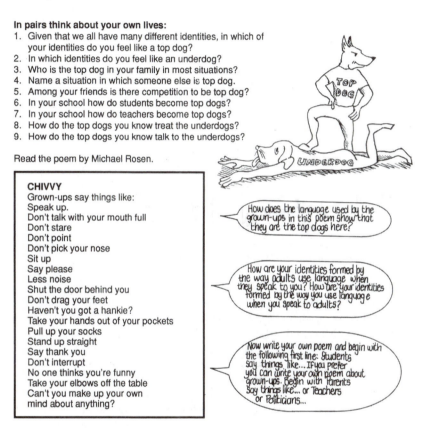

In pairs think about your own lives:
1. Given that we all have many different identities, in which of your identities do you feel like a top dog?
2. In which identities do you feel like an underdog?
3. Who is the top dog in your family in most situations?
4. Name a situation in which someone else is top dog.
5. Among your friends is there competition to be top dog?
6. In your school how do students become top dogs?
7. In your school how do teachers become top dogs?
8. How do the top dogs you know treat the underdogs?
9. How do the top dogs you know talk to the underdogs?

Read the poem by Michael Rosen.

CHIVVY
Grown-ups say things like:
Speak up.
Don't talk with your mouth full
Don't stare
Don't point
Don't pick your nose
Sit up
Say please
Less noise
Shut the door behind you
Don't drag your feet
Haven't you got a hankie?
Take your hands out of your pockets
Pull up your socks
Stand up straight
Say thank you
Don't interrupt
No one thinks you're funny
Take your elbows off the table
Can't you make up your own
mind about anything?

How does the language used by the grown-ups in this poem show that they are the top dogs here?

How are your identities formed by the way adults use language when they speak to you? How are your identities formed by the way you use language when you speak to adults?

Now write your own poem and begin with the following first line: Students say things like... If you prefer you can write your own poem about grown-ups. Begin with Parents say things like... or Teachers or Politicians...

Figure 3.5 Top Dogs and Underdogs.
© 1993 H. Janks. Source: *Language Identity and Power*. Johannesburg, Wits University Press and Hodder and Stoughton.

Table 3.2 summarises the binary oppositions reported in the literature (Wilshire, 1989: 95–96; Davies, 1994). Davies' discussion of these binary metaphors (see Table 3.2) is helpful.

First Davies considers which of the metaphors ascribed to femaleness she 'resonated' with, because they matched how she saw herself, how she would like to see herself, or how society expected her to be as a woman. She

Table 3.2 Male/Female Binary, Adapted from Wilshire, 1989; Davies, 1994

MALE	FEMALE
knowledge	ignorance
higher up	lower down
positive, good	negative, bad
mind	body
rational	irrational
order	chaos
control	laissez faire
objective	subjective
fact	fiction
goals	process
light	dark
written text	oral tradition
public domain	private domain
detached	attached
secular	sacred
linear	cyclical
permanence	change
hard	soft
independent	dependent
individual	social
active	passive

Based on and adapted from Wilshire, D. (1989). *The Use of Myth, Image and the Female Body in Revisioning Knowledge.* New Brunswick: Rutgers University Press.

concluded that overall they make a highly recognisable set of concepts through which femaleness is lived and imagined in our culture (Davies, 1994: 9). She also examined herself in relation to the metaphors attributed to maleness and concluded that she has acquired many of these through education and her professional work. She suggests that this is important

> since it reveals the way in which we can hold intact the idea of maleness and femaleness as binary opposites, even recognise ourselves in that division, at the same time as we know that we can enumerate many examples of transgressions, movements outside the binary.
>
> (Davies, 1994: 9)

Phil Cormack, at the University of South Australia, has an interesting way of working with these binaries. He asks his students to consider which other socially constructed binaries these structured oppositions for male and female can be applied to. It is worth thinking about the extent to which these metaphors resonate for you with the following binaries:

> - Male/Female;
> - Literate/Illiterate;
> - Adult/Child or youth;
> - White/Black;
> - High culture/Popular culture;
> - Heterosexual/Homosexual;
> - Culture/Nature.
>
> It is important to recognise these oppositions as social constructions rather than as biological or natural differences and to think about why this matters.

Fortunately children are smart. Helen Grant (1999) used 'top dogs and underdogs' as the starting point for a whole unit of work on anti-racism with middle and upper primary school students. While many students could articulate when they feel like a top dog and when they feel like an underdog, some of her students decided that they were neither top dogs nor underdogs and invented the concept of 'middle dogs' for themselves, thus refusing the binary (1999: 20).

Foucault argues against overarching conceptions of domination, 'a binary structure with dominators on one side and dominated on the other'. Instead he sees relations of domination as taking many possible forms (1980: 142).

> In speaking of domination I do not have in mind that solid and global kind of domination that one person exercises over others, or one group over another, but the manifold forms of domination that can be exercised within society.
>
> (Foucault, 1980: 96)

It is these ordinary relations between people, embodied in our every day interactions, imbued with power and situated in the local, that 'top dogs and underdogs' asks students to consider.

Foucault and Power

Foucault turns away from a theory of ideology. For him,

> The political question . . . is not error, illusion, alienated consciousness or ideology; it is truth itself.
>
> (1980: 133)

As already discussed in Chapter 1, for him discourses produce truth.

'Truth' is to be understood as a system of ordered procedures for the production, regulation, distribution, circulation and operation of statements. [It] is linked in a circular relation with systems of power which produce and sustain it, and to effects of power which it induces and which extend it. A 'regime' of truth.

(1980: 133)

He is interested in the procedures which constitute discourses and the means by which power constitutes them as knowledge, that is, as truth. Conversely, he is interested in the ways in which these discourses of truth then bolster power. For example, under George W. Bush, quantitative psychometric research on literacy was increasingly viewed as the only valid 'scientific' research – it was the research that received government funding and informed government policy. Constructed as the 'true' discourse about literacy, this effectively excluded qualitative research based on ethnographic research methods and a socio-cultural theory of literacy. Here power was used to sustain a particular discourse and to establish its hegemony. This discourse then has effects of power, setting norms for literacy which can be surveilled, examined, and used to legitimate the Republican party's policy of 'no child left behind'. This policy resulted in 'scripted programmes' designed to produce a quick fix. Larson (2001) provides a critique of these programmes. It is worth noting in passing the way in which the naming of this policy also worked to legitimate it (who in their right mind would want a child to be left behind?), to dissimulate its practices (different and dumbed-down programmes were offered to at-risk children), and to advocate unification while actually producing differentiation. No wonder Foucault thinks that 'discourse is the power which is to be seized' (1970: 110).

Foucault moves away from seeing power as negative, working through the modes of 'censorship, exclusion, blockage, and repression' (1980: 59). Instead, he sees power as strong because it produces effects. In addition to producing effects 'at the level of desire – and also at the level of knowledge' (1980: 59), power infiltrates the minutiae of daily life, affecting the 'processes which subject our bodies, govern our gestures and dictate our behaviours' (1980: 97). This is clearly illustrated in the poster *Rules for good listening* found on the wall of a Grade 1 primary school classroom in South Africa (Dixon, 2004).

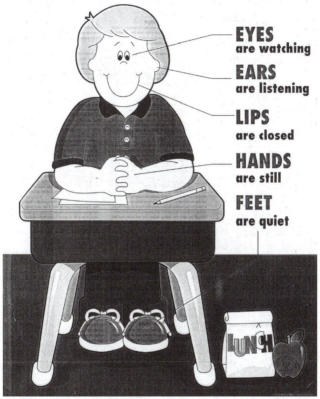

Figure 3.6 Rules for Good Listening.
© Carson Dellosa Publishing CD-6068, Rules for Good Listening. Used with permission.

Therefore, in studying power,

> we should try to discover how it is that [human] subjects are gradually, progressively, really and materially constituted through a multiplicity of organisms, forces, energies, materials, desires, thoughts, etc.
> (Foucault, 1980: 97)

If we take seriously Foucault's view of power as having a 'capillary form of existence' that 'reaches into the very grain of individuals, touches their bodies and inserts itself into their actions and attitudes, their discourses, learning processes and everyday lives' (Foucault, 1980: 39), then this necessitates a focus on the effects of the texts, knowledges, and practices that we bring into our literacy classrooms.

A practical illustration of this can be found by interrogating your practices and unpacking the effects of these practices on your own students.

- What effects do high stakes tests have on your students? Take care to specify which effects for which students.
- What effects does grading have on your students? Which students?

Discipline

- What effects do the furniture and the spatial organisation of your classroom have on students' bodies?
- Look at the Grade 1 *Rules for listening*, Figure 3.6. What are the (unwritten) rules for speaking/writing and listening/reading in your classroom? Think about the management of students' bodies for these activities.
- What are the rules for 'good citizenship' in your classroom? Who decided on these rules? Who monitors them? What happens when students transgress?

The organisation of knowledge

- If the students in your class come from diverse backgrounds would you say that the different funds of knowledge (Moll, 1992) they bring to school are equally validated in your classroom? Give examples.
- What effects does the way power organises knowledge have
  – on you as a teacher?
  – on your students?

Foucault sees modern forms of power as dependent on technologies of self, such as surveillance, examination and confession. Put simply, external forms of surveillance by parents, teachers and other authority figures (with repercussions for bad behaviour) are internalised so that we learn to discipline ourselves. We each acquire a private *flic dans la tête*, a cop in the head,[3] that regulates our own behaviour. Constant examination and reporting of students' behaviour and development produces normalisa-

---

[3] Both *flic* in French and *cop* in English are colloquial expressions for the police.

tion. Students who don't or won't fit the norms are marked as deviant. Conformity is supported by confessional practices such as counselling, therapy and self-evaluation. Comber's research, in which she was a participant observer over a two-year period in four different literacy classrooms, shows how teachers

> deployed a number of normalising techniques to discipline students to be made literate, including frequent 'pep talks', individualised student monitoring or 'patrols' and continual running commentaries or 'voice-over'. The ideal literate student was constituted as an ethical subject: as a self-regulating, productive and socially responsible worker. . . . Teachers stressed the productive use of time and were highly concerned about raising the standards of students' work. To these ends students were trained in technologies of the self, 'self-assessments' where they regularly accounted for themselves in writing across a number of pre-specified domains.
>
> (Comber, 1996: iv)

Here we see Foucault's notion of productive power in operation. The literacy classrooms that Comber observed reveal the practices that produce self-disciplined normative subjects, in operation. The subjectivities that are produced become ingrained dispositions that shape students' bodies, actions and attitudes. This is in turn produces a regulated society. While there is a price to pay, the alternative is an ungovernable society. In the last stages of the liberation struggle in South Africa, the African National Congress adopted a policy of civil disobedience that was designed to make the country ungovernable. It is clearly far more difficult to govern people who will not, and do not, govern themselves. Since independence it has been difficult for the post-apartheid government to re-establish what Foucault calls 'governmentality' ('the conduct of conduct'). South Africans are not compliant citizens. An example of this can be seen in the number of arrests made and fines issued on one weekend in Johannesburg in an anti-crime blitz. See Figure 3.7.

Anti-crime blitz nets 500 in Greater Joburg

Success for law enforcement as police set up 20 roadblocks in and around city

By **Baldwin Ndaba**

It was a tough weekend for criminals in and around Johannesburg. More than 500 suspects were arrested in two large-scale anti-crime blitzes, and stolen and hijacked vehicles, firearms and contraband worth hundreds of thousands of rands were recovered.

In Johannesburg, police on Saturday launched Operation Matrix, a weekend-long action which formed part of National Commissioner Jackie Selebi's ongoing anti-crime initiative, Operation Crackdown.

Johannesburg police spokesperson Inspector Dennis Adriao said more than 300 police officers, assisted by Metro Police and SANDF personnel, conducted 20 roadblocks at which 700 vehicles and 1 900 people were searched.

The Johannesburg operation netted 18 people for crimes including possession of dagga, traffic offences, possession of stolen vehicles, and for being in the country illegally.

A total of 124 people were fined for traffic offences.

"Three stolen vehicles were recovered and three people were arrested while in possession of a stolen car. Another person was arrested for reckless and negligent driving and two others for drinking in public."

Adriao also said the police recovered five hijacked vehicles on Saturday, two of which were found within 30 minutes of having been stolen in Norwood and Wynberg respectively. Another stolen car was found abandoned in Alexandra.

Two people were arrested in Westbury for possession of a stolen car.

Police also apprehended a man for fraud, and another for a murder committed in Randburg.

Other suspects are facing charges of housebreaking, possession of unlicensed firearms and escaping from custody.

On the East Rand, local police conducted their own crime-prevention operation.

They arrested 483 people for crimes such as attempted murder, armed robbery, drunk driving, illegal possession of a firearm, dealing in liquor without a permit, and being in possession of suspected stolen goods.

Figure 3.7 Anti-Crime Blitz Nets 500 in Greater Joburg.
Source: *The Star* newspaper, 7 September 2000. Used with permission.

Discourse and Identity

As we have seen, discourses according to Gee (1990: 142),

> are ways of being in the world, or forms of life which integrate words, acts, beliefs, attitudes, social identities, as well as gestures, glances, body positions and clothes.

For Foucault (1970), they are 'regimes of truth'.

> Every society has its own regime of truth, its 'general politics' of truth: that is the types of discourse which it accepts and makes function as true.
>
> (Foucault, 1980: 131)

'Discourse' is an abstract concept. Socially patterned ways of speaking/writing/designing and constructing truth are not tangible. They only become visible when they are realised in texts. Every text is an instance, hence 'instantiation', of a discourse. They are the material form that discourses take.

We have already seen how one of the effects of power is to constitute us as subjects. Now it is important to consider how who we are and how we think is profoundly influenced by the discourses that we inhabit. We acquire our primary discourse from our family and its extended community. I have chosen to use the word 'acquire' to borrow from Krashen's (1981) distinction between *acquisition* and *learning*. According to Krashen, acquisition is a process whereby we gain knowledge of a language and how to use it, without any explicit knowledge of its grammar, in the same way as infants acquire their home language. On the other hand, when we *learn* a language, it is in response to formal teaching, which gives us explicit knowledge of the grammar, of the structuring rules. By extension, when we *acquire* a discourse, we take on the ways of being in the world constituted by it. We are able to integrate 'words, acts, beliefs, attitudes, social identities, as well as gestures, glances, body positions and clothes' automatically, below the level of consciousness (Gee, 1990: 142). The more natural this way of being feels, the less visible it is to us.

Often when we enter a new community, we discover that our ways of being do not appear natural to members of this new community as their ways are quite different. From their perspective we are able to see our practices with fresh eyes, we become conscious of them. As discussed in Chapter 1, it is easier to see the world otherwise from the standpoint of a different discourse. Acquiring additional discourses can produce a sense of dislocation and confusion as we struggle to take on the new identities constituted by them. It is not enough to learn a new language, we also have to learn a whole new way of being in our bodies, a whole new habitus (Bourdieu, 1991). Michele Aucock's story, written as a contribution to this book, illustrates this well.

Washing Dishes Harmoniously
Michele Aucock

I am a thirty-seven-year-old white western woman recently married to a South Korean man. This past holiday was my first stay in Korea as a member of a Korean family. Prior to this I had lived in Korea for two years working as an English teacher. As the new daughter-in-law, married to the oldest son of the family, I knew that the family had very high expectations of me. In Korean culture, the oldest son is expected to take on the responsibility of the family. His wife is expected to move in to the family home and serve the parents-in-law until she and her husband take on primary roles. The role of Korean daughter-in-law is one that is totally foreign to me. I have grown up in a culture which encourages the daughters in a family to maintain very close bonds with her family of origin. In Korea the daughter-in-law is expected to sever the bonds with her family, in favour of those of her husband's family.

From what I had learned from Eui-Suk (my husband), his mother was a very hardworking and extremely accomplished housekeeper – her greatest strength being her cooking skills. At thirty-seven I am barely able to cook vegetables, let alone the multiple and complex dishes required at a Korean dining room table. Although apprehensive, I decided to take up the challenge and learn to cook/prepare a few Korean dishes under the mentorship of my mother-in-law. The plan was for me to surprise the family with a self-cooked Korean meal by the end of the holiday.

After one morning of being in the kitchen, I realised that the challenge was far greater than I anticipated. In sheer panic I decided that the best thing that I could do, to prove my worth, would be to do the washing-up after each meal. So, as soon as we finished our next meal, I dashed over to the kitchen sink and began the washing-up. The decision to become chief dishwasher wasn't without its problems. I am tall and Korean sinks are designed for shorter people. Prior to washing the dishes Eui-Suk's mother had in fact expressed concern that I would hurt my back. I became aware of a number of onlookers. Eui-Suk's mother appeared slightly distressed at what she saw happening at her kitchen sink. After an exchange of words, all in Korean, which I do not understand, Eui-Suk quietly slipped up behind me and gently informed me that I wasn't washing the dishes 'harmoniously'. It appears that I was splashing water on the outer surfaces of the sink. The fact that I could have used a dishcloth later to absorb any excess water wasn't an issue – the fact that I made a mess while washing was the issue. Eui-Suk then explained to me how to wash dishes in a harmonious and splash-free manner. At the time I was extremely angry at the criticism, I felt humiliated and inadequate, it was as if who I was was not good enough. Ultimately though, I was grateful as I could henceforth wash the family's dishes in an appropriate (and confident) manner . . .

How to wash dishes harmoniously
1 *All the eating utensils are placed in a round basin in the sink.*
2 *A dash of liquid soap is applied to a cloth.*
3 *Each utensil is lifted from the water-filled basin and thoroughly soaped-down. The utensil is then placed in the unoccupied part of the sink.*
4 *Once all the utensils are thoroughly soapy, they are ready to be rinsed under running water. This is the most challenging part of the ritual as each item is rinsed separately and thoroughly under running water.*
5 *Each item is gently shaken before being placed on the dish rack to dry. Should excess splashing occur during the process, the dish-washer is expected to stop the rinsing process and mop-up excess water with a dry dishcloth immediately.*

Aside from not following the set formula, one of my greatest faults was shaking the utensils too roughly and allowing water to splash every-where. Because, as one enters a Korean home, one is expected to take off one's shoes at the front door, any excess water on the floor could create discomfort to a person wearing socks or house slippers.

Notice Michele's feeling of inadequacy when the embodied adult identity that she brings to the menial task of washing dishes is constructed as wrong. It is as if who she is does not fit the new environment, both literally – she is too tall for the sink, and culturally – her splashing ruins the harmony in the home. Even if she could speak Korean fluently, she would still need to acquire a Korean habitus and a different set of beliefs and values in order to become a full member of this new discourse community. In short, she has to acquire a new identity.

I tell a similar story of alienation in Chapter 4, as a new émigré in the UK I felt as though we did not belong. These stories are worth telling.

> Think of situations in which you entered a new discourse community. Describe all the aspects involved in taking on a new identity – language, values, habitus, and the feelings this aroused. Compare this with other people's experiences.
>
> Find examples of students you have taught who are caught between the different worlds of their home and extended community and their school or college. Try to describe moments when you have witnessed their dislocation and sense of alienation.

Notice how the word *dislocation* captures the connection between habitus and habitat – how our identities are tied to place. The theory of multiple identities is important here. If every time we enter a new discourse community we have to give up our old identities, then we are simply assimilated into the new culture. If, on the other hand, we can add identities to the ones we already have, then (much as in theories of additive-multilingualism as opposed to subtractive-multilingualism we maintain our own languages when we acquire new ones), we can become bi- or multicultural. Were Michele able in time to 'be' Korean *in addition* to 'being' who she already is, then she would have both 'Korean-Asian' and 'Western' sensibilities to draw on in reading the world. To the extent that these sensibilities conflict with each other, both are revealed to her as cultural rather than natural formations.

When Gee defines discourses as 'saying (writing)-doing-believing-valuing combinations' (1990: 142), the hyphens are important because they bind saying or writing with doing, believing and valuing. To see literacy as a social practice is to recognise that speaking and writing cannot be separated from embodied action (doing), ways of thinking and understandings of truth (believing), and ethics (valuing). And this is also true when listeners and readers make meaning from texts. We bring who we are and where we come from to the processes of production and reception of spoken, written and visual texts.

Both Marx and Foucault

Both neo-Marxist and Foucauldian perspectives on power are important for critical literacy. While Foucault helps us to understand how discourses work, Marxist approaches help with textual deconstruction and reconstruction. To support my argument that we need both perspectives on power, I turn to the findings of the South African Truth and Reconciliation Commission (TRC).

The TRC, established by an act of parliament, began work in December 1995, under the chairmanship of Archbishop Desmond Tutu. The TRC hearings allowed perpetrators of apartheid violence, both physical and symbolic, to admit to their deeds, to apologise for them and to seek forgiveness. Victims, on the other hand, could provide testimony by telling their stories of loss, degradation, suffering and death. Reparation was promised but fell short of expectations. The process was underpinned by a Christian worldview in which the confession of one's sins and true remorse can lead to forgiveness and redemption. For a period of two and a half years the Commission heard testimony from a great many South Africans, from all sides in the liberation struggle. In his foreword to the final TRC report (1998), its chairman, Archbishop Desmond Tutu, says that the report offers

> [a] road map to those who wish to travel into our past. It is not and cannot be the whole story; but it provides a perspective on the truth about a past that is more extensive and more complex than any one . . . could have hoped to capture [1, 1, 5][4] . . . We have tried, in whatever way we could, to weave into this truth about our past some essential lessons for the future of the people of this country [1, 1, 19] . . . We could not make the journey from a past marked by conflict, injustice, oppression and exploitation to a new and democratic dispensation characterised by a culture of respect for human rights without coming face to face with our recent history [1, 1, 20].

And the stories that we have had to confront as a nation have been more inhuman, more brutal, more profoundly disturbing and more traumatic than we could have imagined. We have all had to deal with the shame of the suffering that we inflicted on one another and the full horror of apartheid's crime against humanity. The final TRC report which was presented to President Nelson Mandela on 29 October 1998, threads its way through multiple perspectives in which truth is elusive, reconciliation a hope and history is written by the oral testimony of ordinary people.

Most of the testimony relates to gross violations of human rights and makes explicit the extensive use of brute power of all kinds. In the chapter which tries to make sense of the causes, motives and perspectives, the Report offers an analysis of the role played by language.

It is a commonplace to treat language as mere words, not deeds, therefore language is taken to play a minimal role in understanding

---

[4] Square brackets are used to indicate the sections in the TRC report where the quotations appear.

violence. The Commission wishes to take a different view here. Language, discourse and rhetoric does things: it constructs social categories, it gives orders, it persuades us, it justifies, explains, gives reasons, excuses. It constructs reality. It moves people against other people. [7, 124, 294]

Language in its many and varied forms, is the central element in ideology as power. . . . In the South African context it is important to understand how multiple discourses combined, intersected and intertwined to create climates of violence. In this respect the ideologies of racism, patriarchy, religions, capitalism, apartheid and militarism all intertwined to 'manufacture' people capable of violence. [7, 131, 296]

In examining the language of the State, the security apparatus and the liberation movement, the commissioners conclude that 'a spiral of discourses increasingly dehumanised the "other", creating the conditions for violence' [7, 125, 295]. What this suggests is that one needs to look at how competing discourses affect and infect one another. It is not enough to look at the language of the oppressor in isolation. Both sides in the struggle used language to support their positions. Here language is portrayed as a powerful and dangerous force. Words can and do harm us.

Embedded in the quotations from the TRC are both Foucauldian and Marxist theories about the nature of language and discourse.

- language is not mere words, a neutral form of communication; language constructs reality;
- discourses manufacture or produce people. They construct subjectivities, both an 'us' and an 'other'; language is a form of action, a deed: it moves people to do things; discourses combine to produce a social climate; language is central to ideology as power.

The TRC findings make it clear that the homily 'Sticks and stones may break your bones, but words can never harm you', which young children are taught to chant, probably as a defence against words designed to hurt, is simply not true. The next chapter, which focuses on reading texts critically, shows how words work to position readers and suggests ways of resisting textual impositions.

CHAPTER 4

Reading Texts Critically

Language Constructs Reality

Although it is possible to view language as a closed abstract system, where each sign, each meaning-bearing unit, is arbitrary and derives its meaning from its place in the system relative to other signs (de Saussure, 1972/1990), this tells us nothing about what happens when language is used. When people use language, they have to select from options available in the system – they have to make lexical, grammatical and sequencing choices in order to say what they want to say.

All these selections are motivated: they are designed to convey particular meanings in particular ways and to have particular effects. Moreover, they are designed to be believed. Texts work to position their readers and the ideal reader, from the point of view of the writer (or speaker), is the reader who buys into the text and its meanings. Another way of saying this is to say that all texts are positioned and positioning. They are positioned by the writer's points of view, and the linguistic (and other semiotic) choices made by the writer are designed to produce effects that position the reader. We can play with the word 'design', by saying that texts have designs on us as readers, listeners or viewers. They entice us into their way of seeing and understanding the world – into their version of reality. Every text is just one set of perspectives on the world, a representation of it: language, together with other signs, works to construct reality. This is as true of nonfiction as it is of fiction.

An examination of the following newspaper text, which appeared in the *Weekly Mail and Guardian*, 14–20 October 1994, can be used to illustrate these ideas. The questions that follow are designed to help readers notice significant uses of language in the 'Egg and Sperm Race' text.

TECHNOLOGY

Egg and sperm race – who's the runner?

Rob Stepney in London

Conventional descriptions of sperm as active, and eggs as passive, participants in fertilisation owe more to gender stereotypes than to true facts of life.

Given the evidence about how sperm and egg really perform it is time we replaced the dead hand of sexist metaphor with something more appropriate.

This at least is the thesis advanced by professor Emily Martin, of the anthropology department in Johns Hopkins University, Baltimore, in the latest issue of the gynaecology journal *Orgyn*.

The standard story runs something like this: having battled its way against overwhelming odds from the vagina to the oviduct, a single valiant sperm succeeds in penetrating the egg, so fertilising it and engendering new life. In contrast this to this heroic endeavour, the egg is shed by the ovary and swept down the fallopian tube to await its date with destiny. For years I have used similar vocabulary in writing about reproduction.

So have many others. A delve into a biology textbook, chosen at random, shows that the sperms' efforts to reach the egg are indeed emphasised: the difficulty of their journey is likened to a man swimming in an Atlantic Ocean of treacle.

In the process of fertilisation, the sperm is also described as the dominant partner, releasing enzymes that dissolve the outer coat of the egg and producing a filament to pierce its membrane.

But at least this is less aggressive vocabulary than that used in a paper cited by Emily Martin, which has the egg being harpooned by the sperm. She also reproduces a cartoon from *Science News* showing sperm attacking the egg with a jackhammer and pickaxe. Such images project cultural values on to the 'personalities' of sex cells, she says.

The biological reality, she argues, is entirely different. According to recent research by biophysicists at Johns Hopkins University, sperm rather than propelling themselves manfully onwards, are ditherers. 'The motion of the sperm's tail makes the head move sideways with a force that is 10 times stronger than its forward movement', Martin reports.

Instead of coming equipped to penetrate, it seems that sperm are designed to avoid attachment - a feature which makes sense given that they are far more likely to encounter cells that are not eggs than they are to meet the ovum.

It therefore falls to the egg to perform the crucial role of cementing the relationship. The ovum's adhesive surface traps the sperm, which is left wiggling ineffectually until the genetic material in its head is engulfed by the egg.

But Martin argues, to describe the events in these terms may simply be to replace one damaging metaphor with another. Instead of sperm as Superman, we have egg as some kind of predatory spider. The most appropriate model, she suggests, is to regard sperm and egg as mutually dependent agents interacting to achieve a common goal.

Instead of active and passive, we have 'feedback loops' and 'flexible adaptation'. This seems appropriate given evidence that molecules on the sperm and the ovum have equal roles in enabling male and female genes to come together.

We are familiar with such ideas of interplay and self-regulation when it comes to biological processes such as the hormonal system. No-one can be sure of how powerfully biological metaphors reinforce social stereotypes, or vice versa.

But we should perhaps now be seeing the conjunction of sperm and egg in terms that do more than simply echo outdated gender roles.

Figure 4.1 'Egg and Sperm Race – Who's the Runner?'
© Guardian Newspapers

Lexical choices

1. Explain how the different choices of words construct either the sperm or the egg as mainly responsible for fertilisation.
2. Look at all the word selections for the sperm and for the egg and decide which ones have positive connotations and which have negative connotations.

Grammatical choices

3. *Voice*: How does the use of the passive voice in 'the egg is shed by the ovary and swept down the fallopian tube to await its destiny' help to construct the egg as a done-to rather than as a doer?
4. *Tense*: Most of this story is written in the present tense. What effect does this have?
5. *Modality*: What is the effect of the word 'seems' in this sentence: 'Instead of coming equipped to penetrate, it seems that sperm are designed to avoid attachment'?
6. *Articles*: Consider the use of 'the', which is the definite article, by comparing the headline with the following possible headline: 'Egg and sperm race – is there a runner?' ('A' is the indefinite article.)

Sequencing

7. The journalist begins the article with the 'standard story'. How might the effect have been different if he had started with the 'biological reality'?

Language constructs reality

8. How many possible versions of reality does this text offer the reader? What are they? Which version does the writer prefer? How do you know?

Visuals Construct Reality

It is important to recognise that visuals and other forms of semiosis (meaning making) are as important as words in the construction of reality. Often a visual text that accompanies the verbal text offers a different version of reality from that of the verbal text, such that the reader is offered contradictory and competing points of view. Newspaper texts have multiple authors: the journalist, the photographer or cartoonist, the editor, the typesetter. In all probability, the journalist who wrote this article did not choose the headline which suggests, contrary to the argument of the text, that fertilisation *is* a race and that there *is* a main contender; nor did he in all probability design or approve the cartoon. In the original text a cartoon is embedded in the article in the top right hand corner of the text, directly under the words 'who's the runner?' It is reproduced as Figure 4.2.

Figure 4.2 'Egg and Sperm Race – Who's the Runner?': Cartoon.
© Dr Jack. Source: *Mail and Guardian*. Used with permission.

> Notice the different version of reality offered by this cartoon and how it is designed and placed to influence one's reading of the argument in the text.

'Egg and Sperm Race – Who's the Runner?' can also be used to explore the idea of a discourse and a counter-discourse. All communities have patterned ways of understanding and talking about the world. As members of these communities, we draw on these culturally encoded repertoires for making meaning which are called discourses. Martin's argument, as discussed in the article, is that the 'standard story' reinforces the gendered binary that constructs men as active and women as passive discussed in the previous chapter (see Table 3.2). This dominant patriarchal representation of reality is often so taken-for-granted that we forget that it is just a version of reality – it has become naturalised, made to seem inevitable and true. Martin could have used the scientific evidence to set up a counter-discourse, one that turns the standard discourse on its head, constructing women as active heroes and men as passive, women as dominant instead of men. In this opposing version, science would simply have been harnessed to service a different set of truths but it would not break the binary construction; it would just reverse the terms along with the power relations they encode. Instead, she argues for a completely different co-operative, rather than oppositional, view of gender relations that refuses the binary paradigm. She rejects the structuring codes of the standard patriarchal discourse and finds a different, more inclusive, discursive location with different beliefs, values and practices, in this case a feminist location, from which to speak.

Discourses Speak Us

So far, I have built up a picture of text designers carefully selecting words and images to position their readers. The idea that speakers and writers choose their words, their grammar and the sequencing of their ideas needs to be qualified in a number of important ways. First, when we are speaking, we usually do not have time to carefully select every word and aspect of the grammar, so we focus on meaning, what we want to say, and let the words choose themselves. When writing, we can be more deliberate, both because we can take our time, and because in the process of writing we can go back and edit our choices. However, because all of us are members of particular discourse communities, our naturalised ways of talking about the world seem to us to be true and appropriate and therefore not in need of editing. We simply draw on the repertoires of meaning available in the discourses we inhabit. For example, the Standard Bank advertisers, drawing on available discourses of literacy/illiteracy, saw nothing inappropriate in comparing Jimmy Khobella with a six-year-old child. In the 1970s Paulo Freire did not edit his use of 'man' as a generic term to refer to both men and women, as in

> [l]iberation is a praxis: the action and reflection of *men* upon their
> world in order to transform it.
>
> (Freire, 1972b: 52, my emphasis)

At the time that he was writing, feminist linguists such as Spender (1980) and Cameron (1985) had not yet done the work needed to destabilise the naturalised assumption that 'men' included women, exactly the kind of work that was needed to shift the conditions of possibility of sexist discourses.

Secondly, even when we are trying to move into a new discourse, old patterns of speaking the world influence our 'choices'. Discourses speak through us. 1994 was the year of the first democratic elections in South Africa. In the same year, the Standard Bank introduced a pension plan designed specifically for domestic workers, called the *Domestic Promise Plan*.[1] That the introduction of this new insurance policy is tied to changes in the socio-historical context is made explicit by six pages in the bank's *Domestic Promise Plan* brochure, addressed to the employer, which give an overview of the new legislation applying to domestic employees. This includes information about salaries and wages, hours of work, meal intervals, annual leave, sick leave, overtime, Sunday work, public holidays, termination of employment. It sets out what is now expected of employers and it gives more information on this than on the pension plan itself. Buying an employee a *Domestic Promise Plan* is thus textually linked to new conditions of service for domestic workers and to post-apartheid labour conditions.

The new labour statutes, notably the Basic Conditions of Employment Act 3 of 1981 extended to domestic workers in 1994, provided domestic workers with some protection against unfair labour practices for the first time. Although it did not include a minimum wage, or pensions and other conditions of service, the bank capitalised on the new political climate by putting the long-term financial security of domestic workers, in the form of a pension plan, on the social agenda. They could frame their new insurance policies within a post-apartheid discourse of workers' rights.

However, the promotional literature developed to sell these policies shows old apartheid discourses at work. Apartheid discourses constructed 'the Boer[2] nation as the senior white trustee of the native ... on the grounds of the cultural infancy of the native' (Rose & Tunmer, 1975: 127–128).[3] Evidence for the continuity of this paternalistic discourse runs through the *Domestic Promise Plan* advertisements, of which Figure 4.3 is one example.

---

[1] This discussion was first published in *Spil Plus*, 29, 1996 and *Discourse*, 18(3), 1997.

[2] Boer: the Afrikaans word for 'farmer', often used to refer to Afrikaners in general. Afrikaners are the descendants of the original Dutch colonisers of South Africa.

[3] Pennycook (1998) provides a detailed analysis of the colonial construction of indigenous people which matches the infantilising constructions in apartheid discourses. His analysis clearly shows that colonial subjects are positioned on the negative side of Wilshire's binary (see Chapter 3).

Sometimes, I stare out the window while baby Jay is sleeping and I wonder where I'll be sleeping when I'm too old to work.

At least I know it will be somewhere comfortable. Ever since Mrs Lambert spoke to me. She showed me this Domestic Promise Plan. Something or other about a retirement policy. She told me she was putting R30 into it each month for me.

But what happens when Jay doesn't need me anymore?

I know what to do when the baby has a cough.
And I know how to prepare a meal for twelve.
But I don't know what happens to me when I'm 65.

She smiled and said the policy could be taken out over 10, 15 or 20 years and I could even take it with me to my next job.

So stop worrying she said. It's all been taken care of.

I turned back to the window. And for the very first time I could see a lot further than my sixty fifth birthday.

Why not give your Domestic peace of mind about retirement? Call 0800 12 4444 toll-free today.

Underwritten by CHARTER LIFE

🏦 Standard Bank
DOMESTIC PROMISE PLAN

With us you can go so much further.

Figure 4.3 *Domestic Promise Plan* Advertisement.
Source: *Weekly Mail and Guardian*, 1994. Standard Bank advertisement. Used with permission.

While the use of personal narrative in this advertisement moves against the dehumanising and othering discourse of apartheid racism, the construction of the woman as an object of our gaze in the visual text does not. Neither does the pattern of lexicalisation. While the employer, Mrs Lambert, and the baby, Jay, are both named, the domestic worker is referred to as 'your domestic'. Her status as a domestic (attribute) worker (nominal) is thus reduced to 'domestic'. If she is a domestic worker, then Mrs Lambert is a domestic employer, but she is not lexicalised by either her attribute 'domestic' or by her status, 'employer'. Finally, in the use of the passive construction, 'It's all been taken care of', the deleted agent is presumably the employer who acts on behalf of her employee without her informed consent, shown by the worker's uncertainty in 'something or other about a retirement policy'. This worker, constructed as unable to take care of herself, is elsewhere in the text shown as capable of performing highly complex and responsible tasks (looking after the employer's sick child and preparing a meal for twelve people). Here one might wish to argue that the advertiser needs to construct the domestic worker as having no agency in order to ensure that the employer will buy the policy for her. The employee is given no say: her employer is 'the senior white trustee' of colonial discourses.

An analysis of the verb processes, what Halliday calls a transitivity analysis, provides further important evidence. In Systemic Functional Grammar verbs are organised into processes as outlined in Table 4.1.

Table 4.1 Description of the Processes in the *Domestic Promise Plan*

Process	Explanation	Examples (see Figure 4.3)
Material	Types of doing, action verbs	showed, was putting, take/n, give, turned, prepare
Mental	Verbs of thinking, feeling, perceiving	wonder, will be sleeping, know, worrying, could see, need
Behavioural	Automatic physiological actions such as breathing, sneezing. Also verbs that are part mental, part material such as 'look', 'listen'	smiled, stare, is sleeping
Relational	Verbs to be and to have: relations of identity and possession	am, has
Verbal	Verbs of saying	spoke, told, said, call
Existential	Things that exist or happen, e.g. 'There is a chance of success'	No examples in this text

Janks, H. (1997). First published in *Discourse. Studies in the Cultural Politics of Education*, 18 (3) p. 337

What is interesting here is not that Mrs Lambert is constructed with predominantly material and verbal processes and the domestic worker with largely mental and relational processes: there is nothing intrinsically superior or inferior about material, mental, verbal or relational processes. What matters here is that the construction of the domestic worker with few material processes suggests that she is unable to act except with the permission or in the service of her employer. It is as if agency is granted to her by her employer. Even more interesting is the patterned alignment between the domestic worker and the baby. They are the only participants whose processes are mental, behavioural and relational. Thus in the transitivity structure one can see the domestic worker constructed along with the baby as someone who needs to be 'taken care of'. The transitivity structure encodes the flip-side of paternalism – infantilisation.

How does this pattern of transitivity happen? Should we imagine advertising copy-writers deliberately working out a careful alignment between the transitivity processes selected for the adult worker and the baby? Because the patterns of transitivity are not apparent simply by reading a text, it is difficult for a writer to detect or control them. That they lie buried in the syntax and are therefore less under the writer's conscious control, suggests that discursive patterns are at work.

While South Africa has negotiated a miraculous political transformation, it is clear that social transformation will continue to be beset by a legacy of old patterns of thinking – tenacious discourses. Even as speakers try to position themselves in new non-racist, post-liberation discourses, old patterned ways of speaking surface. One could argue, with reference to the Jimmy Khobella text, that a deficit discourse of illiteracy combines with a paternalistic racist discourse to infantilise Khobella. What is interesting is that in both these texts, the old discourses speak the bank, at the very moment that the bank is trying to speak a new-democracy discourse of social responsibility.

Like 'Egg and Sperm Race', this text is also multimodal. Here the visual works to reinforce, rather than contradict the written text. Analysis of visual texts is usually conveyed in writing, a mode that cannot do justice to an image. One of the main reasons for this is that the eye is able to take in an image as a whole, all at once – as a gestalt. Words on the other hand are sequential: one word follows another and they have to accumulate to form a picture. This can be illustrated by setting a verbal description of the image in the *Domestic Promise Plan* advertisement against the image itself (see Figure 4.4).

The Standard Bank advertisement for its *Domestic Promise Plan* includes a visual text in sepia blues. Here an African woman in her early thirties, presumably a domestic worker, is portrayed looking to the left out of a window. Her face is lit by the light from the window; the back of her head, neck and shoulders are in shadow. Her hand supporting her chin, in a pose associated with Rodin's *Thinker*, makes her look pensive. She is wearing a collared-dress or shirt and a head-scarf. The window has bars in the shape of a cross.

Figure 4.4 Verbal Description of *Domestic Promise Plan* Advertisement.
Picture adapted from 1994. Standard Bank advertisement. Used with permission.

Notice how writing imposes a sequence on the information in the image: context of the image; colour of the image; race, gender, age, employment and action of the subject in that order; lighting of the image; pose; dress; the shape of the window bars. Because writing is discursive this is inevitable. But there is nothing inevitable about the sequence chosen. Figure 4.5 provides an alternative sequence.

An African woman wearing a collared shirt or dress and a head scarf looks out of a window to her left. Her face lit by the light from the window suggests that she is in her early thirties. Her hand supporting her chin, in a pose associated with Rodin's *Thinker*, makes her look pensive as does the colour of the image, sepia blue. The window has bars in the shape of a cross and the back of her head, neck and shoulders are in shadow. As part of the Standard Bank's advertisement for its *Domestic Promise Plan*, there is the implication that the woman is a domestic worker.

Figure 4.5 Alternative Verbal Description of *Domestic Promise Plan* Advertisement.
Picture adapted from 1994. Standard Bank advertisement. Used with permission.

Alder's method of superimposing written analysis onto an image (2004) obviates some of the difficulties relating to sequencing of information. Hers is an effective and economic way of presenting the image and the analysis simultaneously (see Figure 4.6).

Figure 4.6 Alder's Method of Image Analysis.
Picture adapted from 1994. Standard Bank advertisement. Used with permission.

All description implies some interpretation. Texts are not neutral. Compare the different effects of Figure 4.4, Figure 4.5 and Figure 4.6.

Critical Distance

I have been using spatial metaphors to describe discourses. I have referred to them as 'locations', places that we 'inhabit', as 'positioned' and 'positioning'. I have also shown that if one is 'in' a discourse, it is difficult to escape 'from' it to speak a different discourse. It is equally difficult to resist a text that speaks a discourse that we are comfortable with. Which discourses we are located in and which discourses a text is located in, affect our ability to read with the text or against it.

As a Jew, whose grandparents lost their parents and many of their siblings in the Nazi Holocaust and who has seen the concentration camp tattoos of her great-aunt and her aunt's children, I do not need a course in critical literacy to read against texts produced by the Holocaust deniers. See Figure 4.7. My history provides me with a critical distance.

The Holocaust is an Israeli myth ... to blackmail the world.

The Jews invented the myth of mass extermination and the fabrication that 6 million Jews were put to death in Nazi ovens. This was done with the aim of motivating the Jews to emigrate to Israel and to blackmail the Germans for money as well as to achieve world support for the Jews. Similarly, Zionism based itself on this myth to establish the State of Israel....I continue to believe that the Holocaust is an Israeli myth which was invented to blackmail the world. (*Al-Akhbar*, September 25, 1998)

The Holocaust is a great lie ... to lead the world astray

Most research prepared by objective researchers in connection with what is called the Jewish Holocaust has proven beyond the shadow of a doubt that the Holocaust is a great lie and a myth that the Zionist mind spread in order to lead the world astray. (*Al-Arab Al-Yom*. July 4, 1998)

These and other examples of Holocaust deniers in their own words can be found at http://www.adl.org/holocaust/Denial_ME/in_own_words.asp

---

Figure 4.7 Texts Produced by Holocaust Deniers.

Find a text (it could, for example, be a joke, a movie, a photograph) that offends you because of your own identity investments. It may be elitist, racist, sexist, homophobic, anti-Islam or demeaning in any other way.

In reading texts that offend us, the discourses which structure our own beliefs and values give us the critical distance needed to read against them. It is much more difficult to read against texts that we are comfortable with. If all texts serve interests and entice us into their way of seeing the world, then we need to understand how they work on us – we need strategies for resistant reading.

In my discussion of the *Domestic Promise Plan*, I showed how an analysis of aspects of the language could reveal the ways in which the advertisement was positioning the domestic worker, the employer, the bank, and in the process working to position the reader. To understand how this works, one does need some understanding of both English grammar and visual grammar. *Grammar* – now there is a word to frighten would-be text-analysts who have no training in linguistic or semiotic analysis. I hope to dispel such fears by introducing a few key linguistic features here as simply as possible.

Halliday (1985) describes language as 'meaning potential'. Depending on the choices we make, we realise this potential in one way rather than another. Because our choices are constrained by what the language system allows us to choose from, we have to know something about this system. For example, at times we can only choose between two options: the definite and the indefinite article, the passive and the active voice. At other times, we have to choose between more than two, consider the vast array of synonyms in the lexis of English or the range of tenses that provide us with options.

Over the years I have come to understand which linguistic features are most useful for deconstructing texts. I have developed a table with three columns that lists these concepts, explains them briefly, and illustrates them (see Table 4.2). In this table all the illustrative examples are taken from 'Egg and Sperm Race – Who's the Runner?' (excluding the last three paragraphs).

Table 4.2 focuses only on verbal signs. This is in no way meant to suggest that visual analysis is not equally important. This is well illustrated by an analysis of the cartoon enfolded into the 'Egg and Sperm Race' text (Figure 4.2). Here the humorous depiction of 'ditherer'-sperm looking dopey and half-drugged, even crashing into each other, together with the depiction of the egg looking vicious and trying to get her claws and possibly even her teeth into a panic-stricken sperm, contradicts the words of the text. The visual message undermines the verbal message. The text is also funny. As we shall see in Chapter 9, jokes and humour are a form of legitimation that allow the unsayable, in this case, the sexist constructions of women as predatory.

I shall continue to rely on the key linguistic features summarised in Table 4.2 in the rest of the book to build a cumulative understanding of how they work and how to use them as tools for analysing texts. Each linguistic feature should be seen as just one lens on a text. What matters is not each instance of use, but the patterns that emerge. One cannot look at any particular selection in isolation; instead one has to look at all the occurrences in order to find the patterns of use. Only once the patterns have been established in each of a number of features can one look for continuity or ruptures across the patterns. For example only once one has looked at every process for the sperm and every process for the egg can one say something about the patterns of transitivity (see Table 4.3). A further analysis of voice can then be used to see continuity across both voice and transitivity in the construction of the active/passive gender binary, discussed in Chapter 2, which gives greater agency to the sperm. The sperm is the doer more often than the egg. The egg is 'done to' more often than the sperm.

Table 4.2 Key Linguistic Features for the Analysis of Texts

Linguistic feature	Explanation	Example taken from *Egg and Sperm Race*
Lexicalisation	The selection/choice of wordings. Different words construct the same idea differently.	The lexis constructs sperm first as *valiant* and *heroic* then as *ditherers*. There are more positive lexicalisations of the sperm than of the egg.
Overlexicalisation	Many words for the same phenomenon.	Adjectives for the sperm show overlexicalisation (particularly in comparison to the egg).
Relexicalisation	Renaming.	Both the egg and the sperm are relexicalised to effect the reversal of their positions.
Lexical cohesion	Provides connections across stretches of text by: synonymy (same meaning) antonymy (opposite meaning) repetition collocation (associated words).	Fertilisation and reproduction; egg and ovum active/passive Egg and/or sperm repeated Humour created because an egg and *spoon* race is the usual collocation.
Metaphor	Used for yoking ideas together and for the discursive construction of new ideas.	Like a man *swimming through treacle*; sperm *harpoons* the egg; the egg *cements* the relationship. Sperm as *superman*; egg as *predatory spider*.
Euphemism	Hides negative actions or implications.	*Conventional* descriptions hides that these descriptions are in fact sexist.
Transitivity (see the discussion of the *Domestic Promise Plan*)	Processes: doing – material process being or having – relational processes thinking/feeling/ perceiving – mental saying – verbal processes behavioural – physiological existential.	Sperm are given many more material processes than the egg, thus constructing them as more active and with greater agency, even in a text that works to change our perceptions in this regard.
Voice	Active and passive voice constructs participants as doers or as 'done-tos'. Passive voice allows for the deletion of the agent.	Many more passive constructions are used for the egg (*shed by, swept down, harpooned by*). Even when the egg is given the dominant role it is not by choice: *It therefore falls to the egg* . . .
Nominalisation: a verb is turned into a noun.	A process is turned into a thing or an event without participants, tense or modality.	Fertilisation: the verb *fertilise* has been nominalised. A *delve* into a biology textbook . . .

Quoted speech [DS – Direct speech IS – Indirect speech FIS – Free indirect speech]	Who is quoted in DS/IS/FIS? Who is quoted first/last/most? Who is not quoted? Has someone been misquoted or quoted out of context? What reporting verb was chosen? What is the effect of scare quotes?	Most of what Emily Martin says is reported in FIS, a loose form of IS where the writer's voice merges with that of the person being quoted. She is also quoted with DS. No opposing voices are quoted and the reporter uses his own words to summarise alternative accounts. When she is quoted the framing verb is *reports.* This is stronger than, for example, Martin *surmises.*
scare quotes or 'so-called'	These are used by writers to disassociate themselves from the words chosen, to suggest that they belong to someone else.	Had the headline read: *Egg and Sperm Race – Who's the 'Runner'?*, the quotes around 'runner' would have suggested that the writer doubts that there is a runner.
Turn-taking	Who gets the floor? How many turns do different participants get? Who is silent/ silenced? Who interrupts? Who gets heard? Whose points are followed through? Whose rules for tur- taking are being used given that they are different in different cultures? Who controls the topic?	This category applies more to spoken interaction than it does to written. All it is possible to say here is that the verbal text only presents Martin's views.
Mood	Is the clause a statement, question, offer or command?	The headline poses a question. The text answers it with the use of statements only. Statements are used to give information.
Polarity and tense	Positive polarity – it is. Negative polarity – it is not. Categorical positive or negative statements using tense. Tense sets up the definiteness of events occurring in time. The present tense is used for timeless truths and absolute certainty.	The article relies on the use of the present tense to present the position as categorical truth. Very few statements are hedged or modalised.
Modality Degrees of uncertainty	Logical possibility/probability. Social authority. Modality created by modals (may, might, could, will), adverbs (possibly, certainly, hopefully) intonation, tag questions.	There are only a few examples in this text of the writer using modality to suggest that he is less than certain: Instead of coming equipped to penetrate, it *seems* that sperm are designed to avoid attachment. To describe events in these terms *may* simply be to replace. . . .

(*Continued Overleaf*)

Table 4.2 Continued

Linguistic feature	Explanation	Example taken from *Egg and Sperm Race*
		Seems and *may* introduce notes of uncertainty.
Pronouns	Inclusive we/exclusive we. Us and them. Generic 'he' used to include 'she'. The choice of person: first, second, third.	There is an example here of the use of first-person, which the writer uses to implicate himself along with others. For the rest the article relies on the use of the third person for reporting the story of the egg and the sperm and Martin's argument, as is appropriate for the genre.
Definite article – *the* Indefinite article – *a*	'The' is used for shared information – to refer to something mentioned before or that the addressee can be assumed to know about. Reveals textual presuppositions.	The use of 'the' in the headline assumes that there is a runner in the process of fertilisation.
Thematisation – syntax: the first bit of the clause is called the theme	The theme is the launch pad for the clause. Look for patterns of what is foregrounded in the clause by being in theme position – the first bit of the bit before the verb. Neither the sperm nor the egg appear much in theme position. What is thematised is the argument. Conventional descriptions → given the evidence → the standard story → A delve into a biology textbook → in the process of fertilisation and so forth.	A delve into a biology textbook, chosen at random – suggests any biology textbook, not a specific one.
Rheme – syntax: the last bit of the clause is called the rheme	In written English the new information is usually at the end of the clause. In spoken English it is indicated by tone.	New information relating to the argument appears in the rheme. If we take the text as a whole then rheme appears on the right of a text written in English which is read from left to right, and at the end. Bottom right of the text contains the new information as is the case here. Most newpaper articles put the new information up front – top left.

| Sequencing of information | Sequence sets up cause and effect. | In a text such as this which presents an argument, sequencing and logical connectors are crucial for the structure of the argument. |
| Logical connectors – conjunctions set up the logic of the argument. | Conjunctions are:
additive – and, in addition
causal – because, so, therefore
adversative – although, yet
temporal – when, while, after, before. | Logical connectors establish the following argument: The conventional way of seeing fertilisation is x, but the truth is closer to y, therefore x plus y. Chronology is also used to sequence information. |

Table 4.3 Transitivity Analysis of *Egg and Sperm Race – Who's the Runner?*

Sperm – verb	Sperm – process	Egg – verb	Egg – process
battled	material	is shed	material (done to)
succeeds	material	is swept	material (done to)
penetrating	material	to await	behavioural
fertilising	material	being harpooned	material (done to)
engendering	material	to perform	material
to reach	material	cementing	material
efforts are	relational	traps	material
journey is likened	material (done to)		
is described	verbal (done to)		
releasing	material		
dissolve	material		
producing	material		
to pierce	material		
attacking	material		
propelling	material		
are	relational		
makes	material		
to penetrate	material		
are designed	material(done to)		
to avoid	material		
are	relational		
to encounter	material		
are	relational		
are left wiggling	material (done to)		
is engulfed	material (done to)		
26 processes	20 material	7 processes	6 material (3 passive)

What the systematic description and count of transitivity makes clear in Table 4.3 is that in a text which is trying to correct a previous imbalance, more attention is paid to the sperm, the sperm is constructed with more material processes and the sperm is more a doer than a done-to. The textual attention is on the sperm, not on the egg; the sperm is the runner, the one who acts. Readers' own analyses of the lexical choices should have shown more positive words for the sperm than for the egg, producing a continuity of pattern, with the transitivity analysis. Even the reversal produced by reversing the binary is only partial: more topic space continues to be given to the sperm. Asking the interests question is what makes this analysis critical: Who stands to benefit from the re-production of these gender stereotypes? Why is it that this gendered discourse emerges even in a text that is attempting to disrupt it?

I have chosen two texts that are particularly striking examples of mood and lexical cohesion. Figure 4.8 is an AIDS awareness advertisement and Figure 4.9 is an advertisement for Pick 'n Pay, a national supermarket chain in South Africa. As these are South African texts, I suggest that you make a mental note of anything in these texts that you experiences as alienating or disconcerting. Such responses that you may have will be discussed later.

The use of mood in the AIDS text

According to Halliday (1985), mood describes function of the clause as a statement, a question, an offer or a command. These mood choices construct readers differently: questions assume that readers have answers, statements that readers need information, and commands presuppose the right to tell others what to do. If you look at every clause in the AIDS text, 'Who in their right frame of mind . . .' (Figure 4.8), you will see that the choice of mood moves from questions at the beginning, to statements and then to commands. It is important to think about how this movement positions the reader.

The use of cohesion in the Pick 'n Pay text (Figure 4.9)

Pick 'n Pay is a large national supermarket chain in South Africa. In Figure 4.9 lexical cohesion is used to tie Mandela's name to that of Pick 'n Pay, making him one of Pick 'n Pay's people and associating the supermarket with the Mandela 'brand'. It is worth trying to find specific examples to see how this works in the written text.

It is important to remember that texts are instantiations of discourses. Texts are the material form that discourses take. Texts may of course be hybrid, formed by more than one discourse, as we saw with the *Domestic*

Figure 4.8 'Using Condoms Saves Lives'.
© Gauteng Department of Health. Used with permission.

Promise Plan; the producers and consumers of texts are also likely to be hybrid, formed by the different discourse communities with which they identify (as we saw with Michele). Relating the patterns in texts to the contexts which condition their formation, helps us to find and understand this hybridity.

Figure 4.9 Pick 'n Pay Advertisement.
© Pick 'n Pay. Used with permission.

Texts are also multimodal. Even texts that are predominantly verbal have design features such as the choice of font, font size, and *font style*, colour, $\qquad$ s p a c i n g

$\qquad\quad$ and

$\qquad\qquad$ l-a-y-o-u-t.

In addition to lexical, grammatical, content and sequencing choices, writers and publishers have to decide on the overall design of the page.

> Consider the images that accompany the verbal text in both the Pick 'n Pay advertisement and the Aids Helpline text. What contribution do they make to the meaning of these texts? Use Table 4.4 as a guide.

The key visual features are summarised in Tables 4.4.1, 4.4.2 and 4.4.3[4] which are interspersed with references to illustrative figures. This table is based on the work of Kress and van Leeuwen (1990). Yvonne Reed and I worked together to turn their work into a tool for text analysis, along the same lines as Table 4.2 which summarises the key linguistic features for analysing verbal texts. Neither of these tables is a substitute for working with Halliday's Systemic Functional Grammar, or the literature on other modalities that flows from it. These tables are offered as a starting point for the analysis of visual texts but they do not operate at the level of delicacy needed for research purposes.

It is important to recognise that photographic images are not a neutral 'slice' of the real world, but constructed representations. Not only does the photographer frame and compose the shot, but digital technologies make it easy to 'photoshop' images on screen. Photoshop, an editing programme, is now used as a verb for digital morphing. Figures 4.16, 4.17 and 4.18 demonstrate digital morphing. In 4.15, it is important to know that this is a picture of an African doll that I own and I only have one. In 4.16, when the successive pictures of the lion walking are combined, the lion appears to be charging. In 4.17, two rhino are combined so as to appear to be one rhino with two heads, what I used to call a push-me-pull-you when I was a child. In 4.18, there is no digital morphing, but cropping the picture above the knees gives an entirely different message.

---

[4] I am indebted to Yvonne Reed for permission to use these tables. This is a shortened version of the table that she and I worked on, but the thinking was done together.

Table 4.4.1 Representations of Participants and Processes

	Definition	Meaning	Examples
Narrative	**Narrative images** show actions and interactions between participants with the use of vectors.	**Actional** images use vectors to suggest movement between participants. **Reactional** images use vectors such as the direction of glance and gesture to show the interaction between participants.	In Figure 2.2 (Edge goes to your head), the direction of glance shows no interaction between the participants.
Conceptual: classification	**Conceptual images** represent participants' stable and essential characteristics abstractly. **Classification images** represent taxonomies (classification by type or hierarchy, flows and networks).	**Classification by type** e.g. hierarchical or symmetrical arrangement of participants; flowcharts which show sequencing; non-linear network diagrams which show multiple connections between participants.	The AIDS ribbon in African beadwork (Figure 4.8); the key (Figure 4.9). *Classification* e.g. a table which classifies types of visual meaning-making. *Flows* See Figure 8.5.
Conceptual: analytic	**Analytic images** show attributes that constitute their defining characteristics. These may even be labelled. **Symbolic images** Participants are included in an image because of their suggestive power. Their inclusion requires a symbolic explanation.	Analytic images eliminate colour, details, realism. They tend to be decontextualised and reduced in order to make the essential elements salient. Salience in visual image is produced by features that draw attention to the object or an aspect of it. For the salient aspect to be symbolic it needs to stand for some other meaning. It is a visual metaphor.	In Figure 4.6 the only reduction is size. However, the speech bubbles make the essential elements **salient**. In Figure 4.9 the key, a **symbol** of freedom, is salient because it takes up a significant amount of space. The Lego dolls (Figure 5.2) and the chilli-cricket-ball (Figure 5.4) are **visual metaphors** for sameness and difference.

Table devised by Hilary Janks and Yvonne Reed, based on material in Kress, G., & van Leeuwen, T. (1990). *Reading Images*. Geelong: Deakin University Press.

Table 4.4.2 The Viewer's Relation to the Subject/s of the Image

Many visual features exist on continua, e.g. from extreme long shot to very big close-up or from full colour saturation to the absence of colour. They have to be defined in relation to one another:

	Definition	Meaning	Examples
Gaze	Living subjects look out of the image at the viewer.	They demand a relation with the viewer.	Jimmy Khobella (Figure 1.1)
	Living subjects do not look at the viewer.	They are objectified: they appear as objects for the viewer's gaze, offering themselves for examination.	The domestic worker in Figure 4.3.
The shot	**Close-ups** Concentrate on detail (e.g. face); extreme close-up (e.g. eye).	Close-ups enter the figure's personal space and therefore create a sense of intimacy.	See Figure 4.10.
	Medium shots Show humans from the knees or waist up	This represents the realm of of social interaction.	
	Long shots Extreme long shots show the locale and setting. Long shots show the full figure in space.	Shots indicate the degree of both physical and social proximity or distance.	

(*Continued overleaf*)

Table 4.4.2 Continued

	Definition	Meaning	Examples
Camera angles	**Aerial** – Bird's eye view. **High Angle** – The camera looks down on the subject. **Normal** – The camera is at 'eye level'. **Low angle** – The shot is taken from below the subject. **Tilted** – camera tilted laterally; figure appears likely to fall sideways. **Frontal angles** – the shot is taken from directly in front of the subject. **Oblique angle** – the subject is presented at an oblique angle within the frame.	The viewer is omniscient. Diminishes the subject – makes it look insignificant. Powerful viewer. Creates a sense of realism. No particular power difference. Elevates the subject; makes the subject look powerful/important. The subject is made to appear off-balance. Creates tension and instability. The image maker and viewer are involved with what they see – a visual 'us'. The subject is seen from the sidelines, presented as Other – a visual 'them'.	See Figure 4.11.
Colour	**Saturation:** from full colour to black and white. **Number:** all or few colours. **Variation:** flat (idealised) or natural (lots of variation and shading).	In a **realistic** image, lots of colours, lots of variation and a degree of saturation that looks real create a natural effect. **Scientific** images that reduce an idea to its essential characteristics: black and white (ie no saturation) and reduced colours are valued. **Advertising** images often use hyper-saturation to appeal to the senses (eg food).	The cartoon (Figure 4.2) shows the reduction of an idea to its essentialised characteristics. Here it is used for satirical rather than scientific effects.

Exposure	**Underexposed** – too little light reaches the film; the image is dark. **Overexposed** – too much light reaches the film; the image is washed out.	Creates sinister atmosphere and sense of threat. Suggests that the figure is publically and psychologically exposed.	See Figure 4.12.
Focus	Images can be presented on a continuum from in focus (where the image is crisp) to out of focus where the image is increasingly blurred. Different parts of the image may be in or out of focus.	Less focus provides less detail and appears softer. Soft focus can create feminine, romantic, idealised effects. Sharp focus gives a sense of precision, accuracy, realism even an exaggerated sense of reality. Parts of the image that are in focus have more salience – they attract attention.	See Figure 4.13.
Perspective	Perspective creates three dimensions in an image with a vanishing point determined by the eye of the image maker.	Images with perspective dictate the viewer's point of view. Images without perspective have no built-in point of view and appear less real.	See Figure 4.14.

Table devised by Hilary Janks and Yvonne Reed, based on material in Kress, G., & van Leeuwen, T. (1990). *Reading Images*. Geelong: Deakin University Press.

Table 4.4.3 Salience and Composition of Elements

	Definition	Meaning			Examples
Layout of page	The vertical axis separates information that is **new** for the viewer or **given**, the horizontal axis separates the **ideal** from the **real** (Kress and van Leeuwen, 1996, 108).	*Organisation of the page*			See Figures 4.3, 4.8, 4.9.
		Top left Ideal highly valued given info, some salience	**Top right** Ideal highly valued new info + salience		
		Bottom left the real less valued given info – salience	**Bottom right** the real less valued new info, some salience		
	Centre and margins	This sets up centre periphery relations.			
	Styles: bolding, italicising, underlining, colour.	Styles increase salience and invite the reader's attention.			
	Balance is created by the relative weighting of the elements in a composition.	Weighted elements demand the viewer's attention, and affect the reading path.			

Framing	Reality exists without frames, pictures have edges and the composer has to decide what to include in the frame.	The frame determines what the viewer is allowed to see and not to see. Framing marks off elements within a text from one another.	See Figure 4.18.
Vectors	Vectors are 'lines' which lead the eye from one element to another within the frame. They are created by actual lines, the angling of objects or words, the use of empty space, etc., that direct the path of the viewer's gaze.	Vectors act as pointers. Vectors create an ideal reading path for the viewer. They serve to relate elements in a text or image to one another and create visual coherence or division.	The hand of the domestic worker in Figure 4.3 and the raised leg of the underdog in Figure 3.5 create vectors that direct the eye.

Table devised by Hilary Janks and Yvonne Reed, based on material in Kress, G., & van Leeuwen, T. (1990). *Reading Images*. Geelong: Deakin University Press.

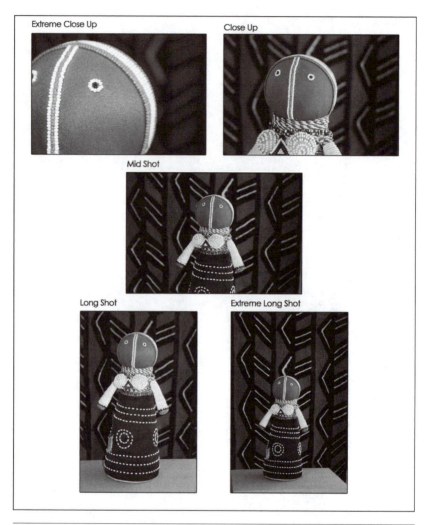

Figure 4.10 Shots.
Photographs by Daniel Janks.

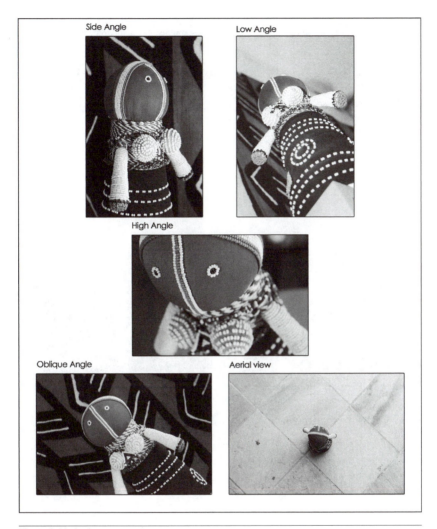

Figure 4.11 Angles.
Photographs by Daniel Janks.

Figure 4.12 Exposure.
Photographs by Daniel Janks.

Figure 4.13 Focus.
Photographs by Daniel Janks.

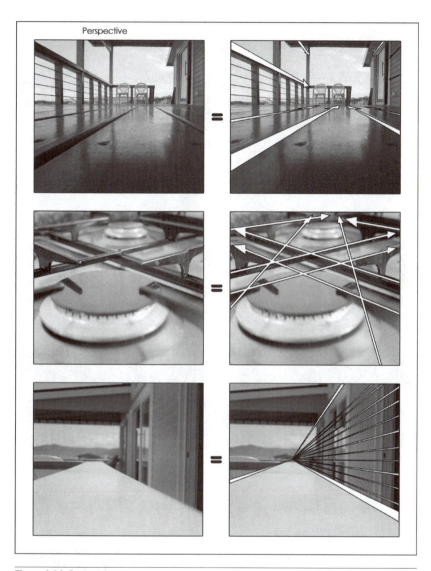

Figure 4.14 Perspective.
Photographs by Daniel Janks.

Figure 4.15 Morphing.
Photographs by Daniel Janks.

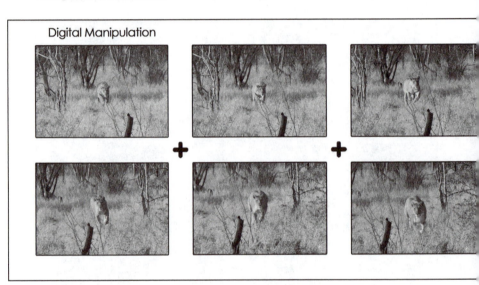

Figure 4.16 Morphing.
Photographs by Daniel Janks.

Figure 4.17 Morphing.
Photographs by Daniel Janks.

2nd Copy   3rd Copy   Final Image

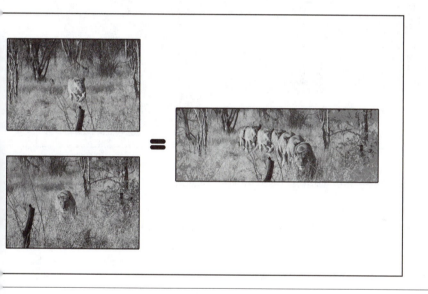

Figure 4.18 Cropping.
© The Bigger Picture/Reuters. Used with permission.

Now more than ever, cameras in combination with computers make it possible for pictures to lie. The film *Wag the Dog* (Levinson, 1997) is a political satire which tells the story of how the media create a fake war with Albania to direct the public's attention away from a sex scandal involving the US President. The bogus news footage, in which a terrified young girl, carrying a fake white cat, is running for her life from a village being bombed, is particularly significant. Here the film shows in detail how each visual detail is chosen to manipulate the public's response. It shows step by step how a news event is visually manufactured so that it appears authentic, even though it never happened. While the media have always been selective in what they choose to tell us and to show us, now, because of the sophistication of digital technology, the public needs the ability to read media texts critically.

Fairclough's (1989, 1995, 2003) model for critical discourse analysis offers us a framework for considering the discussion so far. His model consists of three inter-related dimensions of discourse which are tied to three inter-related processes of analysis. These three dimensions of discourse are:

1 the object of analysis (language: including verbal, visual or verbal and visual texts);

2 the processes by means of which the object is produced (written, spoken,designed) as well as how it is received (read/listened to/ viewed);

3 the socio-historical and contextual conditions which govern these processes and establish what is considered truth.

According to Fairclough each of these dimensions requires a different kind of analysis:

1 text analysis (description);

2 processing analysis (interpretation);

3 social analysis (explanation).

The examination of texts in this chapter illustrates a number of these ideas.

1 Analysing the signs that constitute texts is what Fairclough calls text analysis. In addition to analysing textual signs myself, I designed tools and activities to help readers think about the ways in which language and visual choices have been used to construct reality and to position them. Four texts were considered: 'Egg and Sperm Race', the *Domestic Promise Plan*, an AIDS awareness advertisement and an advertisement for Pick 'n Pay.

2 In discussing the ways in which texts work to position readers, to construct an ideal reading position, I began to explore the processes of production and reception. The multiple authoring of a newspaper text, 'Egg and Sperm Race', was an example of a process of production that had consequences for the overall message that was produced and received.

3 Freire's writing provides a good example of the ways in which socio-historical conditions constrain textual production. His choice of the word 'man', naturalised at his time of writing, could from a later historical moment be read as sexist. Similarly the conditions for the production of the *Domestic Promise Plan* advertisement are unlikely to exist outside of South Africa.

As the context for the discussion of AIDS varies widely, I imagine that readers will have produced very different readings of the AIDS text in Figure 4.8 depending on their own social context. To make this point even more vividly I have included a text written by Grade 7 pupils in Atteridgeville, an African township in South Africa. The students were working on an alphabet book to describe their town and neighbourhood for Australian children as part of an international literacy project on children's representations of place.

H is for HIV/AIDS

HIV/AIDS is a disease that cannot be cured. Many people in Atteridgeville, specially the young ones, are dying of AIDS. People who are suffering from this disease don't want people to know that they are infected and they don't want to talk about it. Some of those who are HIV positive are spreading this disease by infecting others. HIV/AIDS is caused by sleeping around without protection. HIV is spread by someone who is HIV positive who sleeps with others without using a condom. Many people don't have information about AIDS. They still believe in myths. They don't want to shake hands with people who are HIV positive or even touch them. Another myth is that if you (sleep with) rape a child you will be cured of AIDS. This is one of the reasons why child abuse and rape is high in Atteridgeville. When a person is HIV positive that person can lose weight and lose appetite. A person with HIV can look after their body by eating food that build their body and gives energy, and by doing exercise.

Figure 4.19 Alphabet Book.
Used with permission from the children and their parents.

It is important to think about how your reading of this children's text is conditioned by your social context. What might Grade 7 children in your context write about AIDS?

The severity of the HIV/AIDS pandemic in South Africa has necessitated public discussion of sexual practices, explicit billboard and radio advertising and sex education in primary schools. If you live and work in a different context, it is likely that your geographical and social location may distance you from the two AIDS texts. While distance is important for critical reading, it can also prevent readers from engaging with a text, from trying to make sense of a very different world view, from grappling with a dislocating discourse. Critical literacy requires that we both engage with and distance ourselves from texts, which I have described in Chapter 1 as reading *with* a text and reading *against* a text. We have to do both as each on its own is a form of entrapment. Engagement without estrangement[5] is a form of submission to the power of the text regardless of the reader's own positions. Estrangement without engagement is a refusal to leave the confines of one's own subjectivity, a refusal to allow otherness to enter. Without the entry of the other, can we be said to have read the text at all? What then might we be resisting?

I have found that working with both engagement and estrangement makes my literacy teaching more inclusive. If a text for analysis privileges

---

[5] I have taken these terms from Green and Morgan (1992, p. 12) and recast them slightly to fit my own needs.

the funds of knowledge (Moll, 1992) or the cultural capital (Bourdieu, 1991) of a particular group of students, it is often experienced as alienating by other students. I teach students to recognise this sense of alienation as a resource for critical deconstruction. For them the text is not naturalised, they begin from an estranged position and can use their critical distance to refuse the ideal reading position. Their challenge is to make sure that they can also engage with the text in order to make sure that they understand it on its own terms and can see it for what it is. It was for this reason that I suggested that readers made a note of anything in either the AIDS text or the Pick 'n Pay text that they found strange or problematic. It is these reactions that are a resource for resistant reading.

If on the other hand we are the ideal reader of a text, sharing its presuppositions and the positions it takes up, then the text appears natural to us and it is harder to step back from it and to see it as a socially constructed representation. This is when we need analytic tools such as those suggested in this chapter, to enable us to stand outside of the text's structuring codes. Here we start from an engaged position and have to work towards an estranged position. It does not matter, whether we start from an engaged or an estranged position as long as in the end we are able to read both with a text and against it.

One year, I gave my students a text to analyse taken from *House and Leisure*, an upmarket home décor and life-style magazine. The text 'Little Princesses' (*Home and Leisure*, April 2002), an article on young girls' bedrooms, was framed in relation to the fairy tale 'The Princess and the Pea' in which 'a real princess' can feel 'a pea right through twenty mattresses and twenty feather beds [because] nobody but a real princess could be as sensitive as that'. The story is used to justify the excessive luxury advocated for the bedrooms of privileged girls from wealthy families. In addition to naturalising a class-based elitism the text infantilises the young girls and constructs them as agentless dolls, thus reproducing the women-as-passive/men-as-active gendered binary. One of my African students used her own cultural location to read against this text:

> This text is in all respects very strange to me. An ordinary Mosotho woman from a very poor family, I can hardly believe what is portrayed in the text. My culture is very different . . . Such extravagance that is enjoyed by the few, while the rest of the people die of hunger and AIDS. However, I will try to read with the text, although it is very difficult, so that I will be in a better position to analyse it.

Where in many contexts students experience their cultural alienation from classroom material as disempowering, there is evidence throughout this student's essay that she is able to see her own knowledge, her position of outsider to the world of the writer and his or her intended audience, as a resource that she can use with confidence.

While I would argue that all texts are positioned and positioning, I do not see anything sinister in this. It simply is. There would be no point in using language if we did not want people to take our views seriously and be persuaded by them. That is certainly what I hope is happening as you read this book. Why bother otherwise? What matters is not so much that texts work to position readers, but the effects of such positioning. Judgements about whether such effects are good or bad are ethical judgements based on standards of fairness, equity and compassion.

I am often asked whether a critical awareness of language can be used to hone the textual production of already powerful groups in society. There is no question that this is so. It is why businesses employ professional advertisers and governments employ speech writers, communications directors and spin doctors. In *Plan of Attack*, Woodward (2004) discusses the origins and force of the metaphor 'axis of evil' used by Bush to construct Iraq, Iran and North Korea as the countries that threaten the United States. Gerson, his speech writer, changed the phrase 'axis of hatred' to 'axis of evil', broadening the notion, making it more sinister, even wicked. It was almost as if Saddam was an agent of the devil (p. 87).

> Oversimplification was required in a sound-byte culture. . . . In the White House communications shop, Dan Bartlett the director was delighted. What a phrase, a mere five syllables. . . . He could see that the Axis of Evil would become a signature phrase, having a kind of clarity even daring. The starkness of putting it on the table broke through the clutter. The foreign policy priesthood often argued that diplomacy and policy were about nuance – in other words, clutter. Not so. Good versus evil worked.
>
> (Woodward, 2004: 94)

Texts have designs on us. As consumers of textual meanings, we have to be able to see the truths that texts constitute and that constitute them and we have to be able to imagine their effects. Critical reading, in combination with an ethic of social justice, is fundamental in order to protect our own rights and the rights of others.

CHAPTER 5

Diversity, Difference and Disparity

Introduction

Having looked in some detail at language, literacy and power, I turn now to issues of literacy, power and identity and the ways in which teachers work with the diverse identities that students bring with them to school. At the start of the twenty-first century, heterogeneity is the norm in multilingual, multicultural urban classrooms. Students are themselves multiply located across social categories such as gender, race, class, sexuality, ethnicity, religion, ability, which are inflected by their different histories. We need to think of identity as constantly in process, as dynamic rather than fixed, as produced but not determined. Wenger (1998) in recognising the effects communities of practice have on our discourses and literacies – our ways of being in the world – suggests that each of us is formed by our unique trajectory through and membership of these different communities, and that our formation is ongoing. Membership in these communities is further inflected by the social identities (for example, our gendered identity) that we embody. By imagining identity as fluid and hybrid, we resist essentialising people on the basis of any one of the communities to which they belong or to which we assign them. That said, we do have to respect and accommodate people's own knowledges, practices, and identity investments.

> You can ask your students to think of a situation in which an aspect of their identity that was important to them was not respected by

others. They should try to describe the situation and their reactions to it either in writing or with a partner.

It is particularly important to think about how teacher insensitivities and institutional practices with regard to difference impact on children and their families. I offer a story of my own to develop these ideas.

Christmas and the pink rabbit

In 1980 I went with my husband and two children to live in London, England. My older son who was six years old at the time was a student at the local state primary school. It was December and Christmas was everywhere apparent: on television, in trains and buses, in schools, in the streets, at the shops. People celebrate Christmas in South Africa too, but it is not quite as inescapable as it is in England. Schools break up early in December in South Africa, so Christmas is not part of school. As it is the summer holidays, many people are away from work and out of the towns.

My son's teacher in London, Mrs B, set a writing task for the students: they were to write to Father Christmas to tell him what they wanted for Christmas. My son, who knew that as Jews we do not celebrate Christmas, asked his teacher if he could write a story about a pink rabbit instead. She refused, insisting that 'St Nick loves all little children' and she would sort it out with his mother.

That was when all hell broke loose.

It was a long time ago, but I remember the fight I had with her as if it had happened this morning. When I arrived at school, my son told me what had happened and said that his teacher wanted to see me. I was incensed. I remember telling her that we were Jewish and that we did not celebrate Christmas. I remember telling her to take what my son, her student, was saying more seriously. I remember telling her that neither she nor the school could dictate to me, a parent, how I should run my home.

At the time, my son was playing King Melchior in the school Christmas pageant, and the teacher who obviously could not herself tell the difference between play-acting and real life, took this to mean that my husband and I would not object to doing Christmas in our home. I had to tell her that as I did not observe many of the holy days of my own religion, I was not about to observe the high holy days of her religion. Eventually, now fully exasperated with me, she said two things to me that I will never forget. She said 'Mrs Janks, when in Rome do as the

Romans', and she said 'Mrs Janks, you are making your child feel different'.

Here was her educational philosophy in a nutshell: assimilate or brand your child as different. And it was clear that for her different was not a good thing to be. Different was bad. Different was not normal. Different meant exclusion. I remember saying to her in the heat of my anger, 'Mrs B, my son **is** different, and I want to know what you are going to do about it'. We were by this time yelling at each other in the corridor and the principal led me away to her office to contain me. She offered me no support. Nor did she offer any to my son.

For the first time since I had arrived in England, I felt a profound sense of alienation. For the first time I knew that I did not belong. For the first time I did not want to belong. It effected a painful turning point in my attitude to my host country, which I never lost. I understood in a profound way, that it was not, and could not be, my home. At the time, in a new country, I had limited resources both theoretical and practical for dealing with my anger. This resulted in an overwhelming sense of disempowerment. On the positive side, this small episode gave me some understanding of what it feels like to be a displaced person and some understanding of what it feels like to be a parent of a child who is on the outside of what educational institutions construct as the mainstream.

How easy it would have been for Mrs B to let my son write about the pink rabbit. Not many children offer their teachers the gift of a way out. Lots of students simply become disaffected and disruptive, and who can blame them? How I hope that Mrs B (and other teachers like her) get to read this story.

What stands out for me in relation to this story, twenty years later, is how naturalised the practices in 'Rome' were for Mrs B. She did not recognise them as the practices of a socially powerful group. This process of naturalisation, which makes the social constructedness of practices invisible to those who belong, works to constitute the normal.

The Place of Diversity in the Model

In order to understand the place of diversity in the interdependent model for critical literacy, this chapter will develop the arguments contained in the diversity rows of the model (see Table 5.1).

Chapters 3 and 4 focused on the relationship between literacy, text and power, where the emphasis was on power without a full consideration of how power interfaces with diversity, access or design/redesign. It is therefore necessary to consider power in relation to each of these other orientations. In this chapter, I will therefore also discuss the power-without-diversity row in the model (Table 5.2).

Table 5.1 The Place of Diversity in the Model

Diversity without attention to relations of power	This leads to a celebration of diversity without any recognition that difference is structured in dominance and that not all discourses/genres/languages/literacies are equally powerful.
Diversity without access	Diversity without access to powerful forms of language ghettoises students.
Diversity without design	Diversity provides the means, the ideas, the alternative perspectives for reconstruction and transformation. Without design, the potential that diversity offers is not realised.

Janks, H. (1997). First published in *Discourse. Studies in the Cultural Politics of Education*, 18 (3) p. 337

Table 5.2 Power without Diversity

Power without diversity	Power without the recognition of difference and diversity naturalises dominant forms and practices and can lead to both the celebration of sameness and the demonisation of the other. Different perspectives capable of generating innovation and change are lost.

Power without Diversity

Two metaphors are helpful for explaining the naturalisation of socially constructed norms. But first, a well-known riddle:

A man and his son are involved in a terrible motor car accident. Both of them are seriously wounded and are rushed to hospital. The man dies in the ambulance on the way and the son is rushed into the operating room. The surgeon on duty refuses to operate saying, 'I can't operate, this is my son'. How is this possible?

Anyone who struggles with this riddle clearly thinks of surgeons as men, and does not therefore immediately realise that the surgeon is the boy's mother. To prevent this kind of confusion users of language often mark deviation from a supposed norm linguistically, as in '*woman* doctor', '*male* nurse' or '*female* astronaut'. The notion of *markedness* in linguistics is a good example of how one can tell what is considered normal – it takes the linguistically unmarked form. Similarly the normative position can be compared with the default settings on your computer: they are the ones that the computer assumes, unless told otherwise.

One of the ways in which power works is to construct dominant forms as the natural default position, with different forms constructed as other. Discussions of race and racialisation in the literature on critical multicultural education (May, 1999; Sleeter & McClaren, 1995) argue that 'white people "colonise" the definition of the normal' (Haymes, 1995: 111):

> Within the cultural logic of white supremacy difference is defined as the black 'other'. Black identity functions for white culture as a way to mark off difference and define white people as normal. In contemporary society this is how power passes itself off as embodied in the normal as opposed to the superior.
>
> (Haymes, 1995: 110)

McClaren and Torres (1999: 52) quote Wray and Newitz to explain the invisibility of whiteness:

> It has been the invisibility (for Whites) of whiteness that has enabled white Americans to stand as unmarked, normative bodies and social selves, the standard against which all others are judged (and found wanting). As such, the invisibility of whiteness is an enabling condition for both white supremacy/privilege and race-based prejudice.
>
> (Wray and Newitz, 1997: 3)

It is interesting to note how many times during the ceremony to inaugurate Barack Obama he was referred to as the first black president of the United States. In foregrounding his racial identity in this way he was marked as different from his predecessors, in much the same way as Hilary Clinton would have been marked as the first female president of the United States, had she been elected. This establishes white and male as the unmarked forms that would be literally un(re)markable.

In South Africa, because the Population Registration Act[1] legislated the racial classification of every citizen at birth, whiteness is not an invisible category. Nevertheless, many white South Africans fail to understand the full extent to which they have been privileged by their racial classification and the ways in which they continue to benefit:

> Making whiteness visible to Whites – exposing the discourses, the social and cultural practices, the material conditions that cloak

---

[1] One of the cornerstones of apartheid legislation, this Act has now been repealed.

whiteness and hide its dominating effects – is a necessary part of an antiracist project.

(Wray and Newitz, 1997: 3–4)

Enabling students to read forms of power and privilege is as central to a critical literacy project which sets out to help students understand how relations of power are both produced and changed, as it is to an anti-racist project.

The Valorisation of Sameness

The valorisation of sameness is illustrated in 'Spot the Refugee' (Figure 5.1), an advertisement produced by the office of the United Nations High Commissioner for Refugees (UNHCR) and published in *Newsweek* in 1995.

It is one of a series of four UNHCR Lego advertisements, which continue to appear as 'posters' for teachers to download from the UNHCR website (United Nations High Commission for Refugees, 1994–1997). The other three posters are: 'What's wrong here?', 'How does it feel?' and 'What's the difference?'[2] These other posters are discussed briefly in Chapter 8 (see Figure 8.1).

Since 1995, I have used 'Spot the Refugee' for teaching critical literacy to both students and teachers. Despite recognising the excellent work done by the UNHCR, I find the way in which refugees are constructed in these advertisements disturbing. An obvious place to begin analysing this text is with the prominent opening instruction to 'SPOT THE REFUGEE' printed in capital letters and a large bold font. This is the only command in a text that is otherwise made up of statements. If you respond to this imperative by looking carefully at the Lego figures, trying to find the one that stands out as a refugee, the text has already constructed you as someone who thinks of refugees as visibly different, as other. If you refuse this construction, but are nevertheless intrigued by the juxtaposition of Lego dolls and refugees, you may start reading the text. If you then do what the text suggests and look at the figure designated as the refugee, the figure in the 'Fourth row, second from the left. The one with the moustache', you will nevertheless have been reeled in by the text. This is followed by the discovery that you have been cheated, because

---

[2] My analysis of Spot the Refugee, first appeared in *Discourse*, Vol 26, 1, 2005. A more detailed analysis of all four Lego posters can be found there (Janks, 2005).

SPOT THE REFUGEE

There he is. Fourth row, second from the left. The one with the moustache. Obvious really.

Maybe not. The unsavoury-looking character you're looking at is more likely to be your average neighbourhood slob with a grubby vest and a weekend's stubble on his chin.

And the real refugee could just as easily be the clean-cut fellow on his left.

You see, refugees are just like you and me.

Except for one thing.

Everything they once had has been left behind. Home, family, possessions, all gone. They have nothing.

And nothing is all they'll ever have unless we all extend a helping hand.

We know you can't give them back the things that others have taken away.

We're not even asking for money (though every penny certainly helps).

But we are asking that you keep an open mind. And a smile of welcome.

It may not seem much. But to a refugee it can mean everything.

UNHCR is a strictly humanitarian organization funded only by voluntary contributions. Currently it is responsible for more than 19 million refugees around the world.

**UNHCR Public Information
P.O. Box 2500
1211 Geneva 2, Switzerland**

Newsweek

United Nations High Commissioner for Refugees

Models courtesy of The LEGO Group.

Figure 5.1 'Spot the Refugee'.
Source: http://www.unhcr.org/cgi-bin/texis/vtx/template?page=home&src=static/
teaching-tools/tchhr/tchhr.htm

The unsavoury looking character you're looking at is more likely to be your average neighbourhood slob with a grubby vest and a week-end's stubble on his chin. And the real refugee could just as easily be the clean-cut fellow on his left.

In addition, you will have been constructed as someone who assumes that refugees look like 'unsavoury', unshaved 'slobs'. And because you are now someone who sees refugees as both different from and inferior to you, you need to learn that 'clean-cut . . . refugees are just like you and me'.

Each of the four posters repeats this phrase:

- 'You see, he's a refugee. And as you can see, refugees are just like you and me'. ('What's wrong here?')
- *Exactly!* You see refugees *are* like you and me'. ('What's the difference?')
- 'The fact is, refugees are just like you and me'. ('How does it feel?')

'Sameness' is used to 'sell' refugees to local populations. 'Who', one might ask, 'are refugees the same as?' What is the norm on which sameness is based? Is it a Western norm? Is it a linguistic norm? Is it a racialised norm? Is it an ethnic sameness? What about religion?[3] The verbal message of sameness is reinforced by the visual text in which look-alike Lego dolls represent human beings. This construction of human subjects as children's playthings, as manipulatable toys, is a profound objectification that robs us all of life and agency. It is an unfortunate visual metaphor.

> Lego figures are yellow. Consider and discuss the effects of this choice.

---

[3] The use of 'he' in this advertisement presents the refugee as male, despite the fact that 80% of refugees are women and children (www.unhcr.ch, 15 May 2002). The gender stereotyping is reinforced in the visual images, where women tend to be shown without the occupation markers of the male figures and with jewellery. If one looks across the four advertisements, it is possible to see how this is further exaggerated in 'What's wrong here?' where five of the twenty dolls are women, three of whom have cleaning and gardening implements, one of whom has a bicycle and one of whom is carrying what could be tool boxes. The men figures have tools, and motorbikes and megaphones; there is a chef, a barman, a cowboy, a pirate, a cameraman, porters. In 'How does it feel?', although the refugee appears to be a man with a hint of a moustache, there appear to be as many women as men because helmets and occupational headgear have been replaced by caps and hats, which are more gender neutral. To further address the gender imbalance, all the dolls in 'What's the difference?' are identical females, shown with ponytail hairdos and necklaces.

John Thompson's (1984, 1990) five modes of operation of ideology are useful for making sense of this text and in the process its discourse of sameness. 'Spot the Refugee' presents us with a general decontextualised picture of refugees. Using reification, ever-increasing numbers of refugees are presented as a fact of life, not as an effect of human actions. The UNHCR is legitimated as a 'strictly humanitarian organisation', that is 'responsible for more than 19 million refugees'. That it is not state-funded, and that it operates around the world wherever there are refugees, further legitimates it as a non-partisan organisation. Ignoring the differences between people, between, for example, readers of *Newsweek* and refugees living in camps, is a classic example of dissimulation. This dissimulation leaves us unperturbed by the inequalities between the political North and the political South, between rich and poor, between people who have access to food and fresh water and people who do not, between schooled and unschooled, between people on opposite sides of the digital divide, between believers on different sides of a religious war, between men and women.[4] Unification provides the main thrust of the advertisement in which we are repeatedly told that refugees are like us. This construction of an 'us', a collective identity, minimises the fear of the other or others, a 'them' who are different from 'us'. There is no attempt here to think about flesh and blood diversity as capable of producing positive effects and that sees diversity as a 'productive resource', as something to value.

Constructing the Other

All of the UNHCR posters have a fundamental contradiction built into the text. Refugees are the same as you and me:

> Except for one thing.
> Everything they once had has been
> left behind. Home, family, possessions, all
> gone. They have nothing.
>
> ('Spot the refugee')

This refrain also appears with slight variations in each of the posters. What shifts is the agent responsible for the dispossession. In 'Spot the refugee' it is undefined 'others' who 'have taken away' their things; in 'What's wrong here?' there is an agentless passive 'everything they once had has been destroyed or taken away'; in 'What's wrong here?' the agents

---

[4] How are the political North (developed countries) and the political South (under-developed countries) positioned in terms of other binaries? See Chapter 3.

that 'swept away' their things along with their rights are 'violence' and 'hatred', abstract nouns without actors; in 'How does it feel?' there is no agent: 'everything you've known and loved is gone'.

So refugees are just like us, except that they are not. They have nothing. At the very moment that unity is declared, fragmentation emerges.The emphasis on what refugees have lost, by the use of repetition and overlexicalisation, suggests that we are simply the sum of our possessions. This is a fundamentally materialistic view of human worth. In addition, the text exonerates all of us – unnamed others, or neighbours-turned-enemy, are blamed for the plight of refugees. Divorced from history and geography, from socio-political and economic conditions, and from the ugly specifics of racial, ethnic and religious othering, the fact of refugees is presented simply as a state of affairs, with undefined causes and inevitable effects. In the face of this reification, the ever-increasing numbers of refugees is naturalised and there is little we can do. If we think about real refugees in actual contexts, such as Bosnia, Kosova, Rwanda, Zimbabwe, The Democratic Republic of Congo, East Timor, Afghanistan, Palestine, Iraq, rather than as a generalised category of people, this enables us to examine causes and to consider how our own countries are implicated. Which of our activities have produced these effects elsewhere? What activities might be needed to prevent this human suffering? How should our own countries' political and economic policies change so that the world is a safer place for everyone? What small things might each of us do, that could contribute to change?

Adegoke's (1999) research provides us with a critical analysis of representations in the South African press of foreign African countries and of foreign Africans living within or outside South Africa. Her research involved a critical discourse analysis of media texts collected during May 1998 from *The Star*, the *Mail and Guardian* and *The Sowetan*, three South African newspapers with high circulation in the Johannesburg region. These papers are aimed at different race- and class-based readerships. 'The study revealed that the predominant press discourses on foreign Africans in South Africa are systematically negative and xenophobic, as well as racialised' (Adegoke, 1999: iii). Adegoke established a set of conceptual frames for organising the topics of the articles analysed. Table 5.3, taken from Adegoke, lists the ten frames with the highest frequency of occurrence in the 296 articles on foreign African countries (1999: 95).

According to Adegoke, an analysis of these frames 'shows a preoccupation with chaos and anarchy, brutality and violence in African countries' and a 'bestial nature or lifestyle for foreign Africans'. In addition the focus on corruption and crime constructs Africa as a place of 'fraud', and 'self serving interests' (1999: 96).

Table 5.3

Frames	Number of occurrences	Percentage of total
War and violence	37	12.5%
Foreign relations	30	10.1%
Sports	26	8.8%
Economic crisis	20	6.8%
Dictatorship	19	6.4%
Civil unrest and riots	18	6.1%
Economic advancement	16	5.4%
Corruption and crime	15	5.1%
Total	**191**	**61.2%**

Adegoke, R. (1999). Media Discourse on Foreign Africans and the Implications for Education. Master's research report. University of the Witwatersrand, Johannesburg.

Adegoke argues that the generally negative discourse on foreign African countries relates to the xenophobic discourse in relation to foreign Africans in South Africa. Table 5.4 shows immigration and crime as the two frames that make up 76% of the 38 articles on foreign Africans.

Table 5.4

Frames	Number of occurrences	Percentage of total
Immigration and problems	15	39.5%
Crime	14	36.5%
Total	**29**	**76%**

Adegoke, R. (1999). Media Discourse on Foreign Africans and the Implications for Education. Master's research report. University of the Witwatersrand, Johannesburg.

According to Adegoke,

> African foreigners in South Africa are often represented in the South African press as burdens and criminals or as victims of crime. They 'flood' the country and use up resources, creating a social and economic burden for South African taxpayers. Thousands of them come in 'illegally', some 'obtaining citizenship fraudulently'. African foreigners are behind major crimes in South Africa such as drug dealing. . . . Even where a report represents foreign Africans as victims of crime [what is accentuated] is that they are often in the environment of or scene of a crime – 'found dead or injured'.

(Adegoke, 1999: 107)

In 2002, despite Mbeki's vision of an African Renaissance, we witnessed State abuse of asylum seekers and the continued othering encoded in the street construction of foreign Africans as 'makwerekwere'.[5] In 2008, some South Africans went on a rampage against foreign Africans in their local communities, killing many in the process. Adegoke concludes her research with a prescient argument that education needs to address the issues of xenophobia. To do this we need to move away from discourses of both sameness and othering.

> Invite your students to find out about refugees in your country. They could design a poster which represents refugees in a positive light and which is designed to make their fellow citizens value them.

Expurgation of the Other

As discussed in Chapter 2, Thompson (1990: 65) maintains that fragmentation is achieved by differentiation, that is 'the distinctions, differences and divisions between individuals', and by what he calls 'the expurgation of the other'.

> This involves the construction of an enemy within or without, which is portrayed as evil, harmful or threatening and which individuals are called upon collectively to resist or expurgate.
>
> (Thompson, 1990: 65)

Apartheid is an extreme example of differentiation; and the Nazi Holocaust, Bosnia and Rwanda are extreme examples of expurgation as genocide. In the 1980s in South Africa, the State used discursive constructions of oppositional forces to legitimate harsh State action against dissidents. Signs of conflict within the country were attributed to outside others in an attempt to maintain the illusion of a society without internal opposition. Disruption was said to be caused by 'agitators', 'outside agitators', 'insurgents', 'communists' (Janks, 1988).[6] These corrupting influences, which were constructed as entering South Africa from the outside, were blamed for a multitude of forms of resistance: labour disputes, education boycotts, rent strikes, the rejection of constitutional structures.

---

[5] 'Makwerekwere' is an insulting word for foreign Africans. It is derived from the unfamiliar sounds of their languages; 'kwerekwere' refers to the sounds heard by people who do not speak these languages.

[6] The language patterns reported in this research are based on an analysis of newspaper texts collected between 1986 and 1988.

By establishing opposition as emanating from outside, those who disagreed with the apartheid state were constructed as un-South African; with a clear divide established between 'us' and 'them'. Revolutionaries and communists were 'the enemy', the 'they' who try to undermine 'us', the 'them' against whom 'we' could unite. This them-and-us theme runs throughout a full-page advertisement placed in the major national Sunday paper, designed to sell the Apartheid government's reform policy. Figure 5.2 provides excerpts from this text, which took the form of an open letter, signed by P. W. Botha, the then State President of South Africa. I have kept the use of upper- and lower-case as well as the underlining which occurred in the original text. In addition to the underlining, which appears as if hand-drawn, the sections included here, in lower case, are also marked with vertical hand-drawn lines in both the left hand and right hand margins to emphasise their importance. What is chilling is the way this text reverberated for me when I heard President Bush's post 9/11 declaration 'if you are not with us, you are against us' and the ways in which this silenced many oppositional voices within the United States.

REVOLUTIONARIES MAY
STAMP THEIR FEET.
THE COMMUNISTS MAY
SCREAM THEIR LIES.
OUR ENEMIES MAY TRY
TO UNDERMINE US.
BUT HERE IS THE
REALITY.

Those who'd like to take over this country for their own selfish and cruel ideological ends … Well they can shout. They can criticize. They can refuse to acknowledge my sincerity. But, my friends try as they might, they can't deny reality … Peace and prosperity will come about for those who are with us. And despite those who are against us.

Sunday Times, 2 February 1986

Figure 5.2 Political Advertisement.

Here, as in the UNHCR advertisements, 'us' and 'them' pronouns are key to differentiation. It is important to consider who is included in their reference, who is excluded and why. These same revolutionaries, encoded as 'other' by dominant State discourses, were seen as part of 'the community' in counter-hegemonic discourses. Their belonging was encoded by words such as 'comrade', 'brother' and 'sister' (Janks, 1988: 87).

Othering takes place in 'smaller' but significant ways in everyday

Figure 5.3 Advertisement for Topsport.
No ascription allowed. Used with permission.

practices, many of which we see in schools, such as teasing, stereotyping, insulting, joking, in-grouping and excluding, turn-taking, who gets heard, who is silenced. Difference is also constantly constructed in everyday texts. Figure 5.3, a South African Broadcasting Company (SABC) television sports channel advertisement, published in the *Sunday Times*, 18 February 1986, is an example of such a text. The writing under the visual appears enlarged in Figure 5.4.

The writing directly below the picture says

> Direct from the mother continent of killer hot, SABC Topsport brings you live Cricket World Cup coverage. Scalding fresh action from Pakistan, India and Sri Lanka. Exclusive coverage of *all* the South African games, two quarter finals, three semi's (sic) and the finals. But remember no matter how hot it gets, don't drink the water.

Below these two lines of writing is the SABC Topsport Logo and the slogan 'Feel the Action'. To the right and the left of the logo are the schedules of the live broadcasts and the highlights programmes.

Figure 5.4 Text of the Topsport Advertisement.
No ascription allowed. Used with permission.

If you wanted your students to think about this advertisement, they would need to:

- notice all the ways, both verbal and visual, that the text in Figures 5.3 and 5.4 uses to construct 'the east' as other;
- find evidence to show that the other is constructed as dangerous – as a potential threat to us;
- discuss where in the world one has to be for Pakistan, India and Sri Lanka to be 'in the east' and discuss what this tells us about centre/periphery discourses and how they are constructed in relation to geography.

It is important to recognise that this text does not simply construct them, the other; it also constructs us. As *all* texts work to position their readers, it is important in education to include texts that carry the community's commonsense. These are often mundane texts, as it is in these that ideology is naturalised daily and subjects are repeatedly constructed.

Comber and Simpson's (1995) work with children on deconstructing cereal boxes illustrates the use of everyday texts for critical work with young children, as does O'Brien's (2001) work that enabled young children in her Reception classes to see how mothers are discursively constructed by Mother's Day cards. They provide us with powerful examples of how to use mundane texts in classrooms to develop children's understanding of textual power.

Diversity without a Theory of Power

Table 5.5 Diversity without Power

Diversity without attention to relations of power	This leads to a celebration of diversity without any recognition that difference is structured in dominance and that not all discourses/genres/ languages/literacies are equally powerful.

The classic example of the celebration of diversity is what Nieto (1996: 196), after Banks (1991), calls the 'holidays and heroes' approach to multi-cultural education. In this uncritical approach, decontextualised 'bits and pieces of the lived experience of dominated groups' are 'trivialised' when they are separated from larger understandings of their diverse cultures and their diverse histories, and when they are added 'as pieces of exotic content' to the margins of the curriculum (Nieto, 1999, 2002).

Linguistic diversity is often treated in much the same way in educational institutions. A dominant language is chosen as the medium of instruction, lip service is paid to multilingualism, and at best students are allowed to study their home language as a subject. Where multilingual practices are allowed in class, the teacher might use students' languages to explain a difficult concept, or allow one of the students to do so; students might be encouraged to use their own languages when working in groups; resources such as bilingual dictionaries may be available for students to use. In all these cases, students' languages are included but marginalised. This is also true of non-dominant varieties. Students might be allowed to use their own variety in speech but the standard is required in formal contexts and in written work. Students can often use 'non-standard dialects' to create atmosphere or characterisation in drama and 'creative writing', but the 'standard' variety remains the norm.

Many years of socio-linguistic research have now established that all varieties of language are 'equal', that is, they are all highly structured, systematic, rule-governed systems. The standard variety is no less a dialect, than other varieties. It has become the standard by a process of standard-isation, of norming. Usually the language of social elites, the standard's dominance is an effect of power. Labov's (1972) work on the logic of non-standard English, possibly the most cited research designed to counter arguments about linguistic deficit, was able to show that 'non-standard' varieties enable abstract logical reasoning, no less than the so-called standard variety (and that the 'standard' variety is itself not without limita-tions). However, that languages have no inherent linguistic inferiority or superiority does not mean that they enjoy social equality. What counts as acceptable language in different social contexts is tied to the construction of what Bourdieu (1991: 54) describes as a 'linguistic market':

> Linguistic exchange – a relation of communication between a sender and a receiver – ... is also an economic exchange. ... Words, utterances are not only ... signs to be understood and deciphered; they are also *signs of wealth*, intended to be evaluated and appreciated, and *signs of authority*, intended to be believed and obeyed.
>
> (1991: 66, original italics)

> The constitution of a linguistic market creates the conditions for the objective competition in and through which the legitimate competence can function as linguistic capital producing a profit of distinction on the occasion of each social exchange.
>
> (1991: 54)

This means that different varieties of the same language are differently valued. This produces a system of social distinction, providing linguistic capital to those who have access to the distinctive[7] language. For Bourdieu, the different power attributed to different varieties is a form of 'symbolic power' (1991: 72–76). By extension, in a multilingual society different symbolic power attaches not only to different varieties, but also to different languages. It is 'symbolic' because it depends on people's belief in the social distinctions; a language's legitimacy depends on people 'recognising', that is for Bourdieu 'misrecognising', its legitimacy (1991: 170).

Bourdieu calls it 'misrecognition' because he sees it as an example of institutionally manufactured compliance or consent. The education sys-tem is a central institutional apparatus for the privileging of a particular variety (or language) and for legitimating its dominance. Bourdieu draws attention to the fact that while the education system fails to provide

---

[7] Bourdieu plays with the ambiguity. 'Distinctive' means both different and distinguished.

students from subordinated classes with *knowledge of* and access to the legitimate language, it succeeds in teaching them *recognition of* (misrecognition of) its legitimacy (1991: 62, my emphasis).

While Bourdieu refuses to recognise the legitimacy of a dominant language he does not refuse to recognise its real power in socio-economic terms. The linguistic market is tied to the labour market. In South Africa, English has both symbolic value, people attribute status and distinction to those who speak it, and economic value, it increases one's chances of employment. In 'choosing' English-medium education for their children, parents hope to increase their children's linguistic capital. In so doing, they 'collaborate in the destruction of their own instruments of expression' (Bourdieu, 1991: 49). Access to dominant forms tends to come at the expense of diversity. This could be reversed if multilingualism were valued above competence in one dominant language. There is no reason why competence in more than one local or national language should not be a requirement of schooling.

It is interesting to note that speakers of marginalised languages or dialects tend out of sheer necessity to be more multilingual than speakers of dominant languages. In South Africa, Africans who speak one or more African languages are often also competent in one or both of the former official languages, Afrikaans and English. This phenomenon has also been noted by feminist research which shows that women have had to learn male interaction patterns, in addition to their own female styles of interaction, if they wish to be taken seriously by men. This is particularly true in the workplace (Holmes, 2006; Wodak, 1997)

The following activity is based on Orlek's workbook in the *Critical Language Awareness Series,* called *Languages in South Africa.* In the five years prior to the first democratic elections in South Africa there was an ongoing national language debate as educators and activists all over the country tried to envisage a different language policy for the new South Africa. The existing policy recognised only the two colonial languages, Afrikaans and English, as official languages, and limited recognition of the nine African languages spoken by the majority of the population, to the areas allocated for the separate development of ethnic groups, the bantustans. In the process of debating a future policy, we realised that there is nothing fixed or inevitable about a country's language policy and that policies can be contested and changed.

If you wish to imagine other possibilities in your own context, you will first need to find out what your country's national language policy is, and then re-imagine it.

Finding out

- If you live in a country where different states or provinces have their own policy, find out what the language policy is in your state or province.
- Find out the history of language policy in your country.
- What is the language-in-education policy where you live, in your school?
- Are the languages that students in your class speak given equal status and attention?
- What are the consequences of policy choices for speakers of different languages and for their education?
- Are there any signs of resistance to any of these policies? Are there any signs of change?

Re-imagine

- If you could design a new language-in-education policy that valued diversity for your country, what would it be? What languages would be included? How many languages would children be able to learn? What language/s would be used as the medium of instruction? How would this policy change in primary, secondary and tertiary education? Who would benefit from these changes? Who would be disadvantaged?
- What can you do as an individual and collectively to reduce linguistic prejudice?
- Think of one small thing that you can do to accommodate someone who speaks a language different from your own.

One of the main achievements of the New Literacies project[8] has been to successfully pluralise the concept of literacy by looking at literacy practices cross-culturally, in different domains, in different discourses and as they vary in relation to different sign systems and different technologies. It too can be considered in relation to questions of diversity and power. This work poses a challenge to autonomous models of literacy which view writing and text as autonomous modes of communication, independent

---

[8] NLS is embodied in the work of Heath (1983), Street (1984), Barton (1994), and Gee (1996). It has been further developed in edited collections by Street (1993), Barton and Hamilton (1998), Barton, Hamilton and Ivanic (2000), Breir and Prinsloo (1996) and Baynham and Prinsloo (2001).

of social context (Street, 1993). Street quotes Ong to explain his choice of the word 'autonomous' for dominant models of literacy:

> By isolating thought on a written surface, detached from any inter-locutor, making utterance in this sense autonomous and indifferent to attack, writing presents utterance and thought as uninvolved in all else, somehow self-contained, complete.
>
> (Ong, 1982: 132)

In contrast to this approach, the New Literacy Studies turns its attention to how literacy is used in different social and institutional contexts. Using anthropological theories and ethnographic methods, New Literacy Studies attempts to understand literacy events and practices. 'A literacy event is any occasion in which a piece of writing is integral to the nature of partici-pants' interactions and their interpretations of meaning' (Heath, 1983: 196 and 1983: 386, endnote).

While an event takes place in time and place and is an observable phenomenon, the notion of a literacy practice is an abstraction, and it refers to the underlying, regulated, patterned and culture-specific ways of using literacy that are not visible. Literacy practices are shaped by socio-cultural practices and their institutional locations. Understanding literacy as a social practice is very different from seeing literacy as a discreet set of autonomous skills. Street called this the 'ideological model' of literacy to signal that 'literacy practices are aspects not only of "culture" but also of power structures' (Street, 1993: 7).

If students complete tables such as this and add other events and practices that interest them. it will help them to understand these concepts. The idea for tables such as this is taken from Pahl and Rowsell (2005)

Literacy event	Literacy practice	Social practice
Applying for a driving licence	Filling in a form	Driving
Compiling a shopping list with the family	Making lists	Shopping
Discussing an applicant's references		
		Banking
	Letter writing	
Singing a hymn		
	Internet research	
		Watching television

In order to understand the diversity of literacy practices, New Literacy Studies has focused on 'vernacular' or non-dominant literacy practices, in much the same way as Labov investigated and described vernacular or language varieties marginalised as 'non-standard'. These vernaculars, the varieties used by ordinary people, are at best overlooked or ignored by social elites and dominant institutions and at worst denigrated and constructed as deficient. Importantly, work in New Literacy Studies has provided a challenge to dominant discourses about literacy. While it has successfully been able to pluralise our understanding of literacy and to stress the importance of diversity, it has not been able to change the 'distinction' (in Bourdieu's (1984, 1991) sense of the word) that comes with access to educated, school-based literacy, any more than socio-linguists have been able to dent the power of standard varieties of powerful languages. It is not enough to document the vernacular literacies that exist, a danger inherent in ethnographic case studies. One also has to explore the relationship of these literacies to more dominant literacies. It is important to remember that difference, including different literacies, is structured in dominance and that not all literacies are equally powerful.

My analysis is supported by the arguments put forward by Heller (2008). She too sees the connection between the autonomous model and processes of language standardisation and shows how they were both forms of symbolic domination. Both established criteria within nation states for 'determining who counts and who does not, and invite the elaboration of legitimating theories which authorise selection and therefore exclusion' (Heller, 2008: 57). Together with Bourdieu (1977), she argues against views of language as a 'reified system' as this denies an understanding of language as a 'social practice embedded in constructions of relations of power' (2008: 57). While she applauds the New Literacy Studies for its attempt to deconstruct the concept of literacy itself, she argues that this can only be partially successful because 'they fail to engage with its political, economic and social bases' (2008: 64). They do not manage to

> destabilise the notion that there is such a thing, and that mastery of it is a sign of full competence as a member of society and perhaps more importantly as a credible job candidate.
>
> (2008: 63)

The recognition of literacies has to include the recognition that they are not equally valued and they do not offer equal access to symbolic and economic capital.

In her analysis of *Situated Literacies*, the collection edited by Barton, Hamilton and Ivanič (2000), Maybin writes,

The language people use at a local level inserts them into discursive patternings associated with wider social institutions, and ... these wider patternings encode particular conceptions of truth, knowledge, power, subjectivity. The articulation of these discourses at a local level, *therefore* provides a key linkage with broader social structures. In addition, because discourses carry potentials for the positioning of individuals and their subjectivity, their articulation in local activities is also tied up with negotiations and struggles around people's sense of their own identity.

> (Maybin, 2000: 202–203, my emphasis)

Her use of the word *therefore* suggests that the 'linkage' between the local and the social more broadly defined is obvious and logically inevitable. I would argue that these connections need to be made explicit as do the discursive struggles around positioning and identity. The best work in New Literacy Studies does this, exploring the complexity of the relationship between the micro contexts of everyday language use and the macro concerns of society, culture, politics and power (Pennycook, 2001: 172), and in so doing they provide a critical perspective.

The following kinds of activities can be used by teachers to engage students in ethnographic data gathering.

- Choose a place (an office, a restaurant, in a bus or train) and describe all the literacy events that you observe there in a fixed amount of time (one or two hours). In ethnography such a place is called a 'site'.
- Pick a domain (such as your home or your school/university) and list (or photograph) the different kinds of literacy texts that are on display. For the purposes of this activity, I will define a literacy text as a verbal or a verbal/visual text.
- Pick two different school subjects (e.g. English and Science) and describe the kinds of writing expected by one class in these two different disciplines.
- Keep a literacy diary for one day. List all the literacy events that you participate in. Compare your literacy diary with others.

It is important for students to make connections between the data they collect and wider social patterns and structures.

Brouard (2000), Brouard, Wilkinson and Stein (1999) and Pahl and Rowsell (2005) show how a New Literacy Studies approach can be used in classrooms.

Diversity without Access

> **Diversity without access** Diversity without access to powerful forms of language ghettoises students.

It is clear that the more languages one speaks the more speech communities one has access to. The same is true of other kinds of linguistic variation. I would argue that one of the aims of education should be to increase students' linguistic repertoires. Gee stresses the importance of acquiring secondary discourses in addition to one's primary discourse and goes so far as to define literacy as 'mastery of, or fluent control over, a secondary discourse' (1990: 153). Our primary discourse is the language of home and community learnt from socialisation within the family. Secondary discourses belong to the public sphere and are associated with institutions outside the home as well as with the professions and different kinds of employment (Gee, 1990: 152). Without acquiring secondary discourses we remain locked into our local communities. While speakers of a dominant world language such as English, a language with a great deal of linguistic capital, are able to move beyond the confines of the local, monolingualism limits their perspectives. Given Bourdieu's (1991) theory of a linguistic market, the more linguistic capital one has, the greater one's social and economic mobility. Hierarchies of distinction play a central role in determining which languages, literacies, discourses people desire and need.

Vernacular languages and literacies do not give people from marginalised communities access to the mainstream, particularly in contexts where the medium of education is in the standard variety of the dominant language. Delpit (1988; Perry & Delpit, 1998) has been a strong advocate in the US for the use of explicit pedagogies that provide African American children with access to standard forms of English, but not at the expense of children's home language, Ebonics. She sees the value of children's community language in relation to identity, self-worth, standing in the community and enculturation as indisputable, while simultaneously being able to recognise the importance of English for access to the wider society. Delpit's position is shared by other educators in the field of bilingual education (Corson, 2001; Cummins, 2000; Martin-Jones, 2006).

Concerned with making the genres that students need to master to succeed in educational contexts accessible, the genre theorists (Derwianka, 1990; Martin, Christie, & Rothery, 1987) made explicit the features of six genres regularly used in schools – recounts, instructions, narratives, reports, explanations and arguments. Their work made literacy educators question their naturalised assumptions about students' linguistic and cultural knowledge and challenged us to think more carefully about degrees of explicitness that might be needed in teaching students from diverse communities. Their work has been criticised as too didactic, and as uncritically naturalising the status quo. In addition, by reifying the features of these genres they inhibited creativity and possibilities for subversive and/or transformative redesign (Cope & Kalantzis, 1993; Kress, 1999). Although I agree with these criticisms, I also think it is important to recognise that genre pedagogy took questions of access for non-mainstream students very seriously.

While genre theory addresses the literacy needs of students in schools, the field of academic literacy addresses the language and literacy needs of tertiary students. With increased human mobility, university populations worldwide are now more diverse in terms of age, race, class, ethnicity and nationality and one can no longer assume that staff and students share the same kind of schooling, the same cultural capital, the same language. In the late 1980s, when my own institution, the University of the Witwatersrand, began admitting larger numbers of black students in defiance of apartheid laws, the needs of these 'disadvantaged' students put teaching and learning on the University agenda. At first, this led to the development of academic support programmes. Here students 'with deficits' were given additional remedial instruction in study skills and English for academic purposes on a voluntary add-on basis (Starfield, 2000: 27). Staff sent students to the Academic Support Programme (ASP) and to the English Second Language (ESL) course in Communication Studies to be 'fixed up', while teaching in academic departments continued unchanged. The 1990s saw a shift from 'academic support' to 'academic development', a move from student-focused support to support for staff in redesigning their mainstream curricula and pedagogies so as to address the needs of a diverse student body. Discipline-specific, credit-bearing foundation courses were also introduced. Because the discourse requirements of different disciplines are specific to the discipline, generic courses in language and literacy are in any case only of limited value. In addition, it is the interface between conceptual and linguistic development that provides the real challenge to the development of students' literacy in a discourse, rather than language and study skills courses in isolation. Without a focus on academic development in general, and academic literacy in particular, students who gained access to the University would have been denied epistemological access (Morrow, 2008) and might well have been excluded. Many researchers working in the field of academic literacy work at the interface of access, diversity and power (Benesch, 2001; Cadman, 2006; Clarence-Fincham, 1998; Clark & Ivanic, 1997; Ivanic, 1998; Lillis, 2001; Starfield, 1994, 2000).

- Find examples of people who have felt stigmatised by pro-grammes or practices designed to give them access, and suggest how such programmes or practices might be transformed.
- Find examples of classroom practices that make use of the diverse linguistic and cultural resources that students bring to class, so as to give minority students access to dominant languages, literacies and discourses, and students from socially dominant groups access to local languages.

Diversity without Design/Redesign

Diversity without design Diversity provides the means, the ideas, the alternative perspectives for reconstruction and transformation. Without design, the potential that diversity offers is not realised.

Different communities use different symbolic resources for making mean-ing and the differences in meaning across cultures denaturalise our taken-for-granted discourses. Such ruptures are a potential source of innovation. Kostogriz, in a doctoral thesis entitled *Rethinking ESL Literacy Education in Multicultural Conditions*, offers us a way of thinking about diversity as a productive resource. Building on the work of bell hooks (1990), Homi Bhabha (1990) and Edward Soja (1996), he theorises a space of radical openness in which a 'dialogic affirmation of difference' (2002: 155), 'semiotic border crossing' and the dynamics of cultural hybridity (p. 155) provide the resources for imagining new possibilities. He argues for a Thirdspace that cuts across the binaries of 'us' and 'them' and enables the production of new meanings based on our 'diverse semiotic resources and funds of knowledge' (p. 237). He sees cultural collisions as a driving force that enables us to re-mediate and re-present the world (p. 237) and that produces the creative energy necessary for transformation and change. For Kostogriz, as migrants learn new

Figure 5.5 'Einstein was a Refugee'.
Used with permission from the UNHCR with acknowledgement to the Betteman Archive.

languages and assume new identities, they have to find their way through the often incommensurate discourses that they inhabit.

> This tension leads to the articulation of new emergent possibilities of cultural reinvention, transformation and change in educational settings and in wider socio-cultural spheres of life. The productive force of thirding and hybridity then becomes a key issue in the cultural making of new practices, meanings and discourses.
>
> (Kostogriz, 2002: 5)

If we apply Kostogriz's work to the UNHCR Lego advertisements, it is clear that to speak of refugees as having nothing and to imagine that 'nothing is all they'll ever have unless we extend a helping hand', fundamentally devalues the knowledges, skills and values that they have to offer and negates the fullness of the human resources that they bring. A transformative reconstruction is needed.

Figure 5.5, also a UNHCR advertisement, provides us with a very different construction of refugees. Here we have an example of a refugee who has made a significant contribution to his adopted country and to the world. The Albert Einstein advertisement offers a counter argument to the belief that refugees have nothing (see Figure 5.5).

Compare this transformed UNHCR advertisement with the advertisements designed by you and others.

The thought that we might be remoulded into sameness, like Lego dolls, suggests a dull monochromatic world. What we need is a world in which we can learn from our differences, be excited by conflictual perspectives, and all be treated with openness and care.

CHAPTER 6

Access, Gate-Keeping and Desire[1]

The fact that difference is structured according to existing relations of power produces social disparities. Our place in both the social hierarchy and the global economy shapes our life chances and our opportunities for access. While this chapter focuses on access to the languages and literacies of power, it is important to remember that these cannot be separated from access to the kinds of resources that make education possible for children: clean water, food, clothing, care, housing, health services, transport. The relationship between literacy and educational projects that address social needs will be explored in Chapter 8, where the focus is on critical literacy for reconstruction.

We saw in the last chapter that access and inclusion tend to come at the expense of diversity, so efforts to increase access need to be counterbalanced by efforts to maintain and strengthen diverse and marginalised forms and to recognise that all forms are dynamic and open to hybridisation and transformation – to redesign. This chapter will focus on the access dimension of the interdependent model. 'Who gets access to what?' is a key question for critical approaches to education in general. 'Who gets access to which languages, linguistic varieties, literacies, genres, discourses?' is a key question for critical approaches to *literacy* education. This question takes us to the heart of the relationship between access and power, that is, to mechanisms for social inclusion and exclusion.

---

[1] The ideas in this chapter were first published in Janks (2004), The access paradox, *English in Australia*, 12(1): 33–42. Many of the ideas were first developed in Janks, 1995.

The word *access* as it is used in the interdependence model discussed in this book is a noun (as are the words domination, diversity and design). Unlike verbs, nouns do not have actors and the actions are hidden. It is worth thinking about the following questions in relation to your own context.

1. In your context, in relation to language and literacy, what do people need access to?
2. Who gets this access? What do they have to do to get this access? Who provides this access?
3. Which people experience difficulty getting this access? Who or what obstructs their access? What do these people have to do to get access?
4. It is also worth considering which agents and actions are obscured by the other nouns in the model: domination (and power), diversity (and difference), design.

In South Africa, language in education policy since independence entitles learners to education in any of South Africa's eleven official languages. However, the classroom materials needed to make this entitlement more than a policy promise do not yet exist.

The majority of parents want their children to learn English. Because most African parents believe that learning English as a subject is not adequate to ensure full access to English, they believe that it is also necessary for their children to learn through the medium of English (Hendricks, 2006) Parents' 'recognition' of English as a means to an improved socio-economic status continues to increase the dominance of English in schools, despite the government's multilingual language policies and a Constitution that enshrines language rights. That English has extremely high symbolic value (Bourdieu, 1991) in South Africa is not an accident. Rather, as Pennycook (1998) argues with respect to other colonial contexts, it is an effect of powerful colonial discourses which continue into the present. Since independence, many white South Africans desire access to at least one African language. In an urban area like Johannesburg, where speakers switch between African languages, multilingual fluency across Sotho and Nguni language families is what is needed. Very little material exists in print for teaching African languages. The few newspapers, magazines, literary works, textbooks that do exist are not particularly suitable for second or foreign language learners.

Now, despite a constitution which enshrines language rights along with other basic human rights, the increasing hegemony of English has proved to be an obstacle to the formal establishment of multilingualism in high status domains in South Africa. The new national curriculum statements, R-9 and 10–12, published in 2002 and 2003 respectively, together with the *Language Policy for Higher Education* are designed to 'compel transformation' (DOE, 2002a, b, 2003) in terms of the language clauses of the *Constitution*. The school curriculum requires all students to study at least two South African languages. While it is recommended that one of these should be an African language, this is not a requirement. Given the availability of resources for teaching English and Afrikaans, the official languages prior to independence, there is an urgent need to develop modern materials for the teaching of African languages as well as to educate teachers in modern methods for teaching these languages. In addition, until such time as African languages are used for teaching and learning in higher education, African parents will continue to choose English medium of instruction for their children's education.

In my research at Phepo,[2] a primary school in an African township outside of Pretoria where the children speak African languages at home, I am conscious of how using English as the language of teaching and learning inhibits student participation. In this school, students learn through the medium of Setswana from Grade 1 to Grade 4, while learning English as a subject. In Grade 5 they switch to English medium of instruction, although in practice, the teachers regularly code-switch between English and an African language, usually Setswana, in order to facilitate understanding. When the students in a Grade 7 class are expected to respond in English, only about five children out of 43 are confident enough to do so. The rest are mute, robbed of language. In small groups, where these same children are allowed to use an African language, not necessarily their home language, the children come alive. The group dynamics change: different children emerge as leaders and there is a flood of ideas as the children are rescued from the silence imposed by English.

Using a multiliteracies approach with Grade 3 and 4 children, it became clear that the children could convey more meaning with their drawings than they could with spoken or written English.

Figure 6.1 is a Grade 3 child's visual representation of the playground, which shows children skipping, fighting, playing hopscotch, playing a chasing-catching game. Much is happening at once. The child's representations of the space with a tree, walls, tyres used to edge flower beds, and steps between the beds, make it easy to recognise exactly which section of the yard the child has drawn. In addition, the representations of the

---

[2] Phepo is a pseudonym for the school.

Figure 6.1 Grade 3 Child's Drawing of the School Playground.
Used with permission from the children and their parents.

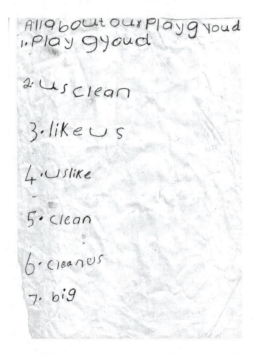

Figure 6.2 Grade 3 Child's Written Description of the School Playground.
Used with permission from the children and their parents.

children's bodies show emotions and movement. Even the tree appears to be running.

The same child's written text (Figure 6.2) is sparse by comparison and appears to bear little relation to the drawing.

The child's linguistic ability – one-word and two-word sentences, unconnected to one another – limits what can be said. The writing shows uncertainty as to the basic word order of English. 'Us clean' and 'us like' uses subject-verb word order, while 'clean us' and 'like us' uses verb-subject order. The child's use of both forms for each meaning suggests an awareness that word order is an issue. In addition, the distinction between the subject and object forms of the pronoun, 'we' and 'us', has not yet been acquired. Here all the child is able to tell us is that children like the playground, they clean it and see it as big. 'Gyound' is a representation of the sound of the word 'ground' as heard by the child. The drawing shows that the child understands the genre of 'telling all about' but as yet is unable to produce it in English. Within 18 months, this child will be expected to cope with English as the medium of instruction.

Access to dominant linguistic forms is not a simple matter. We have to consider both its effects and its conditions of possibility in order to consider our practices in multilingual classrooms. It is important to get access right, because what is at stake is nothing less than students' identities and students' futures. The interdependent model is a means of holding access in tension with different imperatives.

The Place of Access in the Model

This chapter will develop the arguments in the access rows of the interdependent model for critical literacy in order to understand the relationship between access and the other dimensions of the model: power, diversity and design (see Table 6.1).

Table 6.1 The Place of Access in the Model

Access without power	Access without a theory of power leads to the naturalisation of dominant discourses without an understanding of how these powerful forms came to be powerful.
Access without diversity	This fails to recognise that difference fundamentally affects pathways to access and involves issues of history, identity and value.
Access without design	This maintains and reifies dominant forms without considering how they can be transformed.

As discussed in Chapter 4, there is also a need to consider how power interfaces with access by examining the power-without-access row of the model.

Table 6.2 Domination without Access

Power without access	This maintains the exclusionary force of dominant discourses.

Power without Access

We need to think about powerful languages, powerful discourses, powerful literacies and who has access to them. In his inaugural lecture, *The Order of Discourse*, Foucault focuses on how discourse (rather than either language or literacy) is ordered, how

> the production of discourse is at once controlled, selected, organised and redistributed by procedures whose role is to ward off its powers and dangers, to gain mastery over its chance events, to evade its ponderous, formidable materiality.
>
> (1970: 109)

These include

- procedures of exclusion which control who has the right to speak;
- internal procedures which police and constrain discourses according to disciplinary rules, methods, techniques, truths;
- procedures which govern access.

For Foucault

> None shall enter the order of discourse if he [sic] does not satisfy certain requirements or if he is not, from the outset, qualified to do so. To be more precise: not all the regions of discourse are equally open and penetrable; some of them are largely forbidden (they are differentiated and differentiating), while others seem to be almost open to all winds and put at the disposal of every speaking subject, without prior restriction.
>
> (1970: 120)

He goes on to say that

> Ritual defines the qualification which must be possessed by the individuals who speak . . .: it defines the gestures, behaviour, circumstances, and the whole set of signs which must accompany discourse.
>
> (1970: 121)

It is important to recognise that access to discourse is highly regulated and that systems of exclusion produce distinctions which privilege those who get through the discourse gates. Discourses are both differentiated (organised hierarchically, with exclusive discourses having higher status) and differentiating (organising speaking subjects in relation to which discourses they have access to). It is ritual that makes discourses the complex configurations of 'saying (writing)-doing-believing-valuing' (Gee, 1990: 142) that structure access and exclusion. Foucault sees education as the system which is capable of 'maintaining or modifying the appropriation of discourses, along with the knowledges and powers that they carry' (1970: 123).

Foucault's emphasis on the right to speak, which he links to the issue of authority, supports Bourdieu's understanding that cultural and linguistic capital include the power to be heard and believed, the power to impose reception.

> The competence that we have to produce sentences that are likely to be understood might be quite inadequate to produce sentences that are likely to be *listened to* . . . Speakers lacking the legitimate competence are *de facto* excluded from the social domains in which this competence is required.
>
> (Bourdieu, 1991: 55; original italics)

Access is not just about getting access to powerful forms of language; it is also about access to audiences, to platforms, to modes of distribution such as publication, to influential networks. How we teach literacy can make a significant difference to the ways in which the cultural and linguistic capital, associated with powerful discourses, dominant languages, elite varieties and elite literacies, are distributed.

It is important to explore the link between the words *exclusion* and *exclusivity*. Differentiation implies that some people have access where others are excluded. This creates an exclusive system with elite-haves who are insiders and excluded have-nots. Distinction depends in part on exclusivity – as more people gain access to distinctive forms, what counts as distinctive shifts. The goal-posts keep moving and access remains as elusive as world peace.

To illustrate this point, we can think about how the requirements for different forms of employment have changed in our different contexts. For example, having a doctoral degree used to be the height of distinction. Nowadays, in some contexts, *where* one qualified and *who* supervised one's research are additional forms of distinction that are needed to give one an edge in a competitive job market.

According to Shor (1980) the *National Policy and Higher Education: The Second Newman Report* in the United States states that

> because so many have been to college, a college education is now a necessary but not a sufficient condition for social mobility. Not having a degree may block opportunities, but having it will not ensure them.
>
> (Shor 1980, after preface, no page number)

In addition, *Work in America* reports that

> most employers simply raised educational requirements without changing the nature of jobs . . . for a large number of jobs, education and job performance appear to be inversely related.
>
> (Shor 1980, after preface, no page number)

As more people get through the gates, the gates move. This is what is meant by the metaphor of shifting the goal-posts.

In relation to your own context

1. Find examples of discourse 'gates' in your own context.
2. Find an example of how 'the goal-posts' have shifted for teachers and/or students.
3. Foucault says that 'discourse is the power to be seized' (1970: 110). Can you think of any examples in your own context to support or challenge this statement?

Where Foucault works with the order of discourse, we have seen how other theorists work with the ordering of language varieties (Bourdieu, 1991; Labov, 1972) and of literacies.

Language mapping

I regularly ask my students to produce a language map of the class. List all the languages spoken by students on the board and then ask students in groups to rank these languages from high to low status. They should also work out the criteria they need to do this. This activity includes students' heritage languages, such as Urdu, Portuguese, Cantonese or Greek spoken by established communities; religious languages such as Arabic and Hebrew; and foreign languages spoken by new immigrants. In discussion, the students need to consider the different domains in which all these languages are used and to consider the prestige attached to these domains. The ranking usually results in ranked bands, as students often elect to give equal status to some of the languages.

This activity asks students to understand the difference between a language's legal status and its social status and it also makes them aware of their own, often intolerant and prejudiced, attitudes to other languages.

As soon as the mapping and ranking activities have been completed, I ask students to think about how this hierarchy of languages is maintained in their society, whether it needs to be changed, and what they can do to transform current practices.

In the next section, I consider the ordering of languages by focusing on the current power of English in relation to other languages.

Understanding the forces – social, historical, economic, technological – that have produced and that continue to produce the relative power of languages, reduces the symbolic power of English. This in turn helps us to recognise that English is not intrinsically superior to other languages – such a perception is an effect of power. Pedagogies of access need to be tempered by such understanding.

The Power of English

Information on the use of English globally is easy to find on the web. Two significant reports on the status of English were commissioned by the British Council and written by David Graddol (1997, 2006) and published nine years apart. The following information taken from the British Council website summarises the findings of the 1997 research (see Figure 6.3).

What is interesting is that nine years later the picture is different in significant ways. In 2001, for example, English from Grade 3 was made compulsory in China's schools; in 2005 an estimated 137 million children enrolled in primary school; China alone now produces 20 million new speakers of English each year (Graddol, 2006: 95–100). Moreover, learning English as a foreign language has increasingly moved from the secondary school curriculum to the primary school curriculum. According to Graddol's 2006 report,

[i]n the space of the next few years there could be around 2 billion people learning English in many different contexts around the world.

(2006: 100)

Speakers of English	What English is used for	People learning English
English has official or special status in at least seventy five countries with a total population of over two billion English is spoken as a first language by around 375 million people. 375 million people who speak English as a second language probably outnumber those who speak it as a first language There are approximately 750 million speakers of English as a foreign language A quarter of the world's population speaks English, with varying degrees of fluency.	English is the main language of books, newspapers, airports and air-traffic control, international business and academic conferences, science, technology, diplomacy, sport, international competitions, pop music and advertising Over two-thirds of the world's scientists read in English 80% eighty per cent of the world's electronically stored information is in English 36% of the approximately 200 million users of the Internet, communicate in English	By the year 2000 it was estimated that over one billion people will be learning English At any one time there are 130,000 students learning English and through the medium of English in British Council teaching centres worldwide. Children in China have to learn English in school.
http://www.britishcouncil.org/learning-faq-the-english-language.htm, downloaded 16 April 2009.		

Figure 6.3 The English Language.

The historical foundations for the current dominance of English were established during the years of Empire, when communities of English speakers settled in British colonies around the world, beginning in the seventeenth century with the settlement of colonies in America, and consolidated by the end of the nineteenth century with colonies in the West Indies, Africa, the Indian subcontinent and Australasia. Other European languages such as French, Dutch, German, Spanish and Portuguese were also spread by colonial expansion but the pre-eminent position of English was firmly established in the twentieth century by the rise of the United States as a world superpower. The status of English grew alongside the economic, technological, scientific and cultural dominance of the USA. But these historical processes were neither neutral nor inevitable. Critical analysts such as Phillipson (1992) and Pennycook (1994) provide evidence of work done by the British Council, for example, to sell English to the rest of the world for political and economic purposes. As early as 1956, the Ministry of Education in England reported that

> English is a commodity in great demand all over the world. . . . We are, therefore, looking at the language mainly as a valuable coveted export, which many nations are prepared to pay for . . . English is, moreover, an export which is likely to attract other exports – British advisers and technicians, British technological or university

education, British plant and equipment and British capital investment.

(quoted in Pennycook, 1994: 155)

Now, in the first part of the twenty-first century, English is driven by globalisation and it is its current status as the lingua franca that gives those who speak it a competitive advantage. However, were it to become a basic skill for everyone, it would no longer provide its speakers with a competitive edge. Already the increasing number of people learning Spanish and Mandarin suggests that English is no longer enough. Mandarin is now seen as the 'must have' language and 30 million people are registered in Confucius language institutes in key political and economic centres across the globe (Graddol, 2006: 62). Perhaps more important than this is how the use of English as a global lingua franca has produced a 'declining reverence for native speakers as the gold standard for English' (Graddol, 2006: 66). English is used for exchanges between non-native speakers of English where what matters is intelligibility and pragmatic strategies for communication. The language is adapted to the needs of the participants. Often it is native speakers of English who have the most difficulty in using English as a language for international communication (2006: 87). According to Canagarajah, where languages are learnt through the use of

> [p]erformance strategies, situational resources and social negotiations in fluid communicative contexts . . . the previously dominant constructs such as form, cognition and the individual are not ignored, they are redefined as hybrid, fluid, and situated in a more socially embedded, ecologically sensitive, and interactionally open model.
>
> (2007: 291)

In South Africa, Ndebele argued that '[t]eaching English is good [colonial] politics' and he sees the Commonwealth as an 'alliance of users of English' by English-speaking countries (1998: 6). Phillipson (1992) sees 'linguistic imperialism' as an extension of imperialism more generally – structured dominance that produces inequalities between nations. Pennycook (1994) extends this analysis to include 'the cultural politics of English as an international language' – the ways in which the spread of English is tied to the privileging of forms of knowledge and culture. The Hollywood media industry, for example, has succeeded in exporting US culture to the world.

In South Africa, during the time of the liberation struggle, African writers either resisted or appropriated the power of English. Ndebele (1998: 217) maintained that

English cannot be considered an 'innocent' language. The problems of a society will also be the problems of the predominant language of that society. It is the carrier of its perceptions, its attitudes, and its goals, for through it the speakers absorb entrenched attitudes. The guilt of English then must be recognised and appreciated before its continued use can be advocated.

For Mphahlele (2008), in the 1980s, appropriation entails a deliberate rejection of the way in which English encodes Western culture and the domestication of English to express an African sensibility. In *Decolonising the Mind*, Ngũgĩ (1981) argues differently. He believes that African writers should refuse to write in the colonial languages in order to free their own minds and those of their readers. He wrote many of his novels in Gĩkũyũ.

In Janks (1995) I used Arthur's (1988, 1989, 1990) economic theory of increasing returns to understand and explain the increasing power of English. Arthur uses VHS and Beta video tape technologies as an example. Although Beta is the superior product, the one chosen for use in the industry, the public at first bought more VHS video players than Beta players. The demand for movies on VHS in video shops therefore outstripped the demand for Beta tapes so the video shops stocked more VHS videos. People thinking of buying video machines learnt that VHS videos were more available so they chose VHS over Beta and so on. The more this happened, the more VHS increased its dominant position in the market. This snowball effect leads to 'lock in' – one product taking over the market, even if it is inferior. This process is not easy to reverse or halt, but it can be affected by a dramatic shift in technology, such that video tapes are no longer needed. And this is precisely what is happening with the introduction of DVDs and DVD players.[3] In November 2004, a South African radio station, Classic FM, reported that thieves in the European and American metropole, are no longer stealing VCRs; in 2004, my own local

---

[3] Arthur also uses the example of the QWERTYUIOP keyboard to illustrate lock-in. The layout of the keys on this keyboard is now used everywhere. Originally there was a different keyboard that enabled typists to type more quickly. Speed caused the keys on these old-fashioned typewriters to jam. The QWERTY keyboard was deliberately designed to slow typists down. That is, it was specifically designed to be less efficient. Singer manufactured new typewriters using this slower keyboard on a massive scale. By chance, this was the most available keyboard on the market at that time, so many people happened to be trained to use it. This put the inferior QWERTY keyboard into a position of increasing returns: The more people who trained to use it, the more machines were manufactured; the more these machines were manufactured, the more people needed to be trained to use this specific machine. The QWERTY keyboard achieved lock-in and captured the market (Granville *et al.*, 1998).

video rental store in Johannesburg had signs up on every shelf which read 'time to switch to DVD', alerting customers to their intention to stock only DVDs in future.

Although Arthur was working with economic markets, not Bourdieu's metaphorical linguistic market, it is possible to substitute 'language' or 'language variety' or 'genre', or 'discourse' where he refers to 'product'. In considering the idea of increasing returns in relation to the status of languages, one can see that English has already pulled ahead in the marketplace. Images taken from Pennycook which describe the inevitable growth of English, capture what Arthur means by increasing returns. They include images of English as 'spreading like primordial ooze' (1998: 138),[4] and 'eating up, like Aaron's rod, all other languages' (1998: 134).[5] Pennycook (1998: 133–139) provides litanies attesting to the 'wondrous spread' of English, our 'marvellous tongue', that date back to the nineteenth century. These litanies are instantiations of the discourse of the superiority of English and those who speak it. It is this discourse, in combination with colonial discourses, which sets up the inferior other as its binary opposite, that produces the symbolic power of English. It is this 'overvaluing' of the colonial language that induces people 'to collaborate in the destruction of their [own] instruments of expression' (Bourdieu, 1991: 49). This supports Sachs's position that languages need rights 'against English' (1994: 1).

Speaking about South Africa in the mid 1980s Ndebele insisted that colonised people are caught in a dilemma. Given the distribution of economic and political power at that time, English was a means of access to power. But Ndebele maintained that choosing English was 'the necessity of limited choices' (1987: 220), and he blamed colonisation for this 'predetermined pragmatism' (1987: 220). He recognised another danger: where the need for the language is merely functional, 'English in a capitalist society . . . can further reinforce the instrumentalisation of people as units of labour' (1987: 18). What produced and continues to produce a dilemma for colonial subjects learning English is that the desire for the language has to be countered by the simultaneous need to resist it.

Arthur's theory of lock-in, together with Bourdieu's theory of the linguistic market, produces an irresolvable contradiction for English educators (Granville *et al.*, 1998; Janks, 1995). If you provide more people with access to the dominant variety of the dominant language, you perpetuate a situation of increasing returns and you maintain its dominance. If, on the

---

[4] James Alatis, 1977, quoted in Pennycook, 1998.
[5] de Quincy, 1862, quoted in Pennycook, 1998.

other hand, you deny students access, you perpetuate their marginalisation in a society that continues to recognise this language as a mark of distinction. You also deny them access to the extensive resources available in that language; resources which have developed as a consequence of the language's dominance. It is this contradiction that Lodge (1997) has called *the access paradox.*

The access paradox recognises that domination without access excludes students from the language or the language variety that would afford them the most linguistic capital, thereby limiting their life chances. It restricts students to the communities in which their marginalised languages are spoken. As the establishment of ghettoes based on language and ethnicity was one of the main aims of the apartheid state, English in South Africa came to be seen as a way out of the ghetto. On the other hand, access without a theory of domination naturalises the power of the dominant language, English, and devalues students' own languages.

But this is only half the story. Graddol's work (1997, 2006) was designed to enable strategic planning for English into the twenty-first century and to take the necessary steps to protect the British brand in relation to this export commodity. He provides an analysis of the position of English in the world and suggests that its current 'apparently unassailable position'[6] is unlikely to continue. His analyses consider how global trends are likely to affect the use of English in relation to other languages. He focuses on trends in

- demography – how many people there will be in 2050, where they will live and what age they will be;
- the world economy – skills transfer from developed countries is enabling developing countries to increase their productivity and their per capita income. As these countries, particularly Brazil, Russia, India and China (the BRICS) grow richer and provide more opportunities for business and employment, their languages are likely to grow in importance. In addition, changing patterns of trade are likely to increase regional trade along with an increase in the influence of languages such as Chinese, Hindi/Urdu, Spanish and Arabic (Graddol, 1997: 59). There is evidence that the search for new markets is already increasing the use of regional languages. For example, Star TV, based in Hong Kong, offers programmes in Cantonese and Hindi; CNN has launched a 24-hour Spanish News Service and has plans for a Hindi service; CBS plans to develop a Portuguese news service (1997: 46). MTV, 'the music channel which

---

[6] This quotation appears on the first page of the internet book.

has done more than any other to create a global youth music culture, has in the past few years adopted a policy of localisation' (1997: 47);

- the role of technology (in particular changes in computer and communication technologies) – the early systems for text-based communications using computers were originally designed for the English language. Now there are software programmes that accommodate accented languages and non-roman writing systems. Software for voice transcription and translation is becoming increasingly sophisticated. The number of non-English sites and chat rooms on the internet is growing rapidly. 'The close linkage that once existed between computers and English has been broken' (Graddol, 1997: 30);
- flows of people, culture, finance and communication – globalisation has produced an increasingly 'interconnected and interdependent', 'borderless world' (1997: 25) that both requires and enables new forms of communication and exchange;
- the changing nature of work in a knowledge-intensive economy that involves more discursive work – this is evident in the way in which goods are marketed in relation to lifestyle and image, with value added by design and packaging, that is, by semiotic labour. In addition, there has been an increase in document work which is dependent on screen labour: word processing, emailing, information retrieval and the management and use of data bases. 'These technology mediated practices that we think of as literacy, come to the forefront as the means through which workplace competence is judged' (Heller, 2008: 59);
- The growth of the service industries also impacts on language. Many of the new jobs are those found in call centres.

In 1997, Graddol concludes that:

> There is no reason to believe that any other language will appear within the next 50 years to replace English as the global lingua franca. . . . [He argues], however, that no single language will occupy the monopolistic position in the 21st century which English has – almost – achieved by the end of the 20th century. It is more likely that a small number of world languages will form an 'oligopoly', each with particular spheres of influence and regional bases.
>
> (1997: 58)

In 2006, Graddol summarises the key trends that will determine the long-term future of English. These include: the increasing irrelevance of native speaker standards for English; the bleak economic future facing monolingual speakers of English; the increasing competition for educational resources and policy attention from Mandarin and Spanish; the increasing economic importance of the BRICs and their languages; the changes needed in teaching English as a foreign language as learners acquire it for communication rather than cultural purposes; and English's competitive advantage ebbing away if it becomes a near universal basic skill (2006: 14–15).

Meanwhile, English is likely to remain a powerful global language at least for the first half of the twenty-first century. Because of this status it is widely seen as desirable, as the means of access to education, science, technology and the kind of employment that brings material success. English currently is the foreign language of choice. In addition, with the internationalisation of Higher Education and online distance education courses, there is a growing move towards English medium in Higher Education, which Graddol (2006: 14) sees as a trend that is unlikely to reverse. English provides greater access to academic books, to information and research articles. In South Africa, where African parents can choose one of nine African languages as the medium of instruction in schools, most parents choose English.

Access without a Theory of Power

Without a theory of power, one might argue that education should simply aim to give everyone access to whichever language (or genre, or discourse, or variety, or literacy) is powerful at the time to ensure equal life chances for students. Even if such access were not as elusive as the cure for cancer, such an automatic response would simply serve to bolster the hegemonic position of already powerful languages and language forms, contributing to the ever increasing loss of the world's languages. Hegemony is dominance that begins to appear natural or inevitable, commonsensical, such that people support it with their consent (Gramsci, 1971). This is what Bourdieu means when he talks about a language having 'symbolic power' (1991: 163–170). Symbolic power derives from the values that people ascribe to social practices, from the status that they give them. Proficiency in English has become implicated in the structuring of social inequalities in countries where it determines access to information and material advantage. Elite languages and elite literacies often act as gate-keepers that control inclusion and exclusion. The use of English as a global lingua franca is also endangering local vernacular languages, many of which are threatened with extinction. What is needed is a policy of access that works to maintain students' own languages and that promotes and values bilingualism and multilingualism.

> **In your country**
> 1. What languages are used for international communication?
> 2. What languages are used for communication in your region?
> 3. What languages receive national recognition? Is there an official or unofficial hierarchy of these languages. How is this hierarchy established and maintained?
> 4. What are the local vernacular languages? Who speaks them?
> 5. What languages have already been lost?
> 6. What languages are endangered? Who speaks these languages?

We also need to remind ourselves that a dramatic shift in the balance of power in the world, or changes in the flow of people, can, like a change in technology in relation to a material product in the economic market, effect a change in the languages favoured in the linguistic market. Currently the numbers of people electing to learn Mandarin as a foreign language is a case in point. The fate of Latin is a reminder that powerful, imperial languages can die; the advance of Spanish in the United States is proof that patterns of migration can affect the dominance of English; and South Africa's 1996 Constitution shows how politics and the law can empower indigenous languages. It is the job of English teachers to give students full access to English and to its powerful forms – the standard variety for written communication, dominant genres, prestigious registers. But access without an understanding of how the language and these forms came to be dominant reifies them.

In 1997, Graddol alerted us to the possible consequences for English of its status as a world language. First, he asked us to imagine what might happen when there are significantly more second language speakers of English than there are native speakers:

> The widespread use of English as a language of wider communication will continue to exert pressure towards global uniformity … But as English shifts to second-language status for an increasing number of people, we can also expect to see English develop a large number of local varieties. These contradictory tensions arise because English has two main functions in the world: it provides a vehicular language for international communication and it forms the basis for constructing cultural identities. The former function requires mutual intelligibility and common standards. The latter encourages the development of local forms and hybrid varieties.
>
> (1997: 66)

Now research is emerging attesting to the fluid and hybrid nature of lingua franca English (Canagarajah, 2006, 2007; Rampton, 1990).

There are already more speakers of English as a foreign language than of first and second language speakers combined. Already there are more speakers of English who are bilingual or multilingual than there are monolingual native speakers of English. Countries where English is an established second language, are likely to develop their own language teaching materials in order to inflect the language curriculum with local content and local values. They are also likely to favour language teachers who are themselves second language speakers able to speak both the local variety of English as well as the students' native language/s. One can imagine a local standard gaining in status in relation to older British- or American-based standards. The 'standard' is also threatened by the increase in electronic communications, where standardised forms for print are no longer imposed by editors and publishers. Genres such as email are already reducing the differences between spoken and written forms of language. The abbreviated language used for SMS (Short Message Service), that is, text-messaging, on mobile phones, together with new genres and forms of English arising on the internet, are already changing the way English is written (see for example the dictionary of emoticons at http://www.netlingo.com/smiley.cfm).

I wonder how familiar readers are with the meaning of these basic smileys:

☺   ;-)   ☹   :<   :-*   (-:

Or these less common ones:

:-{   ~:o   <:-l   :-!

Students are more likely to use smileys than their teachers. Getting a class to produce a dictionary of smileys that they have seen in use, that they use or that they have made up gives a sense of the extent to which students use the new communications lingo.

Graddol reaches the conclusion that the future will be a bilingual one. Whereas

> yesterday it was the world's poor who were multilingual; tomorrow it will be the global elite. . . . We must not be hypnotised by the fact

that this elite will speak English: the more significant fact may be that, unlike the majority of present-day native English speakers, they will also speak at least one other language – probably more fluently and with greater cultural loyalty.

(1997: 63)

Access without Diversity

Language loss in the world represents a serious threat to diversity. Different languages encode different sensibilities and different ways of apprehending the world, which is why translation is such a complex practice. As discussed earlier, our languages become part of our habitus, our overall embodied ways of being in the world. The languages we speak are tied to the discourse communities that we inhabit and are profoundly connected to our sense of identity (see Chapter 2). No children should have to lose the language/s of their homes as they cross the threshold of the school. The imposition of a foreign language and the denigration of a child's linguistic variety are both examples of what Bourdieu calls symbolic violence (1991: 239).

In the interests of social justice, as educators we need to reduce the power of education to deliver the recognition required for the maintenance of a language's symbolic power, particularly where this recognition is to the detriment of the languages that our students speak. We also need to find ways of rejecting a unitary view of language and a normative view of communicative competence. We need to show that just because a language or a variety or a genre is dominant, it is not 'superior' to other linguistic options that by a different set of historical chances might have been dominant (Arthur, 1990). In addition, we have to understand that difference fundamentally affects pathways to access because this produces a system of fine distinctions where outsiders are easily marked by small deviations from these norms – deviations of posture, proximity, accent, gaze, politeness, grammar, attitude and the like (Bourdieu, 1991: 237). This is particularly difficult when one is learning a non-cognate language, that is, a language that originates from a different family of languages and that provides a different way of construing the world.

In South Africa, I use 'Joe's Beat', a regular column in *Pace* magazine, to work with both multilingualism and multiple discourses in classrooms. It is an excellent example of linguistic hybridity. See Figure 6.4 (Khumalo, 1997).

In order to work with this text students need to

• understand the language. For this they have to rely on those students who understand township slang;

In a room full of shabbily dressed uncles, aunts and oumas, the SUBURBAN youngsters swagger snootily among the RIFFRAFF. Their fatcat parents, SHAMED and AGGRIEVED, berate their brood for not greeting their elderly relatives ...
TYINI, UNZIMA LOMTHWALO!

Joe's Beat

Suburbia? Forget it, mpintshi yam, that's for the new gravy cats. I tell you, broer, life is a real gas in the ghetto. Chicken gizzards, mala mogodu, atchaar, skaapkop and machangaan wors washed down with chibuku and mageu to the backdrop of scamtho and kwaito music. I tell you, mtshana, life is great in the hood. What more could 'n arme darkie want?

Come Friday and it's fill up the table and count the empties because it's pay day and the "weekend tycoons" have money like dust. Ziyamporoma! The airwaves offer eardrum-shattering kwaito and rap sounds as each ghetto household competes with the next for volume supremacy.

On the streets AKs are blazing and the flash guys, the snazzily dressed amagents, are cruising dangerously in their BMs, much to the envy of the girls and All Star sneaker-clad jitas.

Out in the 'burbs the new fatcats who were weaned

on chicken legs and pap are battling to shake down the effects of squawking in tsotsi taal and scamtho, while waging an uphill struggle to get the hang of Mozart and the arts. Big deal! But for 'n fly ghetto laaitie this quiet life is humdrum, mtshana.

Bored with champagne, caviar and ukukhumtsha, they sneak into the dark ghetto in their Pajeros and Audi A4s for their rare dose of soul food, pap and morogo, stokvels, tebellos, amadlozi ceremonies and ever-plentiful mgosi. But there's the rub.

With their kids who have imbibed the suburban culture, going back to the ghetto is a horrific culture shock to the "nose brigade" who express themselves in vogue Oxford accents.

First they will have to contend with the granny, who acquired a smattering of English when she was a "kitchen girl" in the suburbs. Casually they hi and what's-up die arme ouma who is startled by their very English English. "Oh granny, you're so stupid!" Holy Moses — in

Africa nogal! But you ain't seen nothing yet, mtshana.

In a room full of extended family — shabbily dressed uncles, aunts and oumas — the youngsters swagger contemptuously among the riffraff. Shamed and aggrieved, their fatcat parents fumble for words as they berate their brood for not greeting their elderly relatives. But their now Anglicised brood angrily retort: "But folks, why should we greet strangers?" Laf'elihle kakhulu madoda! Cry the beloved country! But there's more ...

While appeasing the ancestors there's ululating and praise-singing as the rustic uncles butcher the sacrificial cow, but the detribalised kids are horrified. "But that's barbaric ... that's cruelty to animals!" they shrill. "Honey, that's for the ancestors. Your uncle had to do it and that's why I'm a bit short of cash this month. They are my family so I had to chip in and help him," whispers the embarrassed dad to his youngest child.

"What? Why didn't he budget for it?" the oldest child asks. "But he's family; it's the custom that I should help," dad points out weakly. "I wouldn't give him a cent! Just because we share a surname doesn't entitle him to our hard-earned money," sneers the teenager as the blushing dad and perplexed relatives look on, mtshana.

"For your information, young lady, you'll be obliged to help with household money this month because I forked out plenty for your uncle to organise the ancestral ceremony." says the fatcat dad to his eldest daughter.

"Damn your brother and his stupid amadlozi ceremony, daddy," the daughter whines. "You won't see a cent of my money! If you and your brother don't know how to budget, then hard luck!" she adds. "Ouch! That hurts," the poor ancestors wince in their graves. Tyini, unzima lomthwalo. Good old ancient Africa — where are you?

Joe Khumalo

Figure 6.4 *Joe's Beat.*

- understand the cultural practices that this language describes – the way of life encoded by the language. Ways of greeting grannies, types of music, food and what counts as a delicacy, *stokvels*, ancestor worship. They need access to the combinations of saying-(writing)-doing-being-believing-valuing that informs this text, the combinations that Gee calls Discourses;
- consider whether or not this text, published in an English-language magazine, is written in English or not; they need to defend their position in relation to context.

I ask my students to rewrite this text in standard South African English to see what is lost and what is gained by this conservative transformation of the text. This method can be used with any text written in a subordinated language variety. I have used cockney texts with students in England and student teachers in South Africa have used this method successfully with texts from African American literature. This is an example of access that embraces diversity. It is worth collecting texts that illustrate the energy and vitality of non-standard varieties and which show how they offer alternative and interesting lenses on the world.

Unfortunately, instead of linguistic diversity being a source of wonder and pleasure, it is often a powerful marker of social difference that can be used to exclude people who we hear and judge as other. John Baugh (2000, 2003) demonstrates conclusively that linguistic prejudices have material consequences in the United States. Baugh is able to speak a number of different varieties of American English. He can produce fluent Ebonics (African American English), Latino English and Chicano English, in addition to the so-called 'Standard'. He responds over the telephone to advertisements offering rented accommodation using these different varieties at different times. Depending on which variety he uses, the accommodation is or is no longer available. Baugh, a Stanford academic, now also works as a forensic linguist providing expert evidence in legal cases based on linguistic discrimination.

Like languages, varieties are also stratified, and teachers have to balance access to prestige varieties with respect for diversity and students' identity investments; access to linguistic capital has to be balanced by the value of linguistic variation. Symbolic value, produced by our attitudes to different varieties, and our linguistic prejudices are shaped by our social prejudices. I demonstrate this to my students by asking them to tell me what they know about people from listening to recordings of their speech. One of the recordings is of a man then in his early seventies, who speaks English with a strong South African accent that is influenced by Afrikaans. In addition to interpreting age and gender, my students often tell me about the man's ethnicity, home language, level of education, intelligence and political affiliations. Those who are prejudiced against Afrikaners read the speaker in terms of their own negative stereotypes and attribute lack of education, low intelligence and political conservatism to him. I am able to tell them that the man is a professional engineer with a university degree; that he is a native speaker of English, not Afrikaans; that he grew up in a small Afrikaans rural town in the Northern Cape; that he is not politically conservative. For some this is enough to make them ashamed of their assumptions; others only begin to confront the effects of their linguistic prejudices when I tell them that in fact, the man is my father.

> Talk radio is a wonderful source for collecting examples of local varieties of a language. Students can be asked to examine what they know and what they assume about the callers, based on the variety of English that they use.

Different language communities also have 'different cultural discourse norms' (Corson, 2001: 36) – different norms for interaction. Whole class teaching, which asks children to respond publicly to questions, may differ from the ways children are expected to behave in their communities (Cazden, 1988). This could as easily account for the reluctance of Grade 7 children at Phepo primary school to volunteer answers as their uncertainty with English. In acquiring the new habitus that comes with learning, and interacting in a new language, it is important that students do not lose their own 'ways with words' (Heath, 1983) – their community's ways of being in the world. If South Africa is to achieve its language in education policy which calls for additive multilingualism, learning additional languages has to mean that a new habitus and identity is acquired *in addition* to that of one's primary discourse. We need to ensure that students' abilities in their home languages and their primary discourses are maintained and developed. At the same time we have to recognise that more often than not languages in contact affect one another as do different identities. We have to be open to the possibility of new hybrid identities, dynamic shifts in language forms and language practices, and entirely new and innovative ways of being in the world. Cultures are not static entities but dynamic flexible forms shaped by new influences and social changes, despite conservative attempts to fix them and box them in.

It is important to mount an argument against monolingualism. The relationships between discourse, habitus and identity are key (see Chapter 2). For Bourdieu, the languages we speak are written on our bodies. He gives the example of the way in which the tiniest movements of the tongue in our mouths create the sounds of our home language, and the national and local varieties of this language (1991: 86). For those of us who have learnt additional languages, we know how difficult it is to get our mouths around what to us are strange vowels and different consonants. Our tongue has to learn new movements and often the ingrained movements of our native tongue leave their mark on our accent in the new language. Old habits die hard. But the micro-movements of the tongue are just one example of how language is embodied. It is also encoded with other uses of the body – hands, eyes, stance, voice – that we have acquired unconsciously as members of the language communities in which we live. These well-established patterns form part of who we are, part of our identity. One of the ways in which we come to 'see' these unconscious behaviours is by learning another language, acquiring an additional habitus, an additional identity. In this way, our taken-for-granted ways of being in the world are denaturalised and disrupted and we come to imagine and own other possibilities.

If one takes seriously the idea that diversity is a productive resource, that hybridity is a 'key issue in the cultural making of new practices, meanings and discourses' (Kostogriz, 2002: 5), and that 'semiotic border crossing' (2002: 155) enables creativity, then as teachers we need to recognise the limitations of monolingualism and the danger of the ever-increasing dominance of English. Saussure (1972/1990) taught us that we can often see what something is, by seeing what it is not. We can help students to understand what English is and what it is not by making use of the wealth of linguistic resources that our multilingual students bring to our English classes. In this way, we might convince all our students that English is not intrinsically superior to other languages, while at the same time teaching them to value linguistic diversity and to respect people who have extensive multilingual repertoires. In my own work with English-speaking student teachers in South Africa, teaching them to hear and reproduce the sounds of the aspirated consonants and the fine tonal distinctions of African languages has helped them to understand why speakers of African languages struggle to hear and make the vowel distinctions of English that do not exist in their own languages.

In response to the new *Language Policy for Higher Education*, which requires universities and technikons in South Africa to develop multilingual language policies, the University of the Witwatersrand adopted a new language policy[7] from 14 March 2003 in which it commits itself to:

---

[7] The policy submitted to the University Senate and Council was written by Dr N. Thwala, Dr D. Swemmer and Prof H. Janks. It was based on language research conducted at the University by van Zyl and Makoe in 2002 and on the advice given by the Senate Language Policy Committee.

- promote multilingualism by supporting the use of all eleven official languages for interaction on the University campus and in ceremonial gatherings, by translating documents and providing interpreting services where necessary and by offering a major in at least one foreign language;
- develop Sesotho by developing language teaching resources and courses in Sesotho for staff and students, and by assisting the government to develop such resources for primary and secondary education. It also proposes to contribute, alongside government, to the development of the language itself, so that it can be used as a medium of instruction in Higher Education;
- develop the linguistic abilities of staff and students in English and Sesotho or IsiZulu by providing courses in these languages and by requiring communicative competence in English and an African language.

Although this policy set the University on a path to introducing a bilingual Sesotho-English medium of instruction in the long term,[8] sadly by 2008 nothing had been done to implement it. Other universities have made more progress. The University of the Limpopo, for example, has introduced a bilingual BA degree (Joseph & Ramani, 2004; Ramani & Joseph, 2006).

The policy recognised African students' desire for access to English[9] while at the same, it requires students and staff who cannot speak an African language to take courses in either Sesotho or IsiZulu. It is the combination of access to English and the requirement that everyone speak an African language that might realise the policy's claim that 'learning the languages of South Africa is a means of enhancing understanding of one another and of overcoming our differences' (University of the Witwatersrand, 2003). The combination also provides a space for holding access in tension with domination, diversity and design/redesign. The dominance of English is reduced by the insistence on competence in an African language and the possibility of introducing a bilingual medium

---

[8] The literature in the field and the *Language Policy for Higher Education* only talks about dual medium of instruction – where some subjects are taught through the medium of one language and some through the medium of another language, and parallel medium of instruction – where all courses are repeated in each language. Instead, the University policy conceptualises a bilingual-medium of instruction which uses oral code-switching. This is the common practice in most South African schools.

[9] Research conducted at the University (van Zyl & Makoe, 2002) 'indicates that there is overwhelming support by all students for improving their English language skills so that they can attain mastery of oral and written competence' and for qualifications to 'include credit-bearing courses in English for students who need them' (University of the Witwatersrand, 2003).

in the long term; diversity is addressed by requiring communicative competence in two languages that are not cognate; regular code-switching between English and Sesotho constitutes a transformation or redesign of existing patterns of interaction at the University. The increased contact between these languages would have produced changes in both languages as well as the development of more hybrid linguistic identities.

Access without Redesign

Access without any possibility of redesign leaves no possibility for transforming the language or its dominant forms. It is here, in bending language to their own purposes and meanings that post-colonial writers have been so successful and colonial subjects, in making English their own, have produced many Englishes as attested to by 21 volumes of the journal *World Englishes*. Like Shakespeare's Caliban, they can say

> You taught me language: and my profit on't
> Is I know how to curse. The red plague rid you
> For learning me your language.
> (Shakespeare, *The Tempest*, Act 1, Sc ii, l 365–368)

As English is used by more and more people who inflect it with their own tongues and use it to express their diverse sensibilities, English has to be open to the possibility of increasing divergence from a fixed metropolitan standard. While the widespread use of English continues to 'exert pressure towards global uniformity' (Graddol, 1997: 56), local hybrid varieties form 'the basis for constructing cultural identities'. According to Graddol (1997: 49), young people, in particular, do identity work with their linguistic choices. In anglophone countries, they choose varieties that are tied to different social identities based on factors such as class, ethnicity, gender, sexuality (Rampton, 2006); in non-English-speaking countries, foreign varieties enable speakers of English to maintain their ethnic or national identities.

Only dead languages do not change. Living languages are moulded and shaped by their users, who bend them to their needs. These needs are never just communicative needs; they are also social, psychological, political. The price native speakers of English have to pay for speaking a global language, is that the language no longer belongs to them. As more and more people gain access to the language, they appropriate it for their own purposes, and in doing so they destabilise it. What native speakers get for free, apart from the linguistic advantage of being born into a powerful world language, is a language that is rich with meanings, filled as it is by words and nuances from all the places that it inhabits and all the people that inhabit it. It is

---

In *The Bone Setter's Daughter*, Amy Tan (2001) is able to capture LuLing's English, the 'choppy talk' (42) that she had taught herself in Hong Kong and China:

> 'Lootie give me so much trouble. Maybe I send her go Taiwan, school for bad children. What you think' (43). Later she says to her daughter Ruth,
> 'You wish I dead? You wish no mother tell you what to do. Okay, maybe I die soon' (46).

An even more playful example can be found in Xiaolu Guo's (2007) novel, *A concise Chinese-English dictionary for lovers*, in which the main character is struggling to master the grammar of English.

> 'London is the Capital of fog'. It is saying in middle school textbook. We studying chapter from Charles Dickens's novel *Foggy City Orphan*. Everybody know Oliver Twist living in city with bad fog. Is very popular novel in China.
> As soon as I arriving in London, I look around the sky but no any fogs. 'Excuse me, where I see fogs?' I ask policemen in street.
> 'Sorry?' he says.
> 'I waiting two days already, but no fogs,' I say.
> He just look at me but no understanding my English (p. 21).

Roberts (2003) similarly captures the cadences of Bombay English in *Shantaram*. Here Prabakar invites Karla to a celebration lunch:

> We will have it a very nice lunches! My good self, I have kept it a complete empty stomach for filling up to fat. *So* good is the food. You will enjoy so much, the people will think you are having a baby inside your dress (p. 246).

Chinua Achebe, rather than using an African variety of English, has instead worked to capture the idiom of Nigeria in English. Here we see time measured by the slow rhythms of the seasons and the crops, belief in the power of potions and the voice of the Oracle, and the importance of the land.

> And so they killed the white man and tied his iron horse to their sacred tree ... This was before the planting season began. For a long time nothing happened. The rains had come and yams had been sown. The iron horse was still tied to the sacred silk-cotton tree ... They have a big market in Abame on every other Afo day and, as you know the whole clan gathers there. That was the day it happened. ... They must have used a powerful medicine to make themselves invisible until the market was full. And they began to shoot. ... Everybody was killed. ... Their clan is now completely empty. Even the sacred fish in their mysterious lake have fled and the lake has turned the colour of blood. A great evil has come upon their land as the Oracle has warned (Achebe, 1958: 125–126).

Figure 6.5 English Varieties Used in Novels.

a language that has been extended by poets and writers across the world who have lent it the cadences of their own tongues and the insights from their different world views, producing an extensive literature in English. Language has an elastic quality that allows it to stretch with new demands and to embrace new concepts. In this, English is no different from any other language; it has simply benefited from the diversity of human experience that it has been called upon to express. If one can tune one's ear to the plenitude of accent, vocabulary, stress, intonation, grammar, across the different varieties of English, then there is much that one can learn and enjoy about people from the ways in which they speak it. The passages in Figure 6.5, taken from literature, show the hybridity and multiplicity of English. I offer them as a start to your own collection of such texts.

To conclude this chapter, I turn to the title: 'access, gate-keeping and desire'. Access is a type of right, the right to enter and get through the gates, the right not to be excluded. Too often language acts as a gate that sorts and selects students, with teachers performing the function of society's gate-keepers. If what is beyond the gates are the elite literacies that are out of reach for most people, then these literacies become highly desirable. This desire is not based simply on symbolic value. Because access is a fundamental instrument of social stratification, it has material consequences that affect people's life chances for generations. Desire is a double-edged sword: becoming what we lack, changes who we are. Something is always lost in the process. As educators, changing people is our work – work that should not be done without a profound respect for the otherness of our students. Desiring what one is not should not entail giving up what one is.

CHAPTER 7

Critical Text Production
Writing and Design

In the model, *design* is the catch-all word that I use for critical text production. It focuses on the production rather than the reception of texts. In the field of critical literacy, less attention has been paid to critical writing than to critical reading, despite the importance of resisting dominant forms and 'writing back' to power. The importance of 'writing back' has been central to the work of post-colonial writers and theorists (for example, Bhabha, 1990; Said, 1994, 1995 and Pennycook, 1998) and has an established tradition in the field of literary analysis and production. Their work was built on the foundations established by feminist writers who theorised and contested patriarchal texts and practices. The work of the feminist linguists (for example, Cameron, 1985, 1990, 1995; Smith, 1993; Spender, 1980; Threadgold, 1997) has been particularly important for work in the area of critical literacy. Street (1984) was the first to raise important questions about the naturalised dominance of essayist literacy in the context of school and Clark and Ivanič (1997: 60) and Ivanič (1998) began to theorise critical writing in their work with mature entry students to higher education, who experienced their subjection to the normative forms of academic writing as oppressive. They took seriously the relationship between writing, identity and power. Where Clark and Ivanič worked with the possibilities for the transformation of academic genres, the genre theorists set out to make explicit the genres required in school in order to ensure access and success for disadvantaged students. More recently, the Multiliteracies Project has paid attention to the importance of teaching students how to produce and design multimodal texts.

155

Control over text production and the means of production are central to the critical literacy project for a number of reasons. The ability to

- produce texts is a form of agency that enables us to choose what meanings to make;
- construct texts gives us a better understanding of how texts are constructed and the affordances and constraints of different modes;
- produce texts enables us to act on the world;
- work actively with the combination and recombination of symbolic forms is a requirement for high-level work in a knowledge economy. It helps us to think about how we are positioning ourselves and our readers by the choices we make as we write;
- produce texts enables us to redesign our texts and the texts of others. It enables us to think about how to transform texts that we have deconstructed to remake the world.

If repositioning texts is tied to an ethic of social justice then writing and rewriting can contribute to the kind of social and identity transformation that Freire's work advocates.

Writing

With the changing communication landscape it is more important than ever that schools encourage students to produce texts that matter to them in different formats and for different audiences and purposes and that they allow them to draw on and extend their range of semiotic resources. There is a lot that we can learn in this regard from the story of Peter.

Peter was a bright young twelve-year-old in my Grade 7 class at a comprehensive school in London, where I was working as a supply teacher in the early 1980s. He was difficult, always finishing first so that he would have time to make a nuisance of himself. Sporting a glass eye, he was a real toughie. When I introduced free-writing journals one Friday afternoon, the students, egged on by Peter, tested me. They wanted to know exactly how free? Could they use swear words? I told them that as far as I was concerned they could fill a page with the worst swear word they could think of, but they would have to take responsibility for what they wrote in their journals if their parents or another teacher found their books. That seemed to satisfy them and no one ever exercised this option.

Peter took his empty exercise book home and on Monday morning returned to school and announced that he had finished. He handed me his journal filled from cover to cover with his writing. Before he could blink, I had pasted a second exercise book into the back of his journal.

His determination to finish ahead of the class, as was his wont, had required him to spend much of his weekend writing. In this concentrated effort, he must have discovered that writing could be pleasurable, because this most unco-operative of students went on to fill five more books with his ideas, his hopes, his concerns, his disappointments.

This was the first time that these students had been given complete control over their writing. Their journals became a safe space where they could write about what mattered to them. It became a space in which they could drop their bravado in front of their peers, and show an interest in school. No one but I would know. For the first time they could use writing to address an interested adult who responded to the meanings they were communicating, rather than to their grammar and form. They had to write at least three pieces of any length every week and although this work was not assessed and did not count 'for marks', most of the students wrote more than the minimum. They begged for time in class to write in their journals. Ironically, for them it was a way of avoiding work.

In this space they had freedom to be whoever they wanted to be and the power to choose what they would write. Many chose to include drawings and photographs of their interests, their families or people with whom they identified – usually pop stars or sporting heroes. Twenty-five years later, I have no difficulty understanding why students, who resist writing in school, will spend hours writing on MySpace or Facebook or on online blogging. Now students can choose their audience from a networked community across the globe and multi-modal text production has become easier and more sophisticated with greater access to the new digital technologies. The contrast with educational settings is extreme. From primary to tertiary education, students' writing is still largely controlled by the teacher and the set-topic essay is still the norm in both language and content subject classrooms, in a range of educational contexts.

The journal-approach to writing is of course not necessarily critical in the Freirean sense of the word. As we saw in Chapter 1, for Freire,

> [i]f learning to read and write is to constitute an act of knowing, the learners must assume from the beginning the role of creative subjects.
>
> (Freire, 1972a: 29)

For Freire's 'creative subject', writing is more than a set of skills, it is about writing the world in order to transform it. Education has to do more than produce fluent writers who enjoy using writing to produce meanings and texts that matter to them. Writers need a critical social consciousness to produce texts that make a difference to the ways in which we 'name' and understand the world. They also need access to schooled literacies – to the standard variety of written language, a range of genres and the social and rhetorical sophistication needed to write for different audiences and purposes. These are harder for students to master if they have no experience of meaningful, pleasurable, fluent writing on which to build.

In the process of writing, we achieve fluency by focusing on meaning rather than form. We concentrate on what we are trying to communicate and allow our brains to find the words we need automatically. It is in this way that words choose us, rather than the other way around. We draw unconsciously on our communities' resources for naming the world, on the discourses that we inhabit (see Chapter 4). When Foucault says that 'discourse is the power which is to be seized' (1970), it is precisely because of this power of discourse to produce us as particular kinds of human subjects and to speak through us.

Designing Writing

In writing, we are more likely to make deliberate choices when we stop to re-read or to edit what we have written and some genres require more deliberation than others. Poets, spin doctors and lawyers are likely to weigh their words more than journalists and copy writers. Writing is a social practice and different practices require different kinds of precision.

I offer an example from my own practice. In 2001, I presented a paper titled 'Critical Literacy Methods, Models and Motivation' at an International Reading Association pre-conference institute on critical literacy. When I first thought of the title for this paper, I wanted to call it 'Critical Literacy: Methods, Models and Motives'. It sounded right. I liked the balance created by the two three-syllable words followed by the three two-syllable words, and the rhythm created by the alliteration. But the word *motives* bothered me. Murderers have motives. The word 'motive' keeps bad company. We think of people as having 'hidden' or 'ulterior' motives. We think of motives as being self-interested more often than we think of them as being pure. The word *motivation*, on the other hand has had a better press. It is associated with a beneficial psychological force that enables us to do good things. We think of people who are 'highly motivated' as achievers, as having positive attitudes. As teachers we all want motivated learners but are likely to distrust students with motives. So, harnessing all the positive connotations of the word 'motivation', I made it a count noun, chose the plural form, and changed my title to 'Critical Literacy: Methods, Models and Motivations'.

Being a linguist, I decided to check my intuitions by referring to the British National Corpus (http:/sara.natcorp.ox.ac.uk/lookup.html). When you type in a word it gives you the number of occurrences of the word in the corpus and fifty random examples of the word in sentences. I searched for *motive* and *motives* and for *motivation* and *motivations*. I then analysed the sample for positive and negative connotations. Any data that was not clearly negative or clearly positive, I discounted. Examples of positive, negative and unclear connotations appear in Table 7.1; the results of the analysis are tabulated in Table 7.2.

From examining the corpus, it became clear to me that people often use the word *motivations* as a synonym for *motives*. It is also interesting that the clearest difference in connotation is in the singular. *Motivation*, in the singular, is the word that carries the positive connotations that I intuited and *motive*, in the singular, carries the negative connotations. So I changed my title again, to 'Critical Literacy: Methods, Models and Motivation'. Critical literacy is not only useful for reading texts – it is also a powerful tool for designing texts. Because I wanted my audience to embrace critical literacy work, I avoided the tainted word *motive* and deliberately chose *motivation*.

In her work with 70- to 85-year-old women on stories of ageing, Kamler (2001: 55–78) capitalises on the ways in which we can re-position our writing by making different choices. Texts are simply versions of reality

Table 7.1 Examples from the British National Corpus

Examples from the corpus of the words used with positive connotations

Instead the eyes settled on her, searching out the motive for such a protective gesture.
With no other interest than glory, and no other motive than a sense of vocation.
If jobs were carefully designed . . . then high levels of satisfaction and motivation would result.
Aspirations, a sense of how we can realise our potential, give us power and motivation.

Examples from the corpus of the words used with negative connotations

All her appeals to the students to end the demonstrations had an ulterior motive.
Even today suggestions are being made as to Judas' motive.
Managers can motivate staff – motivation is at the control of the individual.
. . . subject to allegations of political motivation and partiality . . .

Examples from the corpus of the words used with unclear or neutral connotations

Let us please seek for more stronger motives.
Motive power is provided by No 40092.
There is the same motivation.
The majority failed to understand the motivation of the same characters.

Janks, H. (2008) First published in K. Cooper and R. White (Eds.). *Critical Literacies in Action*. Rotterdam: Sense Publishers.

Table 7.2 Analysis of Examples from the British National Corpus

Word	Number in the full corpus	Positive connotations in the corpus sample	Negative connotations in the corpus sample	Neutral or unclear connotations in the corpus sample
motive	1,043	7	28	15
motives	1,028	9	21	20
motivation	1,524	29	2	19
motivations	237	13	13	24

Janks, H. (2008) First published in K. Cooper and R. White (Eds.). *Critical Literacies in Action*. Rotterdam: Sense Publishers.

and we can, as writers, re-vision our stories. The ability to read texts critically, including our own texts, creates the conditions for transformative redesign:

> The purpose of the project was to confront the narrow range of negative images of ageing pervasive in our culture and to produce new stories written from the perspective of the older women.
>
> (Kamler, 2001: 55)

In this project, older women were given the opportunity to use writing to frame their subject positions differently. According to Lakoff (2004) this act constitutes social change:

> Frames are mental structures that shape the way we see the world. As a result, they shape the goals we seek, the plans we make, the way we act and what counts as good or bad outcomes of our actions. In politics our frames shape our social policies. To change our frames is to change all of this. Reframing is social change.
>
> (Lakoff, 2004: xv)

Whether one see a bucket as half full or half empty, is a well known example of how our frame influences the way we see the world. Kamler is able to help Bella, one of the women in her project, reframe the darkness of her husband's death by the recognition that her 'being with him to the end gave him the strength he needed and that he died surrounded by love and care' (Kamler, 2001: 60). When I became very depressed in 1992 because both my sons 'could have died', one from illness and the other from a serious motor car accident, I was, after some months, able to flip my mood by reframing the events differently. 'Both my sons could have died but they didn't' – our family was, in fact, fortunate.

The ongoing cycle of representation–deconstruction–redesign is captured by Paulo Freire when he says that

> To exist, humanly, is to *name* the world, to change it. Once named, the world in its turn reappears to its namers as a problem and requires of them a new *naming*.
>
> (Freire, 1972b: 61)

In this way Freire links literacy – writing, reading and re-writing the world and the word – to human agency and the power to effect social transformation.

Multimodal Text Production

Design is the concept introduced by Kress and van Leeuwen (Kress & van Leeuwen, 2001; Kress 2003) and taken up by the Multiliteracies Project (Cope & Kalantzis, 2000) to refer to multi-modal text production. I focus first on production, then on multimodality.

- *Production.* Chapter 1 makes the case for the word *design* as the word best suited to the production of texts that use multiple *sign* systems. I therefore use *design* as the overall word for imagining and producing texts, including written texts. *Imagining* sees design as a blueprint for production in which there is a 'deliberateness about choosing the modes for representation, and the framing for that representation' (Kress & van Leeuwen, 2001). In text production, however, there is no clear separation between designing and producing in that the ongoing process of semiotic choice and change, made easy by digital technologies, enables ongoing re-vision and redesign. According to Kress and van Leeuwen, 'The boundary between design and production is . . . blurry' (2001: 55).
- *Multimodality.* Kress and van Leeuwen (2001) and Kress (2003) have stressed the importance of multimodality in an age where new digital technologies have effected a communication revolution. It is now possible to produce permanent records of embodied oral texts, visually sophisticated written texts designed on our laps, as well as multimodal texts which make meaning by combining a number of modes of communication: verbal, visual, aural, spatial, gestural. The New London Group's (2000) work in multiliteracies argues that students have to be taught how to use and select from all the available semiotic resources for representation in order to make meaning, while at the same time combining and recombining these resources so as to

create possibilities for transformation and reconstruction (Cope & Kalantzis, 1997). Stein's (2008) work offers an analysis of classroom practices that use multimodal resources for meaning making in diverse classrooms.

I turn now to two pedagogic interventions in two different research projects to consider multimodal text production in relation to the issues of access, diversity and power.

Fun and Games[1]

The games project was part of a collaborative research project, Critical Literacy, Social Action and Children's Representations of Place, which began in 2001 as a small-scale literacy study initiated by Comber and Thomson at the University of South Australia (Comber, Thomson & Wells, 2001; Janks, 2002a; Janks & Comber, 2006). *Fun and Games* is a book produced by Grade 4 children at Phepo school, a poor school in Atteridgeville, an African township outside of Pretoria for students at Ridley Grove, a poor school in Adelaide, South Australia. The challenge for the teacher was to support young children who speak different African languages and who are learning through the medium of Setswana, to show and explain their games to children in an English-medium school, living in Australia. The occasion for this project was the upcoming visit of their teacher, Emily Langa, to Ridley Grove.

Pat Thomson and Barbara Comber had been working with Marg Wells at Ridley Grove to theorise how children engage with their 'place' in the world and how 'critical literacy' might make new resources available for neighbourhood as a social practice (de Certeau, Giard & Mayol, 1998). They invited me to join them, in the belief that a comparative study across different contexts of poverty would produce a better understanding of the relationship between 'habitus' and 'habitat' (Bourdieu, 1999) that might open the way for thinking about the local in relation to the global. The project on games does not focus on the link between habitat (place) and habitus (embodied subjectivity) as explicitly as in other work based on this research (Janks, 2003). Nevertheless, township games are both embodied and placed. By making them the subject of cultural exchange with children who are differently placed, township children's identities and knowledges are given both recognition and validation. In addition, the movement of educators has enabled staff from these two schools to gain an understanding of what more might be possible in their own contexts at the same time as giving children an opportunity to project and receive the knowledges, rooted in their own places, to children elsewhere.

---

[1] This material was first published in *English Studies in Africa*, 49(1) (Janks, 2006).

When Marg Wells visited South Africa in 2002, she brought two books that her Grade 3/4 students had produced for the students at Phepo school. These books are magnificent. In *A is for Arndale*, each child wrote a text for one letter of the alphabet about their neighbourhood and illustrated it with a painting in bold, striking colours. Careful attention was given to layout and presentation: the texts were typed, the pages were laminated and the book was ring-bound.[2] Similar attention to detail was evident in *Letters from Ridley Grove*. Here each child designed a page to introduce him- or herself to fellow students across the world. In each of their pages, the children's out-of-school lives cross over into their school literacies, enacting what Anne Haas Dyson has called a 'permeable curriculum' (Dyson, 1993, 1997, 2003).

For the teachers at Phepo who had never before produced a book, the splendour of the Ridley Grove books was both a threat and a challenge. Initially they decided that Grade 3/4 children could not produce a book in English, so two teachers and I worked with Grade 7s to produce *A is for Atteridgeville* (Janks & Comber, 2006). In the hope that we might be able to produce a book with Grade 4s, Emily Langa and I set out to establish whether or not this was possible.

We had to overcome the following difficulties:

1. The class had 44 children. The classroom was crowded with little *space* for movement, play, or art work.
2. Children had to produce a book in English, with limited skills in the *language*. Collaboration across continents and the move from the local to the global, necessitated the use of English. The children in Langa's class spoke a range of African languages. Setswana was the medium of instruction in school from Grade 1 to Grade 4, with English increasingly used as the medium from Grade 5.
3. Material *resources* were limited. (Children had little access to picture books, limited materials for producing a book, and at the time no access to digital technologies.)

Langa and I managed to overcome some of these difficulties by working together and pooling our resources. Langa, who speaks the children's languages, worked as the teacher: she negotiated which games the children wanted to demonstrate, she supervised their demonstrations outdoors, she worked with them in class to produce their verbal texts. I did the video recording, typed the students' work, supervised the art production, and provided the materials and the know-how for producing and assembling a low-cost book.

---

[2] Funding for this project was provided by the University of South Australia.

Crucial to the success of the project was the use of multimodal and multilingual pedagogies and the appropriation of alternative spaces in the school for working with the children. The decision to work with three different modalities (performance, drawing and words) enabled us to move from performance to text. We knew that we could capture the games on video. What we hoped was that once we had knowledge of the games, we would be able to scaffold the children's written work. We relied on performance to act as the pedagogic platform for writing.

Bana baka e tlang gae ('My children come home') is a game of catch in which the mother calls the children to come straight home from school because there are 'dangers' on the way. You have to get home without being caught by one of the 'dangers'. This game takes place in response to chanting and singing. What follows is a discussion of the game as represented in each of the three modalities. What this multimodal approach shows is that each of the modalities used affords different possibilities of representation even when the task, to 'explain' the game, remains constant. The three modes required different organisations of resources, space and pedagogical practice.

Video Text

Video is a good medium for representing a game as an embodied perform-

Figure 7.1 Bodies in the Classroom.

ance of an unfolding sequence. The video text demonstrates the game. We watch the children playing and witness their enjoyment. It is clear that it is as least as much fun to be a lion that catches the children on their way home, as it is to be one of the children. The boys in particular delight in being the lions. As the children who are caught become catchers, the number of lions begins to exceed the number of children. Although everyone will eventually get caught, there is pleasure in being clever and fast enough to evade the lions for as long as possible. There is a great deal of laughter and the children enjoy all the different roles. Even the mother, who does not get to run or catch, gets a solo part, and is chosen because she has a big voice.

Because *Bana baka e tlang gae* is an outdoor game of catch that 'needs a big space' we moved outside the classroom for the performance. The teaching at Phepo school remains fairly traditional, as can be seen in Figure 7.1. Bringing play into the curriculum freed children's bodies from the confinement of their desks, their overcrowded classroom and teacher-fronted pedagogy. There is a noticeable shift in how the children comport their bodies (compare Figures 7.1 and 7.2).

Figure 7.2 Relaxed Bodies Making Cars.

The Visual Text

In drawing a game, children have to select a particular moment in the game to represent. Figure 7.3 is the children's drawing of *Bana baka e tlang gae*. The drawings were done collectively by children who chose to work on them. As a group we spent several hours on different days working in the staff room, with the children sharing felt-tip pens. Often the colour selected was based on what was available at that moment. Some children elected to draw, others to outline or colour in. The drawings became a collaborative effort, rather than the vision of one child. As with the video recordings, the spatial constraints meant that this activity was done outside of the more 'formal' space of the classroom. The children worked together around a large central table, made by pushing big tables together. The atmosphere was more relaxed than they were used to in the classroom and the children were clearly having fun.

Figure 7.3 '*Bona baka e tlang gae*'.
Used with permission from the children and their parents.

In their drawing (Figure 7.3), the children capture the moment just before the mother calls, when the children see the 'dangers' that lurk in wait for them on their way home from school. Much of the pleasure of the game is in this moment of anticipation just before the chase. The 'dangers' are portrayed as fierce beasts: a spotted leopard with very red lips and eyes, a brown lion licking its lips in anticipation, a red spotted dog with its tongue salivating. The representation of the people is more ambiguous. Only two children seem perturbed: the one child, bottom left of the frame, who appears to be running away, and another, top left of the frame, who seems to be standing back. The others look fairly aggressive: one child appears to be throwing something at the 'dangers'; most of the children have open mouths and are leaning forward; one is gesticulating at the beasts, one is shouting.[3] Even the student with his hands in his pockets is leaning towards the danger. Only two of the children have school satchels and only one appears to have a tie, indicative of a school uniform. The students look older than primary children and semiotically are shown as Western and hip: purple clothes, bright shoes, and modern clothing create this impression. The representation of the mother in traditional attire, symbolised by her bare breasts, provides a strong contrast. It is as if, despite the representations of the 'dangers' as menacing, this is the mother's old-fashioned fear, which most of the children experience as a challenge rather than as a threat. The over-riding impression, however, is one of engaging humour. Both the people and the animals are cartoon-like caricatures. We are reminded that this is after all a game, which should not be taken too literally.

The Written Text

The written text (Figure 7.4) gives instructions for playing the game. It defines the different roles for participants, the spatial requirements, the script and the sequence of events. It provides the rules that govern the actions and enables one to understand how the game unfolds and concludes. In articulating what children need to play the game, no distinction is made between real players (children) and make-believe roles (mother, lions). Players and 'a large space' are presented as being of the same order of requirement for the game.

This written representation of *Bana baka e tlang gae* includes the words of the game that are shouted as cues for action but it is less easy to see the spatial organisation of the game than in the drawing. The mood in the written text is also different from both the video and the drawing: here the children say that they are scared of the lions that lie in wait for them;

---

[3] The words being shouted are hard to read. The first line says, '*Mama ke tshaba tau*' ('Mama, I am afraid of the lion') and the second line is indecipherable. The words and the child's posture contradict one another.

Bana baka e tlang gae

1
We need 5 lions.
We need children.
We need a mother.
We need a big space.

2
The mother stands at the door of the house and she calls the children.

Mother:	Bana baka e tlang gae. (My children come home).
Children shout:	Re a tshaba (We are scared).
Mother:	Le tshaba eng? (What are you scared of?)
Children:	Re tshaba ditau. (We are scared of the lions).
Mother:	Ba ba nthatang le ba ba sa nthateng e tlang gae! (If you love me or not come home).

3
The children start running home. The lions chase the children who dodge and duck and pull and hide and run away, but the lions catch some children.

4
When the children get home they say to their mother:

Children:	Kabošiga ga go iwo sekolong. (Tomorrow we are not going to school because on the way the lionsare going to chase them).

5
The game starts again. Now there are more lions because the children who were caught become more lions.

6
The game goes on until all the children are lions.

7
At the end the mother is without children.

Figure 7.4 Written Representation of '*Bana baka e tlang gae*'.
Used with permission from the children and their parents.

they describe the struggle that ensues to escape the lions, and they voice their reluctance to go to school. In the end there is no escape: all the children are caught and the mother is left alone. The game itself could be a representation of the fears of both mothers and children in communities where the dangers are real and children have to walk home unescorted. It could as easily reflect children's reluctance to go home when mother calls, or to go to school, when they could be playing with their friends.

In order to support the children in Grade 4 to produce this written text Langa returned to the classroom. She worked with the class as a whole, asking questions with the students responding individually. This breaks with production in the other two modes and marks a return to schooled literacy. First, she established the genre by asking students to answer the following questions in their own languages and to think about what the Australian children needed to know in order to play the game.

- What materials will they need?
- What instructions do we need to give them?
- What is the correct order for the instructions?

Allowing the children to use the full range of their multilingual resources enabled all the children to participate and to hone the information and the instructions before they were translated. Once the class was satisfied with the formulation, someone in the class who could, translated the words into English with help from other children and with help, when necessary, from the teacher. Langa wrote what the children told her in point form on the board and a scribe copied out the instructions. We decided to use point form for two reasons. A numbered list of instructions is appropriate for the genre and short point-form text was more suited to the children's linguistic abilities. Later, I typed the instructions, so that the students would experience the pleasure of seeing their words in professional-looking print.[4] Slowly, step by step, the children built up the instructions for their games.

In addition to using the children's multilingual resources to enable them to produce and then translate their instructions for playing the game, the teacher validated the use and translation of the township chants and songs in the children's written texts. Because the video text includes songs in the children's African languages, their use in the written text was naturalised – they needed to provide the words of these songs for their Australian audience. The inclusion of the children's languages in writing for circulation outside of South Africa, validates linguistic hybridity in written text and becomes an important means for children to display their multilingual identities to their Australian peers. Four of the eight games in the archive include children's songs and chants in African languages.

The Interplay of Design, Power, Access and Diversity in the Games Project

Access, diversity and a theory of power underpin this project which focuses on design – in this instance, multimodal text production. The power vested in knowledge lay with the children as they knew more about their games than we did. In schools that are only beginning to work with child-centred approaches to education, members of staff were able to experience children's expertise as non-threatening and they could see the value of using the knowledge that children bring to school as a resource (Comber & Simpson, 2001; Dyson, 1993, 1997, 2003; Moll, Amanti, Neffe & Gonzále, 1992; Vasquez, 2004). In making their games part of the curriculum, in inviting children to record and share their games, we gave their everyday

---

[4] Now that the school has computers, this work can be done by the children themselves.

out-of-school knowledge a privileged status. That we were interested, and that they were allowed to play these games out of the classroom during school, increased their pleasure. But it was the knowledge that children in Australia were the real audience that gave the work meaning. That children elsewhere might play different games, or the same games

Table 7.3 The Interdependent Model for Critical Literacy

Power without design	The deconstruction of power, without reconstruction or design, removes human agency.

The recognition of power, for example, exclusion from the class of knowledge makers, who contribute to the global flows of information, is interrupted by the circulation of children's texts.

Access without design	This maintains and reifies powerful forms without considering how they can be transformed.

While students are given access to the production of written text, in a genre important for education and in a powerful global language, they are allowed to transform the genre by the inclusion of an African language.

Diversity without design	Diversity provides the means, the ideas, the alternative perspectives for reconstruction and transformation. Without design, the potential that diversity offers is not realised.

The imagined differences between children's games in different countries become a productive resource, which is realised by the production of texts in different modalities.

Design without power	Design, without an understanding of how powerful discourses/practices perpetuate themselves, runs the risk of an unconscious reproduction of these forms.

In South Africa, discourses of schooling often exclude children's funds of knowledge, in the search for quantifiable outcomes. Similarly code-switching, while recognised as natural in oral interactions, is still not encouraged in children's writing. This project does not reproduce these normative practices.

Design without access	Runs the risk of whatever is designed remaining on the margins.

Access to powerful forms, digital technologies and the means of production are key to this project, as is access to new publics and practices of circulation. It matters that these games travel. Where the project is limited is that students did not handle the digital technologies themselves.

Design without diversity	This privileges powerful forms and fails to use the design resources provided by difference.

Students were allowed to use a range of forms to express their local knowledge. (In addition to games, children also made toy cars from wire and demonstrated hair-braiding).

differently inflected, energised the project, and the sharing across diversity offered the possibility of real cultural exchange.

The project gave students access to dominant literacies, powerful technologies, and the means of production. We wanted students to see themselves as knowledge makers, who could produce artefacts (a book, a video) rooted in their own lives that would be valued beyond their own local context. We wanted young Grade 4 children to imagine themselves as agents whose placed and embodied knowledges mattered to their peers on the other side of the world.

Literacy in this project is embedded in a set of relations that positions multimodal textual production as a form of global mobility, with real readers and viewers across the world who without the affordances of text, would otherwise be out of reach. Literacy here is precisely not 'isolated' or 'detached from any interlocutor' or 'somehow self-contained, complete' (Ong, 1982: 132). It enters into practices of circulation which in a modest way help students to see themselves as part of the global flow of information and knowledge. It gives them a glimpse, in Grade 4, of a wider world to which they can belong, and in which they can claim a space for themselves. In the cross-country literacy project we wanted students to begin to imagine themselves as players on a world stage thus increasing their capacity to aspire (Appadurai, 2002). These ideas are summarised in Table 7.3.

The Reconciliation Pedagogies Project[5]

Design articulates differently with power, access and diversity in the Reconciliation Pedagogies project. In this project researchers worked together with teachers to imagine what reconciliation work in South African classrooms might look like ten years after the Truth and Reconciliation Commission (TRC), began its work. Working across the disciplines of English, History and Art in three secondary schools proved productive. What one of the English teachers described as 'art envy' moved the classroom work from written text to multimodality, culminating in students producing postcards to encapsulate their understanding from, or experience of, the project.

Fereira *et al.* (forthcoming) provides an overview of the project, which in 2005 had two distinct phases. In the first phase the teachers encouraged

---

[5] Ana Ferreira, Hilary Janks, Ingrid Barnsley, Charles Marriott, Monique Rudman, Helen Ludlow, and Reville Nussey worked together on this project over a period of a year. Barnsley, Marriott and Rudman are the three secondary school teachers; Ferreira, Janks, Ludlow and Nussey are teacher educators based at the University of the Witwatersrand. This section of the paper is indebted to Ferreira *et al.* (Ferreira *et al.*, forthcoming).

students to work from their own experience of being sorry in order to respond to a range of stimuli such as songs, literature, discussion. The work they produced dealt with individuals' responses to their actions. Where they did offer social commentary this was not tied to a particular South African sensibility. They produced, for example,

- a drawing of a girl feeling sorry for herself;
- a letter from Jennifer Lopez to 'all the animals she's killed by wearing so much fur' accompanied by a collage of women wearing fur coats;
- a letter of apology for a fight at school with a collage depicting male violence, where the photographs are taken from conflicts elsewhere in the world.

In summing up the work of this first phase of the project, we recognised that

we had not engaged with reconciliation in a historically contextualised way. As a result students had taken individual and personal approaches to reconciliation as 'sorry' work in their own lives ... rather than a social and political approach to reconciliation.

(Ferreira *et al.*, forthcoming)

While we were working with new multimodal literacies, the work was not critical. Even where the texts touch on relations of power (as in the collages depicting male violence and women wearing furs) this leads back to the individual and the personal rather than to an analysis of the social. There is little analysis of power, no use of diversity as a resource for new ways of seeing, and little sign of disruption or change. As this was part of an international project on reconciliation pedagogies, the students did have some sense of a wider audience for their work, of greater access to new publics.

These concerns led us in the second phase of the project to collaborate in designing a unit of work on the TRC. Despite our fears that students were resistant to engaging with the past and despite our own reservations about the TRC process,[6] we believed that investigating South Africa's attempt at national reconciliation could produce a more critical pedagogy. The classroom work was based on four pedagogical moves:

1. providing students across the schools with the same basic information on the TRC process;
2. positioning students as researchers who could interview adults in

---

[6] For a fuller discussion of both these points, see Ferreira *et al.* (forthcoming).

their communities to ascertain how the TRC affected people they
knew;

3. requiring students to present their findings to the class;
4. requiring students to reflect on the project by designing a postcard
   that captured in word and image what stood out for them from the
   TRC project. Students were also asked to produce a written
   reflection.

Inviting students to investigate their own communities led to important
learning experiences in those classes where students had differential access
to informed people. Across the different classes, students' access to interesting narratives depended on their identity locations and the funds of knowledge available in their communities. For many students, this was their first
experience of a curriculum that privileged the subjugated knowledges of
their communities. For the first time, who the students were that had
access to the appropriate cultural capital shifted.

> Some of those more privileged children, sort of white suburban
> group,[7] were really disappointed in their parents. They were upset
> that this thing, that they were hearing was so momentous, had been
> ignored.
>
> (Teacher, Research Circle transcript, 17 October 2005)

This displacement was not contested. Because many of the students were
profoundly moved by the stories they were uncovering about what had
happened to members of their own families during the apartheid struggle,
what they had to offer was recognised by the class as valuable for everyone.
One of the teachers reported that

> when they were giving some examples of apartheid atrocities, they
> were the quietest class I've ever had . . . Everyone was listening, even
> the total skater boy hooligans . . . everyone was listening, listening,
> listening.
>
> (Teacher, Research Circle transcript, 17 October 2005)

Not only did some of the children come to see their own families in a new
light but the students and the teachers learnt to see one another differently. In one class in particular, this constituted what Comber and Kamler
(2005) describe as a 'turn-around pedagogy'. Because this teacher was
deeply affected by the story of one of the class 'thugs', who learnt 'life-
changing stuff and was really saying deep things', she came to see him

---

[7] That access to different understandings of the struggle against apartheid is still racialised
in South African classrooms is not surprising. At the same time, it is important to stress that
the split along racial lines was not absolute.

more sympathetically. In the first two pedagogical moves of this unit of work, access to information and knowledge intersected with diversity to change the power relations in the classroom, as the personal intersected with the political. In the one small class where students did not have access to diverse funds of knowledge, there was far less engagement with the project.

By positioning students as researchers of history who could find things out for themselves and share their knowledge with one another, the teachers made it possible for the students to engage with South Africa's oppressive past. In writing about students' reluctance to deal with the past, McKinney argues that

> [w]e . . . need to take seriously the difficulties of young South Africans of living with the legacy of an oppressive past that was not of their making . . . We cannot ignore students' feelings of entrapment, accusation and despair and in doing so we need to find ways of tapping the optimism about being South African that many of these young people express.
>
> (McKinney, 2004b: 71–72)

According to Desmond Tutu in his introduction to the TRC report, the TRC project stands at the crossroads between 'a past marked by conflict, injustice, oppression and exploitation' and the future promise of 'a new and democratic dispensation characterised by a culture of respect for human rights' (TRC, 1998: 20). Because of its location at this specific historic juncture, in their postcards students could choose to look backwards to a painful past or forwards to a born-free future. In addition, because the TRC was itself contentious, the students felt able to take up their own positions in the design of their postcards. It is clear from an analysis of these 71 postcards that these positions are socially rooted and informed by the politics of history, place and identity. Because postcards are spatially condensed multimodal texts, students had to capture their ideas in a single image and an abbreviated text. By and large they used the verbal mode to express an attitude or position, or to describe, narrate or report. The genre of the postcard-picture appears to have freed students to work more symbolically. The visual mode lends itself to abstraction and metaphor and many of the students were able to produce more powerful visual than verbal images. In Figure 7.5, the TRC is represented as 'dry cleaners' that, in removing the blood, 'may cause colours to run'.

'Colour' is a highly suggestive word in the context of reconciliation after apartheid. The metaphor of the colours running suggests an end to segregation. Although this is confirmed by the written text on the other side of

Figure 7.5 Truth and Reconciliation Commission Project.
Used with permission of the teacher, students and parents.

the postcard: 'the background shows how the different races mix', the overall message of the image is discordant. The dry-cleaning metaphor diminishes the work of the TRC and the colours bleed into one another, creating a feeling of unease. This is reinforced by the contrast in the image between the cultural objects and nature. The house and the flag are drawn with sharp lines which contain and control the colour. Nature, on the other hand, is darker and more jagged. There is however hope. In the top right-hand quadrant of the image where ideal, highly valued, new information tends to be placed (Kress & van Leeuwen, 1990: 108), the sky is clearing. Reading the image from left to right also suggests movement from the dark into the light. Dividing the dark from the light is the new South African flag.

The ambiguities in the image are also apparent in the written text (see Figure 7.6 overleaf).

In the first sentence of the postcard, the word 'just' suggests the limitations of the TRC suggesting that it was a process that was designed just to give absolution to people with blood on their hands. 'However' at the start of the second sentence, signals a shift to a more positive view of the TRC process, which established the unity needed for a 'truly New South Africa'. 'Truly' intensifies this achievement which is represented by the new South African flag and racial mixing.

The image in Figure 7.7 is of a person crying for someone that is missing. The use of torn pieces of paper to construct the image powerfully captures a sense of loss and fragmentation. The person's arms are held in a

The building is labled T.R.C

Dry Cleaners as I believe
that the T.R.C was just to
give people the opportunty to
remove the blood of the
people they killed, just as
the sign says. However I do
believe that the T.R.C Helped
unite our country and truly
make a New South Africa. This
is represented by the Flag. The
background shows how the
different race groups mix

To: Janina Kanjee.
121 Indian Street
Lenasia
Johannesburg
Gauteng
South Africa, 2004

Figure 7.6 Truth and Reconciliation Commission Project.
Used with permission of the teacher, students and parents.

Figure 7.7 Truth and Reconciliation Commission Project.
Used with permission of the teacher, students and parents.

position that suggests unanswered questions and they create vectors which direct our gaze to large exaggerated eyes from which tears fall. The object labelled as 'missing' – we assume it is a person from our knowledge of the context – is portrayed as a round featureless shape in a blue-grey that echoes the colour of the blue tears. The shape which mirrors the body of the brown person, has no face and no limbs. The person crying, who could be a man or a woman, is brown and has generalised features so as to represent any black South African whose suffered loss in the struggle against apartheid. Without mouth or ears, we have a clear sense of the mute suffering of a person who has been silenced. The sparseness of this image is a powerful statement of the pain which the TRC wished to acknowledge and heal. The TRC process was specifically designed to enable people to speak and be heard.

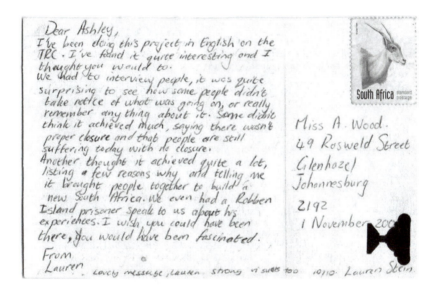

Figure 7.8 Truth and Reconciliation Commission Project.
Used with permission of the teacher, students and parents.

Figure 7.8 shows the writing on the other side of the postcard. It is chatty and provides news as is typical of the postcard genre. Faithfulness to the genre inhibits this student from expressing the depth of feeling that she is able to convey in the image. Her reference to people suffering today because they have been unable to achieve closure explains the image. Part of the aim of the TRC was to find 'the truth' – the disclosures that would allow closure.

The two phases of the project help us to understand how work that is

Table 7.4 Interdependence in the Reconciliation Pedagogies Project

Power without design	The deconstruction of power, without reconstruction or design, removes human agency.

A focus on the abuse of power in the past without the possibility of transformation removes human agency. This leads students to resist learning about South Africa's history. In phase 2 of this project, the TRC faces the past while at the same time offering students a way forward.

Access without design	This maintains and reifies powerful forms without considering how they can be transformed.

Access to knowledge without the ability to remake it creates the sense of entrapment (McKinney, 2004b). The TRC project invites students to understand one another's pasts in order to remake their futures.

Diversity without design	Diversity provides the means, the ideas, the alternative perspectives for reconstruction and transformation. Without design, the potential that diversity offers is not realised.

In phase 1 of the project students rely on their own design resources. In phase 2 diverse funds of knowledge inform what students design.

Design without power	Design, without an understanding of how powerful discourses/practices perpetuate themselves, runs the risk of an unconscious reproduction of these forms.

In phase 1, design is based on interpersonal relations of power within a discourse of humanism; in phase 2, subjugated knowledges enter the classroom to destabilise this dominant discourse.

Design without access	Runs the risk of whatever is designed remaining on the margins.

In phase 1 students' work is based on personal experience and there is no access to a broader community's funds of knowledge. In phase 2, marginalised knowledge moves to the centre and is privileged in the classroom.

Design without diversity	This privileges powerful forms and fails to use the design resources provided by difference.

Phase 1 fails to use the design resources provided by difference. In phase 2 diversity is a resource for a critical engagement with the past while providing possibilities for the future.

critical needs questions of power, diversity, access and design to pull together and counterbalance one another. In the first phase of the project, design is tied to personal experience and individual creativity. It allows students to think about reconciliation in the context of their own lives and their personal relationships. Although not critical, because it remains decontextualised, a-historical and uninflected by questions of power, diversity and access, the focus on 'sorry' work provides a pedagogical platform for phase 2: the TRC project. In this second phase, itself a pedagogical redesign, what counts as valued knowledge disrupts existing relations of power in the classroom. Previously excluded community funds of knowledge enter the curriculum when teachers use diversity in the class as a productive resource. In this way all the students are given access to a range of perspectives and insights from across the racialised divisions in our society and an opportunity to learn from one another. This recognition of the other in itself contributes to the national project of Reconciliation and in a small way to the critical project of social transformation. The interdependence of power, access, diversity and design is summarised in Table 7.4.

Conclusion

It is important to recognise that power, diversity, access and possibilities for redesign manifest themselves differently in different contexts and different classroom projects. Table 7.5 provides a summary of the different articulations of these concepts in these two very different projects.

Table 7.5 Interdependence in the Games Project

	Games Project	Reconciliation Pedagogies Project
Power	This project gives children's local knowledge a privileged status and validates their home languages. Children have the opportunity to see themselves as knowledge makers who can contribute to the global flow of information.	What counts as valued knowledge disrupts existing relations of power in the classroom by changing which students have the appropriate cultural capital. Subjugated knowleges destabilise dominant discourses.
Access	Children are given access to dominant literacies and the means for producing their own book.	All students gain access to a wider range of community funds of knowledge.
Diversity	Here the diversity is provided by the link between a school in South Africa and a school in Australia. Local knowledge is sent abroad and children in Australia are the real audience that children in South Africa have to imagine.	This project only works because diversity within the classroom leads students to an engagement with the past through the narratives of real people, the family and friends of their classmates. Here the personal is constructed within social relations of power and diversity is a resource for seeing history differently.
Design	In using their own languages, the children are able to redesign the dominant monolingualism of South African texts.	Different community funds of knowledge provide the class with other ways of knowing that give them the resources needed for design and redesign.

Power, diversity and access are always inflected by context, so that the conditions of possibility for both design and redesign are always historically and politically specific. When we produce texts, we want readers to enter our world. We can play with the word *design*, and suggest that as writers we have designs on our readers: we work hard to entice them into our way of seeing and understanding the world. We use language in combination with other signs to construct our version of reality and we work to position our readers. Because literacy is at the centre of the politics of text and identity we have a responsibility as educators to create opportunities for students to reflect critically on their world in order to re-imagine and redesign it. As early as 1980, Bolinger described language as a 'loaded weapon'. As text makers we need to recognise that signs can be used in the interests of good or evil. Ultimately it is the values we hold that will determine how we name and rename our world and, in so doing, ourselves. The choice is an ethical one that will be explored further in the next chapter, in which the focus is on redesign and transformative social action that contribute in ways, however small, to a more humane and hopeful future.

CHAPTER **8**

Redesign, Social Action and Possibilities for Transformation

The argument of the book so far is that all texts are constructed and that what has been constructed can be deconstructed. In this chapter the focus is on reconstruction or redesign and the ways in which construction, deconstruction and reconstruction should be thought of as a cyclical process. So, for example, once one has analysed a text in order to understand the interests at play, it is important to imagine how the text could be redesigned so as not to advantage some at the expense of others. We saw in Chapter that the the UNHCR 'Spot the Refugee' advertisement was one of a set of four 'posters' using the Lego theme. I return to these posters in order to explain the concept of redesign. Figure 8.1 gives readers a sense of the similarity in the design of all four of the Lego posters. (See also www.unhcr.org or Google 'UNHCR Lego posters')

Although each poster is different from the others, their similarity is more striking. In addition, each poster is just another instantiation of the discourse that positions refugees as having nothing to contribute. This is not what I mean by redesign because each poster is just a version of one design. To mark its fiftieth anniversary, the UNHCR produced advertisements that are the antithesis of their Lego advertisements. The '50 Million Success Stories' advertising campaign continues the idea introduced in the Albert Einstein advertisement (Figure 5.5). This campaign redesigns refugees as having exceptional skills, knowledge and beauty which they bring to their host country. One of these advertisements features statuesque supermodel Alek Wek, once a refugee from the Sudan, and another portrays Madeleine Albright, the first woman Secretary of State in the United States of America, once a refugee from Czechoslovakia.

Figure 8.1 UNHCR Lego Posters.
Source: http://www.unhcr.org/cgi-bin/texis/vtx/template?page=home&src=static/
teaching-tools/tchhr/tchhr.htm

Here famous people are used to present refugees in a positive light. Again these advertisements are versions of one new design. From the Lego ads, first presented and deconstructed in Chapter 5, to their reconstruction in the success story advertisements, we have one complete cycle of design, deconstruction and reconstruction (Figure 8.2).

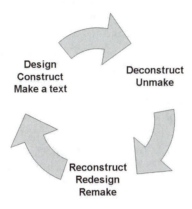

Figure 8.2 The Redesign Cycle.

It is important that this process is conceptualised as cyclical because every new design serves a different set of interests. Because all texts are positioned and positioning, each redesign becomes a new text that requires deconstruction. No design is neutral, and in focusing on exceptional refugees, the success stories advertisements in this campaign, like the Albert Einstein advertisement introduced at the end of Chapter 5, discount the millions of refugees who contribute in smaller ways with their taxes and their labour. These stories also make the countless forced migrants, who work under exploitative conditions, invisible.[1] According to Tollefson (1991: 108),

> Refugees are educated for work as janitors, waiters in restaurants, assemblers in electric plants, and other low-paying jobs offering little opportunity for advancement, regardless of whether the refugees have skills . . . suitable for higher paying jobs.

It is important to recognise that not all redesigns are transformative.

In much the same way, Pat Thomson's redesign of the Edge advertisements (Figure 2.2), discussed in Chapter 2, excluded the less glamorous others who lose their hair for less glamorous reasons than André Agassi,

---

[1] *Dogville* is an excellent allegorical film which explores how an outsider is exploited, in this case by everyone in the community, even the children.

the Dalai Lama or Sinead O'Connor. Some redesigns are conservative in that they seek to maintain dominant interests whereas other strive to transform social relations in order to achieve greater equity.

Even texts that are themselves designed to draw attention to unequal relations of power require analysis and deconstruction. Michael Rosen writes satirical poetry for children that pokes fun at adults. In 'Tea-time' (Rosen, 1988) the family is depicted as sitting at the table for 'tea'. In the first stanza, the father asks his child to fetch the milk. No sooner has the child sat down than the father, in the second stanza, asks the child to fetch the butter, which the child dutifully does. When in the third stanza, the father asks the child to get a teaspoon, the mother intervenes. She says to the father: 'Once you get that bum of yours stuck in a chair you never get it off again, do you?' The poem is fundamentally about power relations in a family: between parents and children (the father expects the child to do his bidding and the adult poet now teases the father), and between the parents (the mother challenges the father's treatment of the child and asserts herself against her husband). Rosen's poem subverts the hierarchy in the family. His use of taboo language – 'bum' – defies social norms and is simultaneously humorous. If the poem is itself a redesign of social relations of power, how might we teach it using a critical approach?

The following questions, which reveal the conditions of possibility of this poem, work effectively with South African students.

- Describe meal times in your family.
- Could your mother talk to your father like this? Explain.
- Do you think the child is a boy or a girl? How do you know?
- Have you ever wanted an adult to side with you in a situation like this? Give examples.

The first three questions quickly allow the cultural diversity in the class to surface. In South Africa, many students live in extended families – this poem suggests a nuclear family. Families who live in small four-roomed houses, referred to as 'matchboxes' in Soweto,[2] do not always have space indoors for sit-down meals. In addition, many parents work long hours or night shifts and are not at home for meals. 'Tea-time', where it exists at all in South Africa, is not a meal – it is a cup of tea, sometimes with a biscuit (cookie). Many traditional and rural African communities are patriarchal: the men do not eat with the women and children, and are served their meals by their wives and daughters; respect for the male head of the family

---

[2] Soweto was built by the apartheid government to house Africans who were not allowed to live in areas designated for other population groups. It has a population of more than a million people.

is inviolate. In Tshivenda there is a saying which translated literally is 'the child is the oil to be sent'. This shows the expectation that children have a duty to run errands for adults. Wives are not permitted to challenge the authority or rights of the head of the house. As a result of all these cultural and material differences, many of my students are shocked by Rosen's poem.

The last question provides a space for the students' fantasies: the desire of the underdog to see the oppressor punished; the wish to triumph over the father; the dream of seeing the tables turned. Fantasy is not culture-bound; poems are not reality. Literature helps us to imagine other possible worlds and to step into them when we read. Seen from this perspective, it becomes possible for students to engage with the poem across their differences.

Critical literacy requires that we engage with and distance ourselves from texts, described in Chapter 1 as reading *with* a text and reading *against* a text. Here, students who are alienated from this poem because it is so 'rude', start from a position of estrangement. They have their own cultural knowledge as a basis for deconstructing and resisting the text. They see that the father has been undermined and they side with him. These students have to endeavour to read *with* the text and to understand it on its own terms. Students who are feminists, on the other hand, are more likely to engage with the text – to accept the power of the mother and to relish her put-down of the father. They are less likely to notice the ways in which specific cultural values and context-dependent assumptions are privileged by the poem. They have to endeavour to work *against* the text's naturalised assumptions. In heterogeneous classes it is possible to use students' different reading positions to generate both perspectives. Some students produce 'ideal' readings, others produce oppositional readings. As discussed in Chapter 3, critical literacy requires both.

The work that I have done with this poem also enables me to illustrate another aspect of redesign. The published version of the poem is accompanied by a witty cartoon-like drawing of the father reclining in an armchair with the child, a boy, fanning him with an oversized leaf. I read this illustration as an ironic reflection on the father's last statement, in response to his wife's challenge, that he 'can't get a moment's peace'. It also provides an intertextual reference to earlier representations of colonial masters being fanned by their colonial subjects, or of pharaohs and emperors being pampered by their slaves. The picture anchors the child in the poem as a boy, and pre-empts discussion of whether fathers expect only their daughters to do household chores.

Wendy Morgan (1994) suggests that 'rubbing' texts up against one another is an excellent way to denaturalise them. This involves providing a similar text as an alternative reference point, as I did with the UNHCR advertisements in this chapter and the Edge advertisements in Chapters 1 and 2. I find that *getting the students to produce these alternative texts* works well. With this poem one can ask students to illustrate the poem before showing them the published illustration. They can then be asked to compare all the illustrations in order to work out how their different designs position the characters in, and the readers of, the poem differently. For example, students could be expected to analyse the different representations of bodies, facial expressions and clothing as well as the relative size of the different figures. It is also possible to give students the published illustration first, and then to ask them to redesign it. Figure 8.3 shows four illustrations of the poem produced by children in Grade 7. With great economy and simplicity, students are well able to depict body language that captures both the emotions of the characters and their own interpretations of the poem.

It is worth comparing these drawings.

- Look at how the father is presented in each drawing. (Look at how the father is positioned; what he is doing; how big he is).
- Notice how the child is represented in each drawing. (What do you notice about size, body language, gender, feelings?)
- How is the mother represented in each drawing?

From its Freireian and Marxist roots, critical literacy has always been conceptualised as a form of social action – as political. Within the model, where design provides the space for action and agency, redesign shows the potential for literacy to contribute to transformation and change. Many teachers fear critical literacy because they think of it as too political. In thinking about power and politics, it is important to draw a distinction between *Politics* with a big *P* and *politics* with a small *p*.[3]

There is an emblematic story of a husband, who on the occasion of his golden wedding anniversary, shared the secret of his successful marriage. 'It's easy', he said, 'my wife makes all the small decisions and I make all the big decisions'. When asked to give examples, he went on to explain: 'My wife decides things like what we should eat, who our friends should be, where we should live, how many children we should have, where they

---

[3] This distinction is indebted to a conversation that I had with Barbara Kamler in which we were playfully applying Gee's (1990, p. 142) notion of little *d*, discourse, and big *D*, Discourse, to the ways in which critical literacy works with the politics of the everyday.

Figure 8.3 'Tea-Time' Drawings.
Drawings by children received as a gift.

should go to school'. And what, he is asked, are the big decisions? The man said that he decided the important things: 'Who should be President of the country, whether or not to go to war, what should be done about the economy'. The story is funny because of the way in which the husband appears naïvely to cede power to his wife on matters that directly affect the quality of his daily life, reserving for himself matters on which he can have an opinion, but over which he can have little direct influence or control. Moreover, the story uses irony to undercut the gendered binary which constructs the domestic domain as the disempowered domain of women, leaving worldliness to men.

Politics with a capital *P* is the big stuff, the worldly concerns of the husband. It is about government and world trade agreements and the United Nations peacekeeping forces; it is about ethnic or religious genocide and world tribunals; it is about apartheid and global capitalism, money laundering and linguistic imperialism. It is about the inequities between the political North and the political South. It is about oil, the ozone layer, genetic engineering and cloning. It is about the danger of global warming. It is about globalisation, the new work order and sweatshops in Asia.

Little *p* politics, on the other hand, is about the micro-politics of everyday life. It is about the minute-by-minute choices and decisions that make us who we are. It is about desire and fear; how we construct them and how they construct us. It is about the politics of identity and place; it is about small triumphs and defeats; it is about winners and losers, haves and have-nots, school bullies and their victims; it is about how we treat other people day by day; it is about whether or not we learn someone else's language or recycle our own garbage. Little *p* politics is about taking seriously the feminist perspective that the personal *is* the political. This is not to suggest that *politics* has nothing to do with *Politics*. On the contrary, the socio-historical and economic contexts in which we live produce different conditions of possibility and constraint that we all have to negotiate as meaningfully as we can. While the social constructs who we are, so do we construct the social. This dialectic relationship is fluid and dynamic, creating possibilities for social action and change. Working with the politics of the local enables us to engage in a different kind of transformative redesign.

The work of Barbara Comber and her colleagues at the University of South Australia is a model of transformative practice that goes beyond designing and redesigning texts to action that makes a material difference to the lives of students and their communities. To give just one example from their large body of work, I focus on their work first with Marg Wells and then with both Marg Wells and Ruth Trimm at Ridley Grove Primary

School. As a teacher, Marg Wells is particularly aware of the social conditions that affect the lives of her early primary students. Her work on neighbourhood began when developers moved in to gentrify the area surrounding the school. Many of the families with children at the school had to move, and children were confronted with large, noisy, yellow bulldozers demolishing the houses of their neighbours and friends. Watching Marg Wells' videos in South Africa of this process, teachers in Atteridgeville and I were struck by the déjà vu experience that took us back to the time of forced removals under apartheid. At that time, so-called African, Indian and Coloured people were taken out of their homes and moved against their will to racially designated townships or rural areas. Bulldozers flattened whole communities.

Rather than pretending that the upheaval in the children's lives was not imminent, Marg Wells undertook projects that showed students how they might be pro-active in the face of change (Comber, Thomson, & Wells, 2001). She negotiated with the developers to give the children a say about the design of a park that was to be built a few blocks away from the school. Not only did her students undo the designs of the developers, they insisted that Australian flora and representations of Australian animals were included in the park. They produced tiles and other artefacts that became part of the new design. They shaped the development and in the process learnt about agency – its limitations and its possibilities.

Following a discussion in which her students identified 'trees' in their neighbourhood as an issue of concern, her class undertook a project in which the students counted the trees and examined their condition. On the basis of a comparison with other wealthier suburbs and using the evidence they had collected, her class successfully petitioned the city council to plant more trees. The recognition of trees in a neighbourhood as a marker of social class is no small achievement for children aged seven and eight in a Grade 2/3 class.

In *Negotiating Critical Literacy with Young Children*, Vivian Vasquez (2004) shows how it is possible to take action on problems that children identify. For example, when her four-year-old students discover during daily news that one of their classmates did not have anything to eat at the school barbecue because there was no food for vegetarians, they were upset. Vasquez talked with them about what they might do. Led by Stephanie, one of the students who had discussed the issue with her family, 'the group decided to act on their concern' (2004: 104). They decided to do some research. They set out to establish how many children in the school were vegetarian and the reasons why people decided to become vegetarian. The absence of books with information in the library resulted in the letter reproduced in Figure 8.4.

> Dear Mr Librarian
>
> Libraries are for kids and all people.
>
> Vegetarians are people but there's no books
>
> about them in the library. There should be
>
> books about all people in the library.
>
> Vasquez (2004, 107)

Figure 8.4 'Dear Mr Librarian' (Vasquez, 2004: 107).
Source: Vasquez, V. (2004). *Negotiating critical literacies with young children*. Mahwah, New Jersey: Lawrence Erlbaum and Associates.

They also wrote letters to the organisers of the barbecue and changed the way the school would provide food in the future, and they wrote to other schools in the neighbourhood telling them about their project so that they too could think about providing food for children with special dietary needs. Vasquez's work is a powerful demonstration of how one can work with the daily politics of inclusion and exclusion.

Since 1994, a watershed year in South African history marked by the first democratic elections, I have been working to conceptualise critical literacy for reconstruction. Having spent the previous decade deconstructing apartheid texts in order to show how they worked to 'sustain relations of domination' (Thompson, 1984: 35), I had to re-imagine my intellectual work in a post-apartheid democracy. I had to shift my emphasis from the *deconstruct* part of the cycle to the design and *reconstruct* part of the redesign cycle (Figure 8.2), so as to contribute to the national project of transformation. I chose the word *reconstruction* to establish an intertextual link with the ANC's *Reconstruction and Development Programme* (RDP) (1994). I also chose it to set up an antonymic opposition with *deconstruction*. Once the liberation struggle was over, it became possible in education for me to focus on the politics of everyday – on curriculum redesign and implementation, on school change, on environmental education and action, on teacher development, on reconciliation. The overall list of possibilities for social action was, and continues to be, endless.

But what does critical literacy for reconstruction look like? Luke (2002), in a paper on Critical Discourse Analysis (CDA), has argued that

> to move beyond a strong focus on ideology critique, CDA would need to begin to develop a strong positive thesis about discourse and the productive uses of power. . . . Particularly in the case of education, the affirmative character of discourse can take many forms.

And he has asked challenging questions such as

> What forms do productive, liberatory political speech take? What are the textual shapes and practices of 'open' and locally enabling social policies? What would a critical or normatively preferable representation of history in a textbook look like? If CDA is avowedly normative and explicitly political, than it must have the courage to say what is to be done with texts and discourse.

I believe that these questions push in the same direction as the question that I asked myself about a critical literacy within a context of post-apartheid restructuring and transformation. With an account of an educational partnership that has produced and is continuing to produce material changes in people's lives, I will attempt to address Luke's challenge.

Working with Barbara Comber and Pat Thomson on an international research project, 'Critical Literacy, Social Action and Children's Representations of Place', funded by the University of South Australia, I based my research at a poor school in Atteridgeville, a township situated west of Pretoria. We focused on place in order to build on the work of Marg Wells and to understand the connections between place and identity, between habitus and habitat.

Phepo school is in an established part of Atteridgeville amidst old-style apartheid housing for Africans. These four-roomed 'matchboxes' are larger and more solid than the RDP houses built by the ANC government. RDP houses have only one room but they include indoor sanitation, water and electricity, which the 'matchboxes' do not. The government has also provided title rights to plots of land with these services. Despite ongoing efforts by the government to address the need for housing, many families still live in crowded informal settlements, in make-shift shacks, often constructed from zinc sheeting. In talking about the models that they built and the pictures they took of the houses they live in as part of the neighbourhood project, the children took pleasure in describing their homes. A home is a place of belonging and children see past the structure to the life within. Nevertheless, many of the children live in extreme poverty and their parents choose to send them to the school because it provides a hot meal every day made from vegetables grown in the school garden.

When the gardens were being established children had to 'pay' for their food by bringing recyclable materials. On different days of the week they were expected to bring vegetable peelings for the compost heap; two litres of 'grey water' – dirty soapy water which acts as an insecticide in an organic garden; tins sold to collect-a-can for recycling; paper for recycling; and half-bricks scrounged from the township for bricking both beds and paths in the garden. The project even made an insecticide 'tea' from cigarette butts. Sethole, the principal, has helped me to understand that what to a middle class household constitutes waste, to her school constitutes resources: empty margarine tubs, polystyrene packaging, paper printed on one side only, empty tins, old magazines, broken toilets, two-litre plastic bottles, plastic bags, old tyres, broken desks, cardboard boxes. I have come to understand that reading one's own litter is an important critical literacy activity.

The students worked in the garden, learnt from the garden and ate from the garden. They put their bodies into the garden and the garden into their bodies. Teachers used the garden to teach mathematics: from counting beds and cabbages, to calculating cubic metres of water. Children measured and recorded water consumption and rainfall, the amounts of recycling material brought by each grade and the money earned from sales. They kept comparative charts and bar graphs. They learnt about earthworms and how to improve the soil – 'the gardens feed us, so we must feed the gardens'.[4] They lived their environmental awareness in their daily practices and they translated these into songs and dramatic performances; they drew and wrote about the gardens and they learnt about the importance of documenting a project through written and visual records. Learning was tied to real needs. In Maslow's hierarchy of needs (1954), physiological needs for air, food, water and bodily comforts form the base, without which self-actualisation and education are impossible.

If we take seriously Foucault's view of power as having a 'capillary form of existence' that 'reaches into the very grain of individuals, touches their bodies and inserts itself into their actions and attitudes, their discourses, learning processes and everyday lives' (1980: 39), then this necessitates a focus on the effects that our pedagogies produce. There is clear evidence that this project changed the corporeal, spatial and material conditions (Luke, 1992) of the children's lives.

The once overgrown school property, at one time a 'a haven of snakes',

---

[4] All unsourced quotations are taken from a lengthy transcribed interview with Sethole, 16–17 February 2002 or subsequent personal communications recorded in field notes. Aspects of this work were first published in *English Teachers at Work*, edited by B. Doecke, D. Homer and H. Nixon (Janks, 2003).

by 2005 had 80 vegetable plots, with a total of 3,840 square metres under cultivation. Each 8 by 6 metre plot is bordered with bricks and covered with hail netting. West of the entrance to the school are the cut flower garden, the Mandela garden – used for teaching students about how Mandela, the tall tree at the centre of the garden, brought people separated by apartheid together, and the Thabo Mbeki garden – where Mbeki, Mandela's successor as President of South Africa – 'a young tree that needs our support to grow' is surrounded by the nine provinces of the new South Africa. East of the entrance is the indigenous garden where every plant is labelled. 'The vegetable garden is for the body, the indigenous garden is for the mind'. Here Sethole speaks of the importance of aesthetics in addition to food; of feeding the children's spirit not just their stomachs. She knows that the birds that are attracted to the indigenous garden enrich the space with both sound and colour.

Alongside this garden is the new media centre built with money donated by the Japanese government. Using her records of the development of the garden project, the principal approached the Japanese for money for three additional classrooms. They were so impressed with what she had achieved that they gave her a media centre in addition. The architecture of the new buildings and the quality of the building materials stand in sharp contrast to the surrounding school buildings, offering the children something distinctive and constructing them as worthy subjects. This is a very different construction from that of the subaltern subjects of apartheid school architecture. Since then a construction company has donated a small feeding centre with a fully equipped kitchen and the school has built two large 'shack' classrooms using construction methods demonstrated by this company. It is called the *Itireleng* Centre which in Setswana means, 'we did it ourselves'. Most recently donor money has enabled the building of three additional science classrooms. The Department of Education has provided fencing.

There is no doubt that the seed garden project supported by BMW has transformed the material conditions of schooling for these children and their teachers. The principal's ability to be proactive in the face of the government's tardiness in addressing the needs of under-resourced schools in African townships, serves as a model for how to combine aspiration, social action and agency. Appadurai (2002) argues that oppressed human subjects need to learn to aspire; this was so for many South Africans living under apartheid rule whose sense of self was brutalised by classifications of racial inferiority and whose hopes for a better future were nullified by structured exclusion. Locating herself in a discourse of hope, Sethole is able to extend the 'horizon of possibility' (Simon, 1992) for her students and her staff.

What is noticeable in the data from the place project is that material conditions matter. Asked to draw and talk about their favourite places at Phepo, the children chose the toilets and the taps. To children who live in shacks, Phepo, with its running water and toilets that 'clik' (flush), does not seem like a poor school. The children say they like the toilets because they can close the door and be alone. Privacy is valued by children who live in communities where most spaces are communal. Similarly interesting is a drawing of a window, done by a boy in Grade 4. The words written in Setswana say

> I like the window because when it is cold we can close it and when it is hot we can open it and so the thieves must not get in the house.

I did not have to be told that this boy lives in one of the informal settlements. Windows are for him a luxury. Children also wrote about how they like the cupboard in the classroom and the shelves on which they can keep their books. Working with the children at Phepo has taught me to notice and appreciate many of the things that I take for granted.

My work on the garden project focused on trying to understand the role played by literacy in contributing to the production of new subjectivities and new futures (Janks, 2003). Key to the overall success of the project were the *School Profiles*. This is the documented record of the project, required by BMW. They show in plans, diagrams, hand-written texts and photographs how this community has visibly transformed its space. These *Profiles* provide a tangible history of the achievement of this school. Every time the principal uses them to talk about the school, she is reminded of where they have come from and what they have achieved. Every time the children see them being used, they are reminded of what is possible. In the use of these profiles to talk about what has been accomplished, the power of a community project to seed much more than food – to seed pride and dignity and independence – is clear. This literacy practice has been key to the school's sense of self.

But this is the work of the adults who have taken up newly empowered subject positions since 1994. My own literacy projects were in the classroom with the teachers and the children. In the first phase of the international project children were invited to produce representations of their school, their homes and their community using a range of modes and media. The children's representation of the school – their 'profile' – is a collage of their photographs organised onto a grid that assists them to position the photographs on a two-dimensional 'map' of the school. Understanding grid lines provides a base for later work on lines of longitude and latitude. To produce the collage, the students had to learn how to use a camera; they had to understand the relationship between a two-dimensional plan and a three-dimensional space; they had to understand directionality. In the process they grasped the idea that maps, like other texts, can be wrong. With all the development and change at the school, the school's 'map' (plan) was outdated and the students took pleasure in telling the principal how to fix it.

The children's individual representations of the school, which depict their favourite places, are full of energy and they convey the pleasure that children find in ordinary things. One drawing transforms a piece of bare dirt into a bright yellow soccer field. In reality, two up-ended bricks serve as goal-posts on an ungrassed piece of ground. Another drawing is more down to earth – here the whole page is coloured brown yet the child's writing makes it clear how much he loves the soccer field.

I love play ground because we play soccer at play ground.
I love play ground bycaus of we play evry thing we want to play it
When we play at play ground Dei (there) is now (no) poeple can
Deistep (disturb) us. When we play at playground we got nyou (new)
freints (friends).

Figure 6.1, in Chapter 6, is a version of a different part of the playground, one that is filled with activity and bursting with life. As older children explain in their alphabet book, 'Poverty does not stop people from enjoying life'.

A is for Atteridgeville, the alphabet book produced by students in Grade 7, and *Fun and Games*, the book about children's games discussed in the previous chapter, were written for children in Marg Wells's school in Australia. From the start we intended that the books would travel. Analyses of globalisation take for granted the ways in which digital communication technologies and twenty-first century modes of transportation have shrunk the world, enabling flows of information and people. What is generally not considered is who has access to this mobility. For teachers and students living and working in poor communities the rest of the world is as far away as ever. Even cyberspace is out of bounds unless their schools are wired and the children and teachers are computer- and internet-literate. We needed to find ways of connecting the local with the global and 'reading and writing have always been tools that take us across borders [and] build bridges across cultures and communities' (Luke, 2003: 20).

In *A is for Atteridgeville* students produced remarkable drawings and texts (Janks & Comber, 2006). The act of deciding co-operatively what aspects of their community to represent using the 26 letters of the alphabet was in itself a significant task. If they chose *A* for *Atteridgeville*, where could they include *AIDS*? If they chose *C* for *churches*, where were they going to discuss *crime*? In the end they chose the following topics: Atteridgeville, *B*MW, *ch*urches, *d*emocracy, *e*lectricity, *f*eed the child, *g*ardens, *H*IV/AIDS, *i*cecream, *J*apan, *K*alefong (the local hospital), *l*anguages, *m*okhuku (tin house), *n*etball, *O*lesang (a local celebrity gospel singer), *p*overty, *Q*uagga centre (the local shopping centre), *r*ecycle, *r*educe, *r*e-use, *s*occer, *t*ransport, *U*buntu (a way of life that values all of humanity), *V*ergenoeg (Far enough – the furthest shack settlement), *w*ater, *x*enophobia, *y*outh, *z*aka (township slang for money).

The alphabet provided useful pegs on which the students could hang their ideas and it enabled them to move between their pleasures (such as ice-cream, sport, gospel singers, Atteridgeville festivities, celebrities), their concerns and fears (AIDS, poor standards of health care, poverty, crime, xenophobia) and their values (environmental awareness and conservation, democracy, religion, multilingualism and the African philosophy of Ubuntu). Every image is about places and people and activities in Atteridgeville and together with the written texts they offer a complex mix of feelings, perspectives and insights.

Figure 8.5 provides the written text of *H is for HIV/AIDS* together with the visual image accompanying this text. Figure 8.6 shows a mural painted on one of the exterior classroom walls at Phepo that goes some way towards making visible the AIDS awareness work that is done with young children in South Africa.

But if HIV/AIDS is an aspect of the dark side of the children's lives, in *B is for BMW*, they offer a a glimpse of both township humour and consumer desires (Figure 8.7).

Like *Fun and Games*, the alphabet book gave children an opportunity to share their local knowledge with children in Australia. Children's lives are both embodied and placed. By making them the subject of cultural exchange with children who are differently placed, township children's identities and knowledges are given both recognition and validation. *A is for Atteridgeville*, produced by the Grade 7s, enacts the fears and the pleasures of childhood. The children's lived experience becomes the focus for a school literacy project, 'bridging the divide between out-of-school literacies and classroom practice' (Hull & Schultz, 2002: Subtitle).

I believe that schools have a responsibility to give students access to dominant literacies, powerful technologies, and the means of production. In both the alphabet and games book projects we wanted students to see themselves as knowledge makers, who could produce artefacts (a book, a video, wire cars) rooted in their own lives that would be valued beyond their own local context. We wanted primary school children to imagine themselves as writers and designers whose placed and embodied knowledges mattered to their peers on the other side of the world. We

H is for HIV/AIDS

HIV/AIDS is a disease that cannot be cured. Many people in Atteridgeville, specially the young ones, are dying of AIDS. People who are suffering from this disease don't want people to know that they are infected and they don't want to talk about it. Some of those who are HIV positive are spreading this disease by infecting others. HIV/AIDS is caused by sleeping around without protection. HIV is spread by someone who is HIV positive who sleeps with others without using a condom. Many people don't have information about AIDS. They still believe in myths. They don't want to shake hands with people who are HIV positive or even touch them. Another myth is that if you (sleep with) rape a child you will be cured of AIDS. This is one of the reasons why child abuse and rape is high in Atteridgeville. When a person is HIV positive that person can lose weight and lose appetite. A person with HIV can look after their body by eating food that build their body and gives energy, and by doing exercise.

Figure 8.5 'H is for HIV/AIDS'.
Used with permission from the children and their parents.

wanted them to begin to imagine themselves as players on a world stage thus increasing their capacity to aspire (Appadurai, 2002).

At a much simpler level I wanted to re-shape the way literacy is imagined in township schools. I wanted to embed it in a set of relations that positions multimodal textual production as a form of global mobility, with real readers and viewers across the world who without the affordances of text, would otherwise be out of reach. Literacy here is precisely not 'isolated' or 'detached from any interlocutor' or 'somehow self-contained, complete' (Ong, 1982: 132). It enters into practices of circulation which in a modest way helps students to see themselves as part of the global flow of information and knowledge. It gives them a glimpse of a wider world to

Figure 8.6 Mural at Phepo School.

Figure 8.7 'B is for BMW'.
Used with permission from the children and their parents.

which they can belong, and in which they can claim a space for themselves. Here redesign works to transform textual practices and subjectivities rather than the texts themselves.

But this is far easier said than done. After five years of working with teachers and the principal in one school, I have to recognise that it is far harder to change habitus than it is to change habitat. I have been struggling to understand why new approaches to educating children are not sustained beyond the intervention itself. Recognising that teachers in South Africa have been 'in-serviced' to the point of resistance in top-down, information-heavy 'workshops', I chose to work with teachers in one school over a number of years in their classrooms. I had hoped that we could together find new ways of effecting change. As part of the international project on place, we raised the money for the teachers, not just the artefacts, to travel. Marg Wells and her principal visited South Africa and Sethole and two of the teachers visited Australia. These educators had the opportunity to experience first-hand each other's schools and to learn from one another. *A is for Arndale* and *Letters from Ridley Grove*, two books made by Marg's students for the children at Phepo, provided the inspiration for the Phepo book projects. The garden project at Phepo inspired the garden design project at Ridley Grove (Comber & Nixon, 2008; Comber, Nixon, Ashmore, Loo, & Cook, 2006). Yet despite the enormous pride that Phepo takes in the books produced in the literacy project and the garden produced as part of the BMW S.E.E.D. project, none of the educational practices associated with these projects has been sustained.

You will have noticed that I used the past tense to describe the educational practices employed at the time that the gardens were being developed. The success of the gardens has led to donors providing rainwater tanks, irrigation systems, smart new bricked beds. The children no longer have to collect water or recycle waste to establish the gardens, so recycling has disappeared as a practice in the school and the children are not allowed into the vegetable or flower gardens unless they are with a teacher. The practices involved in making the garden appear to have been motivated by functional need rather than pedagogical intent. The teachers have asked me to come back to work with them in their classrooms, but as they have never repeated any of the projects we did together in subsequent years with new classes I doubt that this work has had any long-term effects. I know that they can repeat these projects because one of the teachers proudly brought me the alphabet book made by her own children at home. Inspired by the creative work that they saw at Ridley Grove, the teachers came back and made mobiles with their classes. This has not been repeated. Pat Thomson and I established a project which lasted for three years in which newly qualified teachers from Nottingham University spent time at Phepo. Little that these young teachers did with the children has been repeated by the Phepo teachers.

I have struggled to understand this. All that I have to work with is one comment in my field notes. Invited to join the school on the day that the National Minister of Education came to visit, one of the teachers who had been to Australia, proudly invited me to see her classroom. On the wall were the children's drawings: 45 identically coloured-in teddy bears. When I asked the teacher why she had not asked the children to do the kind of visual meaning-making work that we had done together to display, she gave the following reason: 'Because the minister is coming'. What this tells me is that she believes that the minister wants to see identical teddy bears. This must be what she thinks counts as education. I suspect that she and the other teachers must have thought that I was just playing with the children. If this suspicion is correct then it means that the teachers were unable to understand how important pleasure and play are for learning. Although when she saw the completed books, *A is for Atteridgeville* and *Fun and Games*, for the first time, the principal told me that she realised that 'we underestimate our children', she has not encouraged her staff to continue this work. Why?

Adler's large-scale research project which followed teachers back into their classrooms after they had completed a further diploma in education, found that many of the teachers were able to adopt the *form* of the new practices, but not the *substance* (Adler & Reed, 2002). An example of this in my project was the teachers' getting the children to make mobiles, as *seen* in the Australian classrooms. The teachers saw them as decoration rather than as the expression of meaning that they were, as *practiced* in Australia. Not only has the substance of work that I did with teachers in their classrooms on the place project not been taken up, not even the form is a part of their ongoing practice.

The closest that I can come to making sense of this is to use Pahl's (2008) work that explains why teachers on her Creative Partnerships project were unable to recognise what it was that children were learning from the new and different pedagogies they participated in. Like her, I believe that Grenfell's (1996) work on the 'pedagogic habitus' of pre-service teachers provides a means of theorising the difficulties associated with transforming teachers' practices. I would argue that a teacher's literate habitus fundamentally affects how he or she teaches literacy. (See also Albright & Luke, 2008.) 'Habitus' is Bourdieu's concept for explaining our ingrained, unconscious way of being that embodies beliefs, values and ways of doing (1991: 57) discussed in Chapters 3 and 5. It does provide a way of thinking about how resistant our embodied ways of being are to change. I offer my own experience of Alexander therapy as a metaphor for the difficulties involved in re-moulding one's embodied practices.

I became conscious of my own embodiment after injuring my neck from working for long hours at the computer with bad posture. Doctors told me that I had to change the way I stand, sit and lie (even in my sleep). This is easier said than done. With the help of an Alexander therapist, I first had to become aware of my unconscious ways of using my body incorrectly (unconscious incompetence). I had to learn to stop these practices. Once I was able to do that I achieved a level of conscious incompetence as I was not yet able to change the ways I used my body. At the level of conscious incompetence, the mind knows what it should do, but the body does not know how to perform the new understanding. I had to re-learn how to stand and sit and walk. This took a long time during which I had to monitor my practices and consciously perform my new competence (conscious competence). But Alexander therapy aims for automaticity, where correct posture is achieved unconsciously (unconscious competence); where in effect one has acquired a new way of being in one's body. Only in this way can one change the way we sleep, even when we are sleep. Only constant conscious practice leads to an ingrained new habitus, because our old habits lurk just below the surface.

Like our habitus our pedagogic habitus is hard to change. Changing our habitus involves changing who we are and where we have come from, as illustrated in Chapter 3 by Michele Aucock's experience in Korea. Our pedagogic habitus is formed by years spent in school as students, by the teachers who taught us, the books we have read, the education departments and schools we have worked in and the colleagues we have worked with. It is embodied in the way we talk to children, where we position ourselves in the classroom, how we stand, what we do with our eyes, and how we expect our students to comport themselves. Our embodied practices are bound up with ingrained beliefs about education and what we value in students. We have to want to change and we have to work at it. Perhaps this is why some teachers prefer to experiment with a researcher in their classrooms. Perhaps redesigning ourselves and others is too risky to attempt on our own. If the researcher produces only conscious incompetence, then teachers are left profoundly disempowered. If they arrive at a level of conscious competence, then they have to continually use these practices to achieve the confidence that comes from feeling fluent and comfortable with their new pedagogic habitus. This is not a process that happens quickly, which is perhaps why all the short-term in-service teacher training that the government has invested in has produced so little real change in the classroom.

In the final chapter, I turn to a consideration of the unconscious in order to understand the limits of reason and of critical literacy. However, before concluding with the challenge posed by the unconscious, I offer an argument for the continued importance of the critical literacy project.

CHAPTER **9**

The Future of Critical Literacy

In a peaceful world without the threat of global warming or conflict or war, where everyone has access to education, health care, food and a dignified life, there would still be a need for critical literacy. In a world that is rich with difference, there is still likely to be intolerance and fear of the other. Because difference is structured in dominance, unequal access to resources based on gender, race, ethnicity, nationality and class will continue to produce privilege and resentment. Even in a world where socially constructed relations of power have been flattened, we will still have to manage the little *p* politics of our daily lives. This chapter provides a final argument which both defends the need for critical literacy and argues that in a world where the only thing that is certain, apart from death and taxes, is change itself, critical literacy has to be nimble enough to change as the situation changes. The critical literacy agenda is shaped by the socio-historical and political context, the changing communication landscape, teachers' and students' investments, and shifts in theory and practice.

The Ongoing Socio-Historical Imperative for Critical Literacy

With regard to the socio-historical and political context, critical literacy needs to address both global and local issues. Global warming (Gore, 2006), for example, requires both big *P* interventions internationally by governments and little *p* actions locally. It is here that the relation between habitus and habitat is most profound. Unless we move from unconscious incompetence in managing the planet to unconscious competence, where every action of every person is automatically underpinned by

environmental awareness, we risk extinction. If we all take responsibility for our own carbon footprint, individual local action can have a
cumulative global impact.

While global warming has effects across the globe other issues are
more local. In South Africa, for example, the taxi industry is a law unto
itself. Taxi wars over territory and routes continue to endanger passengers
as do reckless driving, unsafe vehicles and unlicensed drivers. Efforts by
government to regulate the taxi industry nationally have met with resistance that is often violent, and bribery is used to avoid law enforcement.
Local action by commuters might be more effective than government
intervention and surveillance.

In the USA, local action in the form of small financial contributions
by ordinary people enabled Barack Obama to change the politics of
election campaign funding. The USA is an excellent example from the
political North of the continued need for critical literacy. Here discourses
of patriotism, fear and the dangerous Other were harnessed to win support
for a war against Iraq based on lies about the existence of weapons
of mass destruction. The bombing of innocent civilians in Afghanistan and
Baghdad and the torture and humiliation of prisoners in Abu Ghraib
prison are classic instances of how dehumanisation of the other can lead
to our own dehumanisation (see Klein, 2007; Lakoff, 2004). Clearly the
hypothetically peaceful world posited earlier does not exist and in a world
of spin critical literacy helps us to understand whose interests are served
by the stories we are told and the stories we tell.

The 2008 US elections have shown how racism and sexism lurk
beneath the veneer of liberal discourses. In South Africa, ugly eruptions of
racial abuse and marginalisation sully the myth of the 'rainbow' nation as
does xenophobic violence. In 2008, white students at the University of
the Free State produced a racist video to protest against the proposed
desegregation of University residences. Shortly thereafter black South
Africans across the country attacked thousands of foreign Africans in an
outbreak of rage fuelled by xenophobia. Similarly policies of gender equality create a façade that hides entrenched patriarchal values that reproduce
male authority. This has an impact on both the domestic and the political
spheres. Violence against women is widespread and in the public sphere
disagreement with men in power is not tolerated. The gap between rich
and poor grows wider. Those of us in the middle class live in luxury
behind electric fences and armed response alarm systems to protect ourselves and our possessions from crime, while the poor eke out an existence
in tin shacks. For some this disparity is uncomfortable, for others it is an
opportunity for display. Conspicuous consumption buys one status.

South Africa and the USA serve as examples of the need for critical literacy in both the political South and the political North respectively. In a world marked by social injustice, critical literacy continues to help us understand the effects of power and the need for redress. Transformative redesign and social action have to ensure that diversity is valued, that there is equity of access and that power is used for the benefit of all.

Current and Future Changes in the Communication Landscape as an Imperative for Critical Literacy

Changes in the communication landscape are captured by a satirical video clip, 'The IT Pro'. The narrative shows a monk living in the middle ages waiting for the IT Pro to arrive to help him with the new technology that he has to master. Used to parchment scrolls, he is struggling to change to books. He is not sure how to open the leather-bound book on his desk and he worries that when he closes the book, the information will disappear. He is more comfortable with a scroll, the older technology that he could operate independently. Now, like many of us today, he is dependent on the IT help-desk. The story is funny because it satirises my generation's uncertainties in the face of the new digital technologies which require a shift from paper to computers, from pens to keyboard, from pages to screens (that in turn require scrolling), from predominantly print-based texts to multimodal texts, to multiple message streams made possible by split screens and hypertext (Snyder, 1998, 2002). The ability to work with these new technologies is now part of what it means to be literate in the twenty-first century. Marsh's work shows how children develop digital literacies from the earliest years (Marsh & Hallett, 1999; Marsh, 2005).

Texts are now more complex than ever and as explained in Chapter 2, readers need to be literate across multiple forms of semiosis to decode multimodal texts. Video texts usually combine visual semiosis with movement and sound, making analysis ever more complex. In multimodal texts, not only does one have to understand how each message stream works, but also how they work together to make meaning. This makes textual deconstruction and re-construction incrementally more difficult. In addition to new forms of text production, the internet provides information at the touch of a button. What matters now is not what information you have but how you evaluate it.

Identity Investments as an Ongoing Imperative for Critical Literacy

It has long been my view that much work in critical literacy has been done by people whose own identity investments have formed their critical literacy projects. In my own case, it was my race and nationality and my shame in the face of the racialised injustices of apartheid that led me to explore the relationship between language, discourse and power. Others have been driven by a feminist project (for example, Kamler, 2001; Smith, 1993; Threadgold, 1997), concerns about masculinity (Martino & Pallotta-Chiarolli, 2003, 2005), class-based consciousness (Comber & Nixon, 2005; Thomson, 2002), or a rejection of heteronormativity (Rofes, 2005; Sumara & Davis, 1998). Our own commitments are often the starting point for the work we do in teaching and research.

Teachers also respond to the needs of their students and their students' identity locations. McKinney (2004a) worked with the positions of her Afrikaans students at the University of Stellenbosch, Norton (2000) with the language and identity issues of her Chinese students newly immigrated to Canada, and Haas Dyson (2003) with the popular culture worlds of the children she studied. González, Moll and Amanti (2005) brought community funds of knowledge into the classroom. Vivian Vasquez took her lead from the concerns of her four-year-old students (2004). For Foucault, power is productive because it produces human subjects. Subjectivity is therefore a theoretically sound starting point for critical literacy practice and research.

Current and Future Changes in Theory as an Imperative for Changes in Practice

Different theories enable different critical literacy practices. A Freirean approach to critical literacy provides the basis for Vasquez's problem solving work with young children and Brian Morgan's (1998) work with Chinese immigrants in Canada. Fairclough's work on CDA (1989, 1995) and CLA (1992) informs *Language and Position*, the workbook that I wrote for the CLA series (1993) and the centrality of visual semiosis underpins Newfield's *Words and Pictures* (1993) in the same series. Orlek's (1993) workbook on language variation and language policy flows from sociolinguistic research. The Chalkface Press workbooks by Mellor *et al.* (1987, 1991, 1996), and Wendy Morgan's classroom work on Ned Kelly (1994) rely on post-structuralist theory. The workbooks in the *First Australians New Australians* series (Martino, 1997; Kenworthy & Kenworthy, 1997) use post-colonial theory. Bourdieu's work on habitus lays the foundation for the work of Luke (1992) and Dixon (2004, 2007) on literacy and the body. Dixon adds theory from Foucault to the mix. Dixon's focus on the body has enabled us to understand how children's bodies are regulated by literacy routines and their organisation in time and space. Leander and Sheehy's (2004) edited collection on spatialising literacy as well as work in the area of critical geography more broadly have influenced work on literacy and space (for example, Gregory & Williams, 2000; Pahl & Rowsell, 2006). New Literacy Studies provides the framework for Pahl and Rowsell's (2005) book on classroom practice. Stein's (2004) work on multimodal pedagogies is indebted to the work of both Gunther Kress and the New London Group.

It is precisely because critical literacy is open to a multitude of theoretical orientations that its practice is both rich and flexible. My argument in this book is that these theories are not just add-ons. It is the complex inter-relationship of theories of domination and power, identity and social difference, equity and access as well as multimodal design and redesign that make critical literacy a rigorous and dynamic multidisciplinary space.

Past and Future Applications of the Interdependent Model

Analysing and Designing Curriculum

The integrated model can be used for the analysis of curriculum. If one were to analyse the school project on diversity education recorded in the documentary film *Paperclips* (Berlin & Fab, 2003)[1] using the model, we could answer the question of whether or not this is critical literacy work. The problem confronting the principal of the school in Whitwell, Tennessee, was how to do multicultural education in a school with homogeneous students in a homogeneous rural town in the southern USA. The school decided to engage with the Holocaust as a way of understanding the politics of othering and how processes of dehumanisation can lead to genocide. The project was repeated every year with each Grade 8 class putting its own stamp on the work. In order to grasp the magnitude of the number of people killed, one of the Grade 8 classes decided to collect six million paperclips. The students chose the paperclip when they discovered, from their own research, that Norway invented the paperclip and used it as a symbol of opposition to the Nazis. The task of collecting, recording and storing six million paperclips was a mammoth endeavour that gives one a sense of the determination and organisation necessary to deliberately murder Jews, gypsies, homosexuals and other 'deviants'.

The collection process was slow until the project caught the attention of two German-born journalists based in New York who gave it media coverage. Their ongoing involvement with the school and the project

---

[1] I have chosen to use *Paperclips*, distributed by Hart Sharp videos, as readers can buy or hire the DVD of this documentary and 'see' for themselves.

helped the students to understand that not all Germans are Nazis. Holocaust survivors visited the school, told their stories and enabled the students to imagine the people symbolised by each paperclip. Most people in that community had never before encountered either a German or a Jew. The project succeeded in bringing diversity into the lives of the students and the wider community.

Millions of paperclips take up a great deal of space and the principal wanted a permanent and meaningful place to house the collection. The idea of a Holocaust museum was born. With the help of the journalists, the school managed to secure one of the railway carriages used during the Holocaust to transport Jews to the gas chambers and both the students and the community contributed to its transformation.

In this ongoing school project power, access, diversity and design/redesign come together to create a meaningful learning experience for successive classes of students. Intending to raise students' consciousness about the dangers of othering, the school provided students with access to people who were different from the only people they had ever known. The power of the Nazis to label, exclude, ghettoise and murder people they constructed as deviant was an intrinsic part of the project. Even the adults talk about how this project made them confront their own prejudices. The curriculum was designed every year to build on the work that had gone before and it was underpinned by students' online research, multimodal literacy projects, presentations to the school, and the need to solve problems as they arose. Transformative social action continued throughout the life of the project: events with Holocaust survivors; engagement with German journalists and the media; presentations to the school and community culminating in the redesign of a German death-carriage as a memorial to those who died.

This is a critical literacy project, but it is critical literacy at a distance. Whether or not students are invited to examine constructions of Muslims, Latino/as, African Americans, native Americans, immigrants, communists, gays and lesbians or even gender discrimination in their own context is not shown in the documentary. Difference is not only somewhere else. Questions of access, power and transformation in their own country and their own community is a silence in the film. This is brought home by the coincidence inscribed in the moment in the film when the death-carriage is off-loaded from a boat in Boston. The date is 9/11.

If the model can be used to analyse curriculum it can also be used to design curriculum. In using the model to build curriculum one has to decide whether to cover the different theories separately or to work with each theoretical field in relation to each of the others. What is important is that students understand their interdependence. At the same time it is inevitable that at times one dimension comes into focus more than another. In my own work under apartheid, the focus was more on power as domination, differences in race and gender and how together they affect access. With my more recent focus on reconstruction, the emphasis has been more on redesign and equity in relation to access.

Analysing Research Data

The interdependent model is useful for analysing research data. Two examples are included here. In 'Redesigning Romance: The Making and Analysis of a Critical Literacy Comic in South Africa', Shariff and Janks (2001) used the model as an analytic tool to examine the stories in *Heart to Heart*, a comic that Shariff developed with high school students as part of her research (1994). What our analysis shows is that in each of these stories all of the orientations to literacy education feature, but in each case one of the terms was privileged. In the first story included in the comic, 'Dream Love', the students produce a story that privileges patriarchal power. In the second story, 'True Love', the voices of the women students are elicited and used to transform 'Dream Love' in order to offer an alternative version of what happens. Here diversity in the group is used as a resource for redesign. The story that links 'Dream Love' and 'True Love' is a meta-narrative about the process of production that enabled the alternative version of the story to emerge. The linking story provides the design solution that enables both love stories to be told. The final comic, *Heart to Heart*, which includes the three stories, weaves power, diversity and design together in complex moves from construction to deconstruction and reconstruction, holding them in productive tension. And the project as a whole gives students in a remote rural village access to publication.

The second example looks at the work of Jerome Harste and his colleagues at Indiana University (2007).[2] They used the model as a way of analysing the artwork produced by pre-service and in-service teachers in response to the question '*What changes do you wish to see in our society's conceptions of literacy?*' (see Figure 9.1). The researchers coded each picture independently as to which dimensions of critical literacy were addressed in the different paintings. The most interesting finding was that 93% of the sample produced pictures that were read as dealing with multiple aspects of critical literacy. Although the coders were able to establish which aspect was highlighted in each painting, what they

---

[2] This section of the book would not have been possible without the generosity of Jerome Harste, who generously allowed me to use his research data which has enriched this final chapter immeasurably and provided the cover illustration for the book.

Figure 9.1 Literacy Posters.
Produced by Jerome Harste's postgraduate students. Used with permission.

noticed is that the different aspects tended to co-occur. This gives weight to the theory of interdependence that the model argues for. Figure 9.1 includes five of the paintings in Harste's collection. Readers might like to consider which aspects of the model they can see addressed in each painting.

Analysis of Current Events

In 2008, the racist video produced by students at the University of the Free State revealed the resilience of apartheid discourses. In this video, young white male students are shown humiliating black workers; particularly shocking is a sequence in which the workers are depicted eating food into which a student had urinated. Here apartheid attitudes to racial difference create an abuse of power. In addition, lack of knowledge or respect for African cultural values, where older people are venerated, increases the insult. What was at stake for these white students was the proposed access of black students to their whites-only residences. Fourteen years after the transition to a non-racial democracy, this incident shows the power of discourses to speak through us. These students were three years old when Mandela was released from jail. No doubt, when the father of one of these boys declared, 'My son is not a racist', he believed it. In this incident we see how difference, power, access and resistance to redesign come together to remind us that despite change, racist discourses endure.

Adegoke's (1999) research examined representations of foreign Africans and their countries in the South African press in order to mount an argument for including xenophobia in a critical literacy curriculum. The research was driven by her own experiences of being othered as a Nigerian living in South Africa. This research, discussed in Chapter 5, was prescient. In the same year that witnessed the ugliness of white racism in the Free State, black South Africans living in poverty turned on the foreign Africans living in their communities. Anger at having to compete with foreigners for access to scarce jobs and scarce resources combined with xenophobic hatred erupted in horrific acts of violence in which many people were injured or killed, and many lost their homes and all their possessions. Adegoke's work is a reminder that education directed at achieving social justice always has both a present and a future perspective.

The Limits of the Model

While the interdependent model of critical literacy is useful as a means for thinking about how theories relate to one another in a multidisciplinary space, it is not meant to be totalising. Even without any further developments in theory, the model is not able to bring all that we know now into play. In focusing on the socio-cultural, it ignores the psychological. Because critical literacy is essentially a rationalist activity it does not sufficiently address the non-rational investments that readers bring with them to texts and tasks.

If one considers the way in which I theorised the interdependent model (Table 2.1) by considering each theoretical dimension without each of the others, the logocentric theorising which underpins such analysis is clear. Here, I want to step outside of this framework to raise some difficult questions for critical literacy education and for critical pedagogy more generally. These questions confront the profoundly rationalist underpinnings of critical deconstruction. Fairclough's model of critical discourse analysis, for example, depends on three inter-related forms of analysis: text analysis, processing analysis and social analysis which he calls description, interpretation and explanation (Fairclough, 1989, 1995). All of these depend on logical reasoning and argument in relation to evidence in both text and context. What is missing from this model is the territory beyond reason. The territory of desire and identification, pleasure and play, the taboo and the transgressive – what Giroux (1994) calls 'disturbing pleasures', what Kenway and Bullen (2001: 157) call 'the profane', and what Comber (1997) notices when children in classrooms are 'given permission to be other than sensible and serious'.

It is necessarily to consider the territory beyond reason in order to avoid a problematic disjunction between critical deconstruction and students' affective engagement with texts. In teaching students to deconstruct advertisements, we examine the words and the images to see what political work they are doing. We expose the faulty logic, look for the silences in the text, criticise the values that underpin the text and reveal the underlying assumptions. When we have finished, students can produce a reasoned critique that is not in any way transformative. This is how the problem manifested itself to a group of English teachers at an all girls' school. One of the teachers, Weber (1999), had completed a small research project on fruit juice advertisements which appeared in two different magazines aimed at differently racialised youth markets. Expecting to find different constructions of race, the teacher/researcher found different constructions of gender instead. When men were used to sell the product, they were constructed as energised by drinking pure fruit juice, thus enhancing their sporting prowess. When women were used to sell the product, they were constructed as objects of our gaze. The advertisement reproduced the unsurprising active/passive binary in gender construction. Moreover, from month to month the gorgeous, slim women models were progressively identified with the product (with the aid of digital morphing, they moved from drinking the product, to wearing the product to becoming the product) and they were progressively sexualised. While students had no difficulty in deconstructing the visual and verbal semiotics of these advertisements, what bothered the teachers was that despite all this work, many of the girls still had their favourite model, the one they identified with, the one they wished they could be. Where identification promises the fulfilment of desire, reason cannot compete. Students could produce the required deconstructive reading of the text, what Thompson and Janks have come to call dominant deconstructions, without any change in either their aspirations or their practices.

Beyond Reason[3]

If desire and identification work against reason, are there other psychological processes that do the same? Freud, in *Jokes and their Relation to the Unconscious* (1916: 85), says

> If one laughs at a joke really heartily, one is not precisely in the mood for investigating its technique.

I will use Freud's work on jokes to introduce the concepts of pleasure and play and then I will return to the unconscious process of identification, to show that the terrain of the non-rational provides a challenge that work in critical literacy education needs to address.

Nando's is a South African-based international food business that sells Portuguese-style grilled chicken, flavoured either with lemon and herb or with piri-piri, to a relatively small niche market. Piri-piri, which literally means small chilli, is a hot sauce made from a blend of chillies, herbs and spices first discovered in Portuguese East Africa. Nando's has outlets in 16 countries, including Australia and New Zealand. Nevertheless, Nando's is small compared to big mass-market companies like McDonalds and Kentucky Fried Chicken. According to the South African *Ad Index*, their above-the-line per annum advertising budget is less than a third of what the competition spends.

In South Africa, Nando's employed a multi award-winning advertising agency to sell their products. In describing their brand personality, Josie McKenzie, the Nando's marketing director for South Africa says, 'It's fun, irreverent, cheeky, humorous and above all intelligent' (Interview, 2001). Nando's advertisements are worth investigating because they teach us how to combine critique with pleasure and play, how to use irreverence as a rebellion against authority and how to transgress the restraints of political correctness. They make the intelligent pleasurable.

Their humour is apparent in their short, punchy sports cricket advertisements. A good example is the advertisement that is shown when a batsman in cricket goes out without scoring (known as going out 'for a duck'). The picture of the animated yellow duck that moves across the bottom of the screen (in a squeezeback), while the batsman leaves the field, is followed by a Nando's advertisement saying, 'Why go out for a duck when you can go out for a chicken?'. Freud would describe this as an innocent verbal joke in which we derive pleasure from the play on words, from the joke technique. Both 'go out' and 'duck' have double meanings which the joke exploits.

---

[3] This section first appeared in *The Australian Educational Researcher*, 29(1), 2002, as a paper entitled 'Critical Literacy: Beyond Reason'.

Nando's also makes use of satire. The following advertisement parodies direct marketing advertisements and is in fact an anti-ad that makes us laugh at the silliness of advertising per se. The joke is carried by the voice-over script that is accompanied by appropriate visuals.

Voice-over script

Need excitement? Well here's the Nando's box. This fantastic recyclable receptacle comes with an all-white interior, fully functional lid and stylish designer-designed logo. Now how much would you pay for such an ornament? Sixty rand? Fifty rand? Thirty rand? Now we're giving the box away for a stunning twenty rand fifty. But that's not all. We also throw in a genuine Nando's flame-grilled chicken leg in your choice of lemon and herb or mild or hot piri-piri. And there's more. If you come in, we also give you a chicken wing, attached to the leg by a complimentary breast and thigh. Still not enough? Then we'll fill the box with our old-style chips. So, that's the box with white interior, designer logo, chicken leg, matching wing, breast, thigh, chips [french fries] and to top it all, this small till slip printed with figures that you can show your friends. So don't hesitate, call this number now.

This extended joke allows Nando's to exploit something ridiculous in other advertisements to enhance our pleasure in the Nando's ads.

This is an example of what Freud calls a tendentious joke. Tendentious jokes have additional sources of pleasure to that occasioned by the wordplay of innocent jokes. These jokes, which have a social purpose,

> make possible the satisfaction of an instinct (whether lustful or hostile) in the face of an obstacle that stands in its way.
>
> (Freud, 1916: 144)

By

> making our enemy small, inferior, despicable or comic, we achieve in a roundabout way the enjoyment of overcoming him [sic].
>
> (1916: 147)

Joke-work often happens below the level of consciousness. It helps us to overcome psychic inhibitions (internal obstacles), and our psychic relations to external obstacles, such as authority figures or enemies. We do not always know why we are laughing or what the source of the pleasure is.

In addition to being witty, the Nando's advertisements are also often risqué, transgressive and politically incorrect. They play with taboo topics and transgress boundaries, flirting with the 'forbidden' (Freud, 1916: 150).

The following transgressive advertisement (Figure 9.2) begins with a written message that unfolds frame by frame, accompanied by a voice reading the words together with background music. Each paragraph represents one frame that rolls up onto the screen, and the frames follow in quick succession. The font is an approximation of the font used in the advertisement.

It's been a secret

for hundreds of years

A secret brought to Africa by our

Portuguese ancestors

This closely guarded secret

is the mystery behind our delicious

flame-grilled peri-peri chicken

Now, at last, we're ready to

show the world

The secret of how

Nando's chicken is made.

Figure 9.2 Nando's Advertisement.
Nando's advertisement. Used with permission.

As the message moves into its last frame, the music starts building to a climax. The camera then cuts to a picture of a hen scratching around in the ground, followed immediately by a shot of a cock flying in and mounting her to inseminate her, as the music reaches its peak.

This advertisement breaks a number of rules. First, it shows the food that we eat running around live. It foregrounds the fact that the animals we eat were once living creatures. Secondly, it explicitly focuses on the sex act, transgressing the way we habitually think about ready-to-go prepared food, or sanitised polythene-wrapped animal protein in supermarkets. It plays with the words 'are made'. This really is how chickens 'are made' as distinct from how they 'are prepared' as food. In the context of food, this advertisement works with the unsayable. And we laugh. Jokes work against repression and the amount of pleasure derived from them corresponds to the amount of psychic expenditure that is saved (Freud, 1916: 167). Energy is released from the work on inhibition and suppression. In evading the psychic censors, jokes open sources of pleasure that have become inaccessible (1916: 147).

Had any animal rights activists stepped up to have the advertisement taken off the air, Nando's might have countered with the slogan which appears on another of their advertisements: 'No animals were harmed in the making of this advertisement, they were just eaten'. This political incorrectness points to the hypocrisy of bunny-hugging meat eaters.

'Political correctness' is an obvious example of discursive policing and an endeavour to organise the field of both the sayable as well as ways of saying. Although the term is mainly used pejoratively by conservatives as a form of resistance to the transformation of their discourse practices, it can also be harnessed by the left to silence opposition. Because what is deemed politically correct is often associated with self-righteousness it is an easy target for satirists; it invites transgression.

In his introduction to *Politically Correct Bedtime Stories*, Garner takes a pot shot at many of the cows that some of us hold sacred:

> If, through omission or commission, I have inadvertantly displayed any sexist, racist, culturalist, nationalist, regionalist, ageist, lookist, ableist, sizeist, speciesist, intellectualist, socioeconomist, ethnocentrist, phallocentrist, heteropatriarchalist, or other type of bias as yet unnamed, I apologise and encourage your suggestions for rectification.
>
> (1994: x)

So, is it funny or just bad taste? And how much are funny and taste determined by our own identifications, our own reading positions, our own ability to enjoy the transgressive or not, our own ability to allow play, even in relation to matters that for us are important and serious? How much is taste (Bourdieu, 1984) related to our own cultural and class-based schooling? Freud says that

> only jokes that have a purpose, run the risk of meeting with people who do not want to hear them.
>
> (1916: 132)

Where are the boundaries? Which borders may not be crossed? For whom? And what does this have to do with education? Many of the Nando's advertisements raise awareness of social issues in South Africa which, with the use of intelligent humour, make us both laugh and think. Irreverent and transgressive reframing make the social issues visible.

In the next example, Nando's perversely uses women with eating disorders to sell food. In this advertisement, mournful, wafer-thin women wearing T-shirts inscribed with the word 'model', are shown slavering over a Nando's advertisement on television. We see and hear them rewinding the tape to replay the pictures of the food which the advertisement allows them to enjoy vicariously as they munch on their celery sticks. Thin models are the norm in advertising. 'Fat', as we know, is a feminist issue. Here, Nando's make the thinness, and the eating disorders that they point to, visible in such a way as to construct the thinness as deprivation. In celebrating its food, rather than the thin models, it provides a critique of the way in which other advertisements exploit women.

In the second example, Nando's makes disability visible. Here, tempted by the enticing smell of the chicken, a guide dog leads its blind mistress into a pole so that it can eat the chicken which it has made her drop. The dog enjoys the food, while its mistress, a little grey-haired old lady, lies unconscious on the pavement. The music accompanying this film is jaunty, upbeat and frivolous. This was the most controversial of all Nando's advertisements, and many viewers believe that it is cruel and not at all funny. For Freud,

> An impulse or urge is present which seeks to release pleasure from a particular source and if it were allowed free play, would release it. Besides this, another urge is present which works against this generation of pleasure – inhibits it, that is, or suppresses it. The suppressing current must, as the outcome shows, be a certain amount stronger than the suppressed one.
>
> (1916: 186)

At the time Nando's thought that this was a 'sweet ad'.

McKenzie: We didn't think that it was going to particularly cross the boundary. We knew there was a sector who would find it offensive but nothing to the level that it went. I mean it went international even. It went around the world in a matter of days ... we didn't realise how far the line was crossed. In retrospect you see what people will find acceptable and what they won't. And something like that is not acceptable. Clearly, on a world platform, never mind South Africa.

Interviewer: Why? How did it cross the line?

McKenzie: [It was] offensive in terms of the fact that it is someone who is disabled.

Interviewer: Laughing at someone who is disabled.

McKenzie: Laughing at someone who is disabled . . . it's the thing that when you were at school, you'd laugh heartily at and then you'd be reprimanded by your teacher or your mother. Actually that's not funny and why it's not funny. It then makes you squirm.

(Interview, October 2001)

In the end McKenzie's assessment is that it was schoolboy humour, not the intelligent humour that is the brand personality. She says that without the intelligence, the advertisement is hard to defend. She distinguishes Nando's advertising from the Benetton ads, which have been accused of appropriating social issues to create brand visibility using shock tactics. Her view is that Nando's advertisements are not sensationalist, but that they work instead with intelligent humour on taboo topics in a socially responsible way.

You're saying 'think about it'. You've got to use your head about it.

(Interview, October 2001)

However, while Nando's advertisements in South Africa have satirised crime, prostitution, poaching, political corruption, homeless children, beggars, gambling, drugs, racial stereotyping, unemployment, there is still material that remains unsayable. McKenzie, for example, thinks that AIDS and rape are 'desperately serious issues' in South Africa. South Africa has the highest rape statistics in the world, projections are that millions of South Africans will die of AIDS in the next ten years; child abuse is widespread, there are 58 cases of child rape a day (*The Star*, 5 November 2001) including horrifying instances of infant rape that defy comprehension. For McKenzie, it is clear that serious social issues are not suitable for irreverent treatment. How does she know where the line is?

It's always a gamble . . . At the end of the day it's intuitive and it's what [it] feels like here. (She places her hand over her heart) . . . What you do with your head is try and anticipate negative reactions, who will complain. Does it fit with the Advertising Standards Authority's code? . . . But the initial concept, [you ask yourself] does it sit right here? (She places her hand over her heart again.)

(Interview, October 2001)

In this statement, McKenzie articulates the relationship between her intuitive knowledge, what she feels with her heart, and her rational analysis, what she does with her head.

Lessons for Teaching Critical Literacy

According to Freud successful jokes make possible what is forbidden by reason (1916: 179):

> The thought seeks to wrap itself in a joke because in that way it recommends itself to our attention and seems more significant and more valuable but above all because this wrapping bribes our powers of criticism and confuses them. We are inclined to give the thought the benefit of what has pleased us in the form of the joke; and we are no longer inclined to find anything wrong that has given us enjoyment and so to spoil the source of the pleasure. If a joke has made us laugh, moreover, a disposition most unfavourable to criticism [reason] will have been established. . . . Where argument tries to draw the hearer's criticism over on to its side, the joke endeavours to push the criticism out of sight. There is no doubt that the joke has chosen the method which is psychologically more effective.
>
> (Freud, 1916: 82–83)

Freud sees jokes as freeing us from sexual inhibitions, from disciplined control of our aggressive instincts, and from the tyranny of logic and reason. Freed, we are able to regain pleasure and to 'recapture the mood of our childhood' (Freud, 1916: 302). What critical deconstruction of a joke does, is it refuses the bribe and insists on reason. It enables us to see the powerful interests at work, but it robs us of laughter and play. More importantly, it refuses the release of psychic energy bound up in repression. To insist on criticism is to lose the joke. This can be related to the critical work in classrooms that applies rational analysis to the popular cultural forms that our students enjoy. In many instances, the project of schooling asks students to police their pleasures (Buckingham, 1998; Comber, 1997; Giroux, 1994; Kelly, 1997; Kenway & Bullen, 2001).

But according to Thompson,

> [j]okes . . . are continuously engaged in recounting the way that the world appears and in reinforcing through laughter which profits at another's expense, the apparent order of things.
>
> (1990: 62)

In this way

> we may be drawn into a symbolic process which may serve, in some
> circumstances, to create and sustain relations of domination
>
> (1990: 62)

where humour is used to legitimate them.

For this reason I am reluctant to abandon the critical literacy project, to agree with Kenway and Bullen (2001) that we are now in a post-critical moment. With Comber (1998), I want to ask,

> [i]n what ways might humour and play be productive in literacies in classrooms? How can we keep the space for powerful, critical, satisfying and socially responsible literate practices and at the same time have fun? Is it possible, allowable?

Nando's provides some of the answers. Social action can take the form of parody, satire and caricature. Jokes and humour allow us to rebel against authority, to attack powerful institutions or views of life (Freud, 1916: 153) and to unmask deception (1916: 262). We could ask students to think of an offensive joke that they know. They could think about who they could never tell the joke to and what makes the joke 'forbidden'. They could consider the consequences of telling this joke. They could work out who would be offended by the joke and why. They could be asked to imagine contexts in which the joke might be tellable and how they would assess or know this. In these ways, students can begin to think of how they respond to jokes in terms of their own identity investments and their own upbringing.

Working with the pleasure of jokes and the transgressive need not preclude an understanding of what is at stake. At the end of the day, Nando's branding and its advertising are designed to sell chicken meals. Television advertisements are expensive to produce. A low-level flighting chews up a large proportion of the advertising budget. Nando's is a business and every marketing initiative has objectives; each store has a target to reach. Nando's knows what the 'upsell' is from every campaign. Advertising works. Mistakes cost money. However, negative publicity is not necessarily detrimental. Nando's feels that because they handled the public outcry over the blind lady advertisement sensitively 'they turned what could have been a huge negative into a positive'. According to McKenzie, the story was covered by 'every newspaper, every daily, every weekly, every radio station, every talk station' and 'the sales for that period were phenomenal, absolutely phenomenal' (Interview, October 2001).

In the early 1990s when I explored what happened when my Critical Language Awareness materials were used in schools, I came to understand that in much the same way as Nando's cannot predict which of their risqué advertisements people will find offensive, the teacher cannot predict which text will erupt in class. The research produced evidence that when texts or tasks touch something 'sacred' to a student, critical analysis is extremely threatening. I came to define as sacred, meanings that were constitutive of students' identities, meanings that if challenged, attacked what one teacher described as 'the fibre of their belief' (Janks, 1995: 364, Interview 15). In that research, first it was a task that asked students to consider

> Who should look after the children? Do you think that men and women are likely to have the same or different positions about this? Why?

Secondly it was an alternative version of the Noah's ark story[4] that touched raw nerves in different classrooms. Then, while I recognised the power of identity investments, I failed to realise how helpless rationality is in the face of them. This finding of my own research is confirmed by that of Granville (1996) and McKinney and van Pletzen (2004), in my own context, by the work of Kenway and Willis (1997) in Australia, and Ellsworth (1989) in the United States, amongst others. McKinney and van Pletzen, in explaining their findings, quote from Britzman *et al.* who argue that

> the commitment to rationality – and to rational persuasion – . . . actively erases the complex, contested and emotionally charged investments students and teachers confront when their subject positions are called into question. It does this by positioning all participants as equal as if one could choose to be unencumbered with the larger dynamics of domination and subordination.
> (Britzman, Santiago-Valles, Jiménez-Muñoz, & Lamash, 1993)

I have come to understand that we cannot know in advance which texts are dangerous for whom or how they will impinge on the diverse and multiple identities and identifications of the students in our classes.

Beyond Reason: Identification, Projection and Desire

Identification is a non-rational process that affects our desires below the level of consciousness. I remember once sharing a hotel room with a

---

[4] In *Tooth and Nail* (Junction Avenue Theatre Company & Orkin, 1995), a South African play, the story of Noah is told from the perspective of the drowned. This story told from below, sees Noah as the privileged class with access to the materials needed to build an Ark. Students who did not understand the politics and the hypothetical and fictional nature of this change in perspective, thought the story was challenging the literal truth of the biblical account and was therefore blasphemous.

woman colleague. I had packed all my brightly coloured summer clothing. She had brought a suitcase full of sophisticated black. I regretted not bringing my own black clothes and my chunky jewellery to match hers. Unbeknown to me, she wanted my fresh lime green, my purple and my white clothes. Only when she confessed this to me, was I able to work out that our mutual admiration had produced an unconscious desire in each of us to be like the other with whom we identified. We needed to name it to bring it back into the realm of language and reason in order to laugh at ourselves and regain our respective senses of self.

I remember at the time of 9/11 how I was gripped by my identification with people in the World Trade Center and on the hijacked planes that were used as living bombs. I had just returned from the USA with my extended family to attend my son's wedding. All of us had been on planes; all of us had flown from Boston; many of us had flown through New York. Just the week before, my son and his new wife had flown on a United Airlines flight from Boston to Los Angeles. I was glued to the television, absorbing the terror, feeling vulnerable, overcoming my disbelief. For days I was gripped by an irrational, unconscious, all-consuming identification with the United States. As my usual stance in relation to the American foreign policy at the time was critical, it took me days to understand why I could not engage intellectually with the issues. Only by recognising that what I was experiencing was an unconscious identification, could I recover my critical abilities.

Our projections are equally unconscious and opaque. Perhaps the best known manifestation of this phenomenon is our ability to get rid of aspects of ourselves that we do not like by projecting them on to others. This psychological mechanisms fuels the process of othering and constitutes the other as not us; as the undesirable and dangerous other.

Desire too confounds reason and it relates to each aspect of the model in important ways. Power is both the object of and the means to attain one's desires. Conflict often relates to differential access to things we desire that give us sexual, institutional or political power. These 'things' can be material wealth (money, designer labels, fancy cars, works of art), personal attributes (beauty, intelligence, skill, qualifications), or influential social networks. These correspond to Bourdieu's (1991) different forms of capital: economic, cultural and social. In addition there is symbolic capital that is the socially produced system of valuing that determines what specific things count as capital in different historical contexts. Desire is also tied to identity. The desire for access to new ways of doing and being is what enables us to aspire to new identity positions. Access alone is not enough; desire is the force that drives change. But desire does not guarantee equal access to opportunity. The media universalise desire and create

Figure 9.3 'Fab Shoes' by Matthew Kemp, © Paperlink 2009.
© Mat Kemp. Source: http://www.welovecards.co.uk/product/fab-shoes.html. Used with permission.

consumer lust that most people cannot afford to fulfil. Yet ongoing design and production, epitomised by fashion, produces ongoing desire, consumption and debt.

The situation depicted humorously in Figure 9.3 shows how a concern for social issues fades in the face of consumer desire.

While desire can consume us, pleasure can renew us. Critical literacy work in classrooms can be simultaneously serious and playful. We should teach it with a subversive attitude, self-irony and a sense of humour.

References

Adegoke, R. (1999). *Media discourse on foreign Africans and the implications for education.* Johannesburg: University of the Witwatersrand.

Adler, J., & Reed, Y. (2002). *Challenges of teacher development: An investigation of take-up in South Africa.* Pretoria: van Schaik.

African National Congress. (1994). *The Reconstruction and Development Programme.* Johannesburg: Umanyano Publications.

Alba, A., Gonzalez-Gaudiano, E., Lankshear, C., & Peters, M. (2000). *Curriculum in the postmodern condition.* New York: Peter Lang.

Albright, J. and Luke, A. (Eds.). (2008). *Pierre Bourdieu and literacy education.* London: Routledge.

Alder, D. (2004). *Visual identity texts: A case study in the English classroom.* Unpublished Honours research essay, Witwatersrand, Johannesburg.

Althusser, L. (1971). Ideology and ideological state apparatuses. In *Essays on ideology.* London: Verso.

Appadurai, A. (2002, August). The capacity to aspire: Culture and the terms of recognition. Paper presented at the WISER Seminar Series, Johannesburg.

Apple, M. (1979). *Ideology and curriculum.* London: Routledge and Kegan Paul.

Arthur, W. B. (1988). Self-reinforcing mechanisms in economics. In P. W. Anderson, K. J. Arrow, & D. Pines (Eds.), *The economy as an evolving and complex system.* Santa Fe Institute Studies in the Sciences of Complexity Proceedings. Boulder, CO: Westview Press.

Arthur, W. B. (1989). Competing technologies, increasing returns and lock-in by historical events. *The Economic Journal,* 99 (March), 116–131.

Arthur, W. B. (1990). Positive feedbacks in the economy. *Scientific American,* 80, 92–99.

Banks, J. A. (1991). *Teaching strategies for Ethnic Studies* (5th ed.). Boston: Allyn and Bacon.

Barnes, D. (1976). *From communication to curriculum.* Harmondsworth, UK: Penguin.

Barnes, D., Britton, J., & Rosen, H. (1969). *Language, the learner and the school.* Harmondsworth, UK: Penguin.

Barthes, R. (1972). *Mythologies.* London: Paladin.

Barton, D. (1994). *Literacy: An introduction to the ecology of written language.* Oxford: Wiley-Blackwell.

Barton, D., & Hamilton, M. (Eds.). (1998). *Local literacies: Reading and writing in our community.* London: Routledge.

Barton, D., Hamilton, M., & Ivanic, R. (2000). *Situated literacies.* London: Routledge.

Baugh, J. (2000). *Beyond Ebonics: Linguistic pride and racial prejudice.* New York: Oxford University Press.

Baugh, J. (2003). Linguistic profiling. In S. Makoni, A. Ball & G. Smitherman (Eds.), *Black linguistics: Language, society and politics in Africa and the Americas.* London: Routledge.

Baynham, M., & Prinsloo, M. (Eds.) (2001). New directions in literacy research: Policy, pedagogy, practice. *Special Issue Language and Education,* 15(2 & 3).

Benesch, S. (2001). *Critical English for academic purposes: Theory, politics and practice.* Mahwah, NJ: Lawrence Erlbaum and Associates.

Berlin, E., & Fab, J. (Directors) (2003). *Paperclips* [Film]. J. Fab, M. Johnson & A. Pinchot (Producer). One Clip at a Time and Hart Sharp Video (Distributor).

Bernstein, B. (1996). *Pedagogy, symbolic control and identity: Theory, research, critique.* London: Taylor & Francis.

Bhabha, H. (Ed.). (1990). *Nation and narration.* London: Routledge.

Bolinger, D. (1980). *Language the loaded weapon.* London: Longman.

Bourdieu, P. (1984). *Distinction* (R. Nice, Trans.). Cambridge, MA: Harvard University Press.

Bourdieu, P. (1991). *Language and symbolic Power* (J. B. Thompson, Trans.). Cambridge: Polity Press.

Bourdieu, P. (1999). *The weight of the world: Social suffering in contemporary societies* (P. P. Ferguson, Trans.). Stanford, CA: Stanford University Press.

Bourdieu, P., & Passeron, J. (1977). *Reproduction in education, society and culture.* London: Sage.

Breir, M., Matsepela, T., & Sait, L. (1996). Taking literacy for a ride: Reading and writing in the taxi industry. In M. Breir & M. Prinsloo (Eds.), *The social uses of literacy.* Cape Town: Sached Books and John Benjamins Publishing Co.

Breir, M., & Prinsloo, M. (1996). *The social uses of literacy.* Cape Town: Sached Books and John Benjamins.

Britton, J. (1970). *Language and learning.* Harmondsworth, UK: Penguin.

Britzman, D. K., Santiago-Valles, A., Jiménez-Muñoz, G. M., & Lamash, L. M. (1993). Slips that show and tell: Fashioning multiculture as a problem of representation. In C. McCarthy & W. Crichlow (Eds.), *Race, identity and representation in education.* New York and London: Routledge.

Brouard, A. (2000). *Students as ethnographers: Understanding literacy practices outside of school.* Unpublished Master's research report. University of the Witwatersrand, Johannesburg.

Brouard, A., Wilkinson, L., & Stein, P. (1999). 'Literacy is all around us': Literacy ethnography and curriculum 2005 in three Johannesburg classrooms. *SAJALS,* 7, 11–26.

Buckingham, D. (1998). *Teaching popular culture: Beyond radical pedagogy.* London: Taylor & Francis.

Buckingham, D. (2003). *Media education: Literacy, learning, and contemporary culture.* Oxford: Blackwell Publishing.

Buckingham, D., & Sefton-Green, J. (1994). *Cultural Studies goes to school: Reading and teaching popular media.* London: Taylor & Francis.

Cadman, K. (2006). *Trans/forming 'The King's English' in global research education: A teacher's tale.* Unpublished Doctoral thesis, University of Adelaide, Adelaide.

Cameron, D. (1985). *Feminism and linguistic theory.* Houndsmills, UK: Macmillan Press.

Cameron, D. (Ed.). (1990). *The feminist critique of language.* London: Routledge.

Cameron, D. (1995). *Verbal hygiene.* London: Routledge.

Canagarajah, S. (2006). Negotiating the local in English as lingua franca. *Annual Review of Applied Linguistics,* 26, 107–208.

Canagarajah, S. (2007). Lingua Franca English, multilingual communities and language acquisition. *The Modern Language Journal*, 91, 921–937.

Cazden, C. B. (1988). *Classroom discourse: The language of teaching and learning.* Portsmouth, NH: Heinemann Educational Books.

Clarence-Fincham, J. (1998). *Voices in a university: A critical exploration of black students' responses to institutional discourse.* Unpublished Doctoral thesis, University of Natal, Pietermaritzburg.

Clark, R., & Ivanic, R. (1997). *The politics of writing.* London: Routledge.

Clark, R., Fairclough, N., Ivanic, R., & Martin-Jones, M. (1987). Critical language awareness (Part 1). *Language and Education*, 4, 249–260

Comber, B. (1996). *The discursive construction of literacy in a disadvantaged school.* Unpublished Doctoral thesis. James Cook University, North Queensland.

Comber, B. (1997). *Pleasure, productivity and power: Contradictory discourses on literacy.* Paper presented at the Combined National Conference of the Australian Literacy Educators and Australian Association of Teachers of English, Darwin.

Comber, B. (1998). *Productivity, pleasure and pain.* Unpublished work, University of South Australia.

Comber, B., & Kamler, B. (Eds.). (2005). *Turn-around pedagogies: Literacy interventions for at-risk students.* Newtown, NSW: PETA Press.

Comber, B., & Nixon, H. (2005). Re-reading and re-writing the neighbourhood: Critical literacies and identity work. In J. Evans (Ed.), *Literacy moves on: Using popular culture, new technologies and critical literacy in the primary classroom* (pp. 115–132). London: David Fulton.

Comber, B., & Nixon, H. (2008). Spatial literacies, design texts, and emergent pedagogies in a purposeful literacy curriculum. *Pedagogies*, 3, 221–240.

Comber, B., Nixon, H., Ashmore, L., Loo, S., & Cook, J. (2006). Urban renewal from the inside out: Spatial and critical literacies in a low socio-economic school community. *Mind, Culture and Activity*, 13(3), 228–246.

Comber, B., & O'Brien, J. (1994). Critical literacy: Classroom explorations. *Critical Pedagogy Networker: A Publication on Critical Social Issues in Education*, 6(1 and 2).

Comber, B., & Simpson, A. (1995). *Reading cereal boxes: Analysing everyday texts* (Vol. 1 Texts: The heart of the curriculum). Adelaide: Curriculum Division, Department for Education and Children's Services.

Comber, B., & Simpson, A. (2001). *Negotiating critical literacies in classrooms.* Mahwah, NJ: Lawrence Erlbaum and Associates.

Comber, B., Thomson, P., & Wells, M. (2001). Critical literacy finds a 'place': Writing and social action in a neighborhood school. *Elementary School Journal*, 101(4), 451–464.

Cope, B., & Kalantzis, M. (1997). Multiliteracies, education and the new communications environment: A response to Vaughn Prain. *Discourse*, 18(3), 469–478.

Cope, B., & Kalantzis, M. (Eds.). (1993). *The powers of literacy: A genre approach to teaching writing.* London: Falmer Press.

Cope, B., & Kalantzis, M. (Eds.). (2000). *Multiliteracies.* London: Routledge.

Corson, D. (2001). *Language, diversity and education.* Mahwah, NJ: Lawrence Erlbaum and Associates.

Cummins, J. (2000). *Language, power, and pedagogy: Bilingual children in the crossfire.* Clevedon, UK: Multilingual Matters.

Davies, B. (1989). *Frogs and snails and feminist tales.* Sydney: Allen and Unwin.

Davies, B. (1993). *Shards of glass.* St Leonards, NSW: Allen and Unwin.

Davies, B. (1994). *Poststructuralist theory and classroom practice.* Geelong, VIC: Deakin University.

de Certeau, M., Giard, L., & Mayol, P. (1998). *The practice of everyday life, volume 2: Living and cooking* (T. Tomasik, Trans.). Minneapolis: University of Minnesota Press.

de Groot, M., Dison, L., & Rule, P. (1996). Responding to diversity in university teaching: A case study. *Academic Development Journal*, 2(1), 25–36.

de Saussure, F. (1972/1990). *Course in general linguistics* (R. Harris, Trans.). London: Duckworth.

Delpit, L. (1988). The silenced dialogue: Power and pedagogy in educating other people's children. *Harvard Educational Review,* 58, 280–298.

Department of Education (2002). *National curriculum statement R–9.*

Department of Education (2003). *National curriculum statement 10–12.*

Department of National Education (2002). *Language policy for higher education.*

Derwianka, B. (1990). *Exploring how texts work.* Newtown, NSW: Primary English Teaching Association.

Dixon, K. (2004). Literacy: Diverse spaces, diverse bodies? *English in Australia,* 139(1)(Joint IFTE issue), 50–55.

Dixon, K. (2007). *Literacy, power and the embodied subject.* Unpublished Doctoral thesis, University of the Witwatersrand, Johannesburg.

Dyson, A. H. (1993). *Social worlds of children learning to write in an urban primary school.* New York and London: Teachers College Press.

Dyson, A. H. (1997). *Writing superheroes: Contemporary childhood, popular culture, and classroom literacy.* New York and London: Teachers College Press.

Dyson, A. H. (2003). *The brothers and sisters learn to write: Popular literacies in childhood and school cultures.* New York and London: Teachers College Press.

Eagleton, T. (1991). *Ideology.* London: Verso.

Ellsworth, E. (1989). Why doesn't this feel empowering? Working through repressive myths of critical pedagogy. *Harvard Educational Review,* 59(3), 297–324.

Fader, D. (1976). *The new Hooked on Books.* New York: Berkeley Publishing Corporation.

Fairclough, N. (1989). *Language and power.* London: Longman.

Fairclough, N. (1995). *Critical discourse analysis.* London: Longman.

Fairclough, N. (2003). *Analysing discourse.* London: Routledge.

Fairclough, N. (Ed.). (1992). *Critical language awareness.* London: Longman.

Ferreira, A., Janks, H., Barnsley, I., Marriott, C., Rudman, M., Ludlow, H., et al. (In Press). Reconciliation pedagogy in South African classrooms: From the personal to the political. In P. C. R. Hattam, P. Bishop, J. Matthews, P. Ahluwalia, & S. Atkinson (Eds.), *Pedagogies for reconciliation.* London: Routledge.

Foucault, M. (1970). The order of discourse. Inaugural Lecture at the College de France. In M. Shapiro (Ed.), *Language and politics.* Oxford: Basil Blackwell.

Foucault, M. (1975). *Discipline and punish.* New York: Vintage Books.

Foucault, M. (1978). *The history of sexuality, volume 1* (R. Hurley, Trans.). London: Penguin.

Foucault, M. (1980). *Power/knowledge: Selected interviews and other writings 1972–1977.* New York: Pantheon Books.

Fowler, R., Hodge, B., Kress, G., & Trew, T. (1979). *Language and control.* London: Routledge and Kegan Paul.

Fowler, R., & Kress, G. (1979). Critical linguistics. In R. Fowler, B. Hodge, G. Kress & T. Trew (Eds.), *Language and control.* London: Routledge and Kegan Paul.

Freebody, P., & Luke, A. (1990). Literacies programmes: Debates and demands in cultural contexts. *Prospect: A Journal of Australian TESOL,* 11, 7–16.

Freire, P. (1972a). *Cultural action for freedom.* Harmondsworth, UK: Penguin.

Freire, P. (1972b). *Pedagogy of the oppressed.* Harmondsworth, UK: Penguin.

Freud, S. (1916). *Jokes and their relation to the unconscious.* Harmondsworth, UK: Penguin.

Garner, J. F. (1994). *Politically correct bedtime stories.* New York: Macmillan.

Gee, J. (1990). *Social linguistics and literacies.* London: Falmer Press.

Gee, J. (1994). Orality and literacy: From *The savage mind* to *Ways with words.* In J. Maybin (Ed.), *Language and literacy in social context.* Milton Keynes, UK: Open University Press.

Gee, J., Hull, G., & Lankshear, C. (1996). *The New work order.* Sydney: Allen and Unwin.

Gilbert, P. & Rowe, K. (1989). *Gender, literacy and the classroom.* Carlton, NSW: Australian Reading Association.

Giroux, H. (1981). *Ideology, culture and schooling.* London: Falmer Press.

Giroux, H. (1994). *Disturbing pleasures.* New York: Routledge.

González, N. (2005). Beyond culture: The hybridity of funds of knowledge. In N. González, L. Moll & C. Amanti (Eds.), *Funds of knowledge: Theorising practices in households and classrooms* (pp. 29–46). Mawah, NJ: Lawrence Erlbaum and Associates.

González, N., Moll, L., & Amanti, C. (Eds.). (2005). *Funds of knowledge: Theorising practices in households and classrooms.* Mawah, NJ: Lawrence Erlbaum and Associates.

Gore, A. (2006). *An inconvenient truth: The planetary emergency of global warming and what we can do about it.* New York: Melcher Media.

Graddol, D. (1997). *The future of English.* Retrieved 6 February 2009, from http://www.britishcouncil.org/learning-elt-future.pdf

Graddol, D. (2006). *English next.* Retrieved 6 February 2009, from http://www.britishcouncil.org/learning-research-english-next.pdf

Graff, H. J. (1978). *The literacy myth: Literacy and social structure in the nineteenth-century city.* New York: Academic Press.

Gramsci, A. (1971). *Selections from prison notebooks* (Q. Hoare & G. Nowell-Smith, Trans.). London: Lawrence and Wishart.

Grant, H. (1999). Topdogs and underdogs. *Practically Primary,* 4(3), 40–42.

Granville, S. (1996). *Reading beyond the text: Exploring the possibilities in Critical Language Awareness for reshaping student teachers' ideas about reading comprehension.* Unpublished Master's dissertation, University of the Witwatersrand, Johannesburg.

Granville, S., Janks, H., Joseph, M., Mphahlele, M., Ramani, E., Reed, Y., et al. (1998). English with or without g(u)ilt: A position paper on language in education policy for South Africa. *Language and Education,* 12(4), 254–272.

Green, B. (2002). *A literacy project of our own?* Unpublished manuscript.

Green, B., & Bigum, C. (1993). Aliens in the classroom. *Australian Journal of Education,* 37(22), 119–141.

Green, B., & Morgan, W. (1992). After *The tempest,* or, Literacy pedagogy and the brave new world. Paper presented at the Third Whole Language Umbrella Conference, Niagara Falls.

Gregory, E., & Williams, A. (2000). *City literacies: Learning to read across generations and cultures.* London: Routledge.

Grenfell, M. (1996). Bourdieu and initial teacher education: A post-structuralist approach. *British Educational Research,* 22(3), 287–303.

Hall, S. (1997). *Representation: Cultural representations and signifying practices.* London: Sage.

Halliday, M. A. K. (1985). *An introduction to functional grammar.* London: Arnold.

Harste, J. C., Leland, C. H., Grant, S., Chung, M., & Enyeart, J. A. (2007). Analyzing art in language arts research. In D. W. Rowe, R. T. Jimenez, D. L. Compton, D. K. Dickerson, Y. Kim, K. M. Leander, & V. J. Risko (Eds.), *56th Yearbook of the National Reading Conference* (pp. 254–265). Oak Creek, WI: National Reading Centre.

Haymes, S. (1995). White culture and the politics of racial difference: Implications for multiculturalism. In C. E. Sleeter & P. L. McClaren (Eds.), *Multicultural education, critical pedagogy and the politics of difference.* Albany, New York: State University of New York Press.

Heath, S. B. (1983). *Ways with words.* Cambridge: Cambridge University Press.

Heller, M. (2008). Bourdieu and 'literacy education'. In J. Albright & A. Luke (Eds.), *Pierre Bourdieu and literacy education.* New York and London: Routledge.

Hendricks, M. (2006). *Writing practices in additional languages in Grade 7 classes in the Eastern Cape Province.* Unpublished Doctoral thesis, University of the Witwatersrand, Johannesburg.

Heugh, K., Siegruhn, A., & Pluddemann, P. (1995). *Multilingual education for South Africa.* Johannesburg: Heinemann.

Holmes, J. (2006). *Gendered talk at work: Constructing gender identity through workplace discourse.* Oxford: Blackwell hooks, b. (1990). *Yearning: Race, gender and cultural politics.* Boston: South End Press.

Hull, G., & Schultz, K. (Eds.). (2002). *School's out! Bridging out-of-school literacies with classroom practice.* New York and London: Teachers College Press.

Ivanic, R. (1998). *Writing and identity.* Amsterdam: John Benjamins Publishing Company.

Janks, H. (1988). *'To catch a wake-up': Critical Language Awareness in the South African context.* Unpublished Master's dissertation, University of the Witwatersrand, Johannesburg.

Janks, H. (1993a). *Language and power.* Johannesburg: Hodder and Stoughton and Wits University Press

Janks, H. (1993b). *Language and identity.* Johannesburg: Hodder and Stoughton and Wits University Press

Janks, H. (Ed.). (1993c). *Critical Language Awareness Series.* Johannesburg: Hodder and Stoughton and Wits University Press.

Janks, H. (1995). *The research and development of Critical Language Awareness materials for use in South African secondary schools.* Unpublished Doctoral thesis, Lancaster University, Lancaster.

Janks, H. (1998). Reading *Womanpower. Pretexts*, 7(2), 195–212.

Janks, H. (2000). Domination, access, diversity and design: A synthesis for critical literacy education. *Educational Review*, 52(2), 175–186.

Janks, H. (2001). We rewrote the book: Constructions of literacy in South Africa. In R. de Cilla, H.-J. Krumm & R. Wodak (Eds.), *Loss of communication in the Information Age.* Vienna: Verlag der Österreichischen Academie der Wissenschaften.

Janks, H. (2002a). *The politics and history of the places children inhabit.* Paper presented at the American Educational Research Association Annual Meeting, New Orleans, Louisiana, April 1–5.

Janks, H. (2002b). Critical literacy: Beyond reason. *The Australian Educational Researcher*, 29(1), 7–26.

Janks, H. (2003). Seeding change in South Africa: New literacies, new subjectivities, new futures. In B. Doecke, D. Homer & H. Nixon (Eds.), *English teachers at work* (pp. 183–205). Kent Town, SA: Wakefield Press in Association with the Australian Association for the Teaching of English.

Janks, H. (2004). The access paradox. *English in Australia*, 12(1), 33–42.

Janks, H. (2005). Deconstruction and reconstruction: Diversity as a productive resource. *Discourse*, 26(1), 31–44.

Janks, H. (2006). Fun and games. *English Academy Review*, 49(1), 115–138.

Janks, H., & Comber, B. (2006). Critical literacy across continents. In K. Pahl & J. Rowsell (Eds.), *Travel notes from the New Literacy Studies: Instances of practice.* Clevedon, UK: Multilingual Matters.

Joseph, M., & Ramani, E. (2004). Academic excellence through language equity: Case study of the new bilingual degree (in English and Sesotho sa Leboa) at the University of the North. In H. Griesel (Ed.), *Curriculum responsiveness: Case studies in higher education.* Pretoria: SAUVCA.

Junction Avenue Theatre Company, & Orkin, M. (1995). In *At the junction: Four plays by the Junction Avenue Theatre Company.* Johannesburg: Witwatersrand University Press.

Kamler, B. (2001). *Relocating the personal.* Albany, NY: State University of New York.

Kamler, B., Maclean, R., Reid, J., & Simpson, A. (1994). *Shaping up nicely: The formation of schoolgirls and schoolboys in the first month of school.* Geelong, VIC: Deakin University.

Kelly, U. (1997). *Schooling desire.* London and New York: Routledge.

Kenway, J., & Bullen, E. (2001). *Consuming children: Education–entertainment–advertising.* Buckingham, UK, and Philadelphia, PA: Open University Press.

Kenway, J., & Willis, S. (1997). *Answering back: Girls, boys and feminism in school.* St Leonards, NSW: Allen and Unwin.

Kenworthy, C., & Kenworthy, S. (1997). *Aboriginality in texts and contexts, volume 2.* Fremantle, WA: Fremantle Arts Centre Press.

Khumalo, J. (1997). Joe's beat. *Pace*, March, 112.

Klein, N. (2007). *The shock doctrine: The rise of disaster capitalism*. New York: Metropolitan Books.

Kostogriz, A. (2002). *Rethinking ESL Literacy Education in multicultural conditions*. Unpublished Doctoral thesis, University of New England, New South Wales, Australia.

Krashen, S. D. (1981). *Second language acquisition and second language learning*. Oxford: Pergamon.

Kress, G. (1995). *Making signs and making subjects: The English curriculum and social futures*. London: Institute of Education, University of London.

Kress, G. (1999). Genre and the changing contexts for English language arts. *Language Arts*, 32(2), 185–196

Kress, G. (2003). *Literacy in the New Media Age*. London: Routledge.

Kress, G., & van Leeuwen, T. (1990). *Reading images*. Geelong, VIC: Deakin University Press.

Kress, G., & van Leeuwen, T. (2001). *Multimodal discourse*. London: Arnold.

Kritzinger, M., Steyn, H., Schoonees, P. & Cronje, U. J. (1963) *Groot Woordeboek*. Pretoria: JL Van Schaik.

Labov, W. (1972). The logic of non-standard English. In P. Giglioli (Ed.), *Language and social context*. Harmondsworth, UK: Penguin.

Lakoff, G. (2004). *Don't think of an elephant*. White River Junction, VT: Chelsea Green.

Lankshear, C. (1997). *Changing literacies*. Buckingham, UK: Open University Press.

Larson, J. (2001). *Literacy as snake oil: Beyond the quick fix*. New York: Peter Lang.

Leander, K., & Sheehy, M. (Eds.) (2004) *Spatialising literacy research and practice*. New York: Peter Lang.

Levinson, B. (Director) (1997). *Wag the dog* [Film]. USA: New Line Productions.

Lillis, T. (2001). *Student writing: Access, regulation, desire*. London: Routledge.

Lodge, H. (1997). *Providing access to academic literacy in the Arts Foundation Programme at the University of the Witwatersrand in 1996: The theory behind the practice*. Unpublished Master's dissertation, University of the Witwatersrand, Johannesburg.

Luke, A. (1992). The body literate: Discourse and inscription in early literacy training. *Linguistics and Education*, 4, 107–129.

Luke, A. (2002). Beyond science and ideology critique: Developments in Critical Discourse Analysis. In M. McGroaty (Ed.), *Annual review of applied linguistics*. Cambridge: Cambridge University Press.

Luke, A. (2003). Literacy for a new ethics of global community. *Language Arts*, 81(1), 20–22.

Luke, A., & Freebody, P. (1997). The social practices of reading. In S. Muspratt, A. Luke & P. Freebody (Eds.), *Constructing critical literacies*. St Leonards, NSW: Allen and Unwin.

Marsh, J. (2005). *Popular culture, new media and digital literacy in early childhood*. London: Routledge.

Marsh, J. & Hallet, E. (Eds.). (1999). *Desirable literacies: Approaches to language and literacy in the early years*. London: Sage.

Martin-Jones, M. (2006). *Bilingualism*. London: Pearson Education.

Martin, J., Christie, F., & Rothery, J. (1987). Social processes of education: A reply to Sawyer and Watson (and others). In I. Reid (Ed.), *The place of genre in learning: Current debates*. Geelong, VIC: Deakin University.

Martino, W. (1997). *From the margins, volume 1*. Fremantle, WA: Fremantle Arts Centre Press.

Martino, W., & Pallotta-Chiarolli, M. (2003). *So what's a boy? Addressing issues of masculinty and schooling*. Maidenhead, UK: Open University Press/McGraw-Hill Education.

Martino, W., & Pallotta-Chiarolli, M. (2005). *Being normal is the only way to be: Adolescent perspectives and gender and school*. Sydney: UNSW Press.

Maslow, A. (1954). *Motivation and personality*. New York: Harper.

May, S. (Ed.). (1999). *Critical multiculturalism*. London: Falmer Press.

Maybin, J. (2000). NLS: Context, intertextuality, discourse. In D. Barton, M. Hamilton & R. Ivanic (Eds.), *Situated literacies*. London: Routledge.

McClaren, P., & Torres, R. (1999). Racism and multicultural education: Rethinking 'race' and 'whiteness' in late capitalism. In S. May (Ed.), *Critical multiculturalism*. London: Falmer Press.

McKinney, C. (2004a). 'It's just a story': 'White' students' difficulties in reading the apartheid past. *Perspective in Education*, 22(4), 37–45.

McKinney, C. (2004b). 'A little hard piece of grass in your shoe': Understanding student resistance to critical literacy in post-apartheid South Africa. *Southern African Linguistics and Applied Language Studies*, 22(1&2), 63–73.

McKinney, C., & Van Pletzen, E. (2004). 'This apartheid story . . . we've finished with it': Student responses to the apartheid past in a South African English Studies course. *Teaching in Higher Education*, 9(2), 159–170.

Mellor, B., & Patterson, A. (1996). *Investigating texts*. Scarborough, WA: Chalkface Press.

Mellor, B., Patterson, A., & O'Neill, M. (1987). *Reading stories*. Scarborough, WA: Chalkface Press.

Mellor, B., Patterson, A., & O'Neill, M. (1991). *Reading fictions*. Scarborough, WA: Chalkface Press.

Misson, R., & Morgan, W. (2006). *Critical Literacy and the aesthetic: Transforming the English classroom*. Urbana, IL: National Council of Teachers of English.

Mphahlele, Es'kia, Ogude, J. & Raditlhalo, S. (2008). *Es'kia: Education, African humanism and culture, social consciousness, literary appreciation*. Cape Town: Kwela Books

Moll, L. (1992). Literacy research in community and classroom: A sociocultural approach. In J. G. R. Beach, M. Kamil & T. Shanahan (Eds.), *Multidisciplinary perspectives on literacy research*. Urbana, IL: National Council of Teachers of English.

Moll, L., Amanti, C., Neffe, D., & Gonzále, N. (1992). Funds of knowledge for teaching: Using a qualitative approach to connect homes and classrooms. *Theory into Practice*, 31(2), 132–141.

Moon, B. (1992). *Literary terms: A practical glossary*. Scarborough, WA: Chalkface Press.

Morgan, B. (1998). *The ESL classroom*. Toronto: University of Toronto Press.

Morgan, W. (1992). *A post-structuralist English classroom: The example of Ned Kelly*. Melbourne: The Victorian Association for the Teaching of English.

Morgan, W. (1994). *Ned Kelly reconstructed*. Cambridge: Cambridge University Press.

Morrow, W. (2008). *Learning to teach in South Africa*. Pretoria: Human Sciences Research Council.

Ndebele, N. (1987). The English language and social change in South Africa. In D. Bunn & J. Taylor (Eds.), *From South Africa: New writings, photographs and art* (pp. 217–235). Evanston, IL: North Western University Press.

Ndebele, N. (1998). Memory, metaphor, and the triumph of narrative. In S. Nuttall & C. Coetzee (Eds.), *Negotiating the past: The making of memory in South Africa*. Cape Town: Oxford University Press.

New London Group. (2000). A pedagogy of multiliteracies: Designing social futures. In B. Cope & M. Kalantzis (Eds.), *Multiliteracies* (pp. 9–42). London: Routledge.

Newfield, D. (1993). *Words and pictures*. Johannesburg: Hodder and Stoughton and Wits University Press.

Ngũgĩ wa Thiong'o. (1981). *Decolonising the mind: The politics of language in African literature*. Nairobi: Heinemann.

Nieto, B. S. (1999). *Affirming diversity: The Sociopolitical context of multicultural education*, third edition. London: Longman.

Nieto, S. (1996). From brown heroes and holidays to assimilationist agendas: Reconsidering the critiques of multicultural education. In C. E. Sleeter & P. L. McClaren (Eds.), *Multicultural education, critical pedagogy and the politics of difference*. Albany, NY: State University of New York Press.

Nieto, S. (2002). *Language, culture and teaching critical perspectives for a new century*. Mahwah, NJ: Lawrence Erlbaum and Associates.

Nixon, H. (1999). *Creating a clever, computer-literate nation: A cultural study of the media, young people and new literacies.* Unpublished Doctoral thesis, University of Queensland, Brisbane.

Nixon, H. (2003). Textual diversity: Who needs it? *English Teaching Practice and Critique,* 2(2), 22–23.

Norton, B. (2000). *Identity and language learning.* London: Longman.

O'Brien, J. (2001). Children reading critically: A local history. In B. Comber & A. Simpson (Eds.), *Negotiating critical literacies in classrooms.* Mahwah, NJ: Lawrence Erlbaum and Associates.

OED department. (1980). *The shorter Oxford English dictionary on historical principles,* third edition. Oxford: Clarendon Press.

Ong, W. (1982). *Orality and literacy.* London: Methuen.

Orlek, J. (1993). *Languages in South Africa.* Johannesburg: Hodder and Stoughton and Wits University Press.

Pahl, K. (2008). *Seeing with a different eye: How can the New Literacy Studies help teachers to understand what children bring to texts?* Paper presented at the American Education Research Association, New York.

Pahl, K., & Rowsell, J. (2005). *Literacy and education: Understanding the New Literacy Studies in the classroom.* London: Sage.

Pahl, K., & Rowsell, J. (Eds.). (2006). *Travel notes from the New Literacy Studies: Instances of practice.* Clevedon, UK: Multilingual Matters.

Partridge, B., & Starfield, S. (2007). *Thesis and dissertation writing in a second language.* London: Routledge.

Pennycook, A. (1994). *The cultural politics of English as an international language.* London: Longman.

Pennycook, A. (1998). *English and the discourses of colonialism.* London: Routledge.

Pennycook, A. (1999). Introduction: Critical approaches to TESOL. *TESOL Quarterly,* 33(3), 329–348.

Pennycook, A. (2001). *Critical Applied Linguistics.* Mahwah, NJ: Lawrence Erlbaum and Associates.

Perry, T., & Delpit, L. (Eds.). (1998). *Power, language and the education of African American children.* Boston: Beacon Press in collaboration with Rethinking Schools.

Phillipson, R. (1992). *Linguistic imperialism.* Oxford: Oxford University Press.

Ramani, E., & Joseph, M. (2006). The dual-medium BA degree in English and Sesotho sa Leboa at the University of Limpopo: Successes and challenges. *LOITASA,* 4, 4–18.

Rampton, B. (1990). Displacing the English language speaker. *ELT Journal,* 44, 97–101.

Rampton, B. (2006). *Language in late modernity: Interaction in an urban school.* Cambridge: Cambridge University Press.

Rofes, E. E. (2005). *A radical rethinking of sexuality and schooling.* Lanham, MD: Rowman and Littlefield.

Rose, B., & Tunmer, R. (1975). *Documents in South African education.* Johannesburg: Ad. Donker.

Rose, N. (1989). *Governing the soul.* London: Free Association Books.

Rosen, M. (1988). *The Hypnotiser.* New York: Scholastic.

Sachs, A. (1994). *Language rights in the new Constitution.* Cape Town: South African Constitutional Studies Centre, University of Cape Town.

Said, E. (1994). *Culture and imperialism.* London: Vintage.

Said, E. (1995). *Orientalism.* London: Penguin.

Scribner, S., & Cole, M. (1981). *The psychology of literacy.* Cambridge, MA: Harvard University Press.

Shariff, P. (1994). *Heart to heart.* Johannesburg: Storyteller Group.

Shariff, P., & Janks, H. (2001). Redesigning romance: The making and analysis of a critical literacy comic in South Africa. *English in Australia,* 131(July), 5–17.

Shor, I. (1980). *Critical teaching and everyday life.* Chicago: Chicago University Press.

Simon, R. (1992). *Teaching against the grain.* Toronto: The Ontario Institute for Studies Education Press.

Sleeter, C. E., & McClaren, P. L. (Eds.). (1995). *Multicultural education, critical pedagogy and the politics of difference.* Albany, NY: State University of New York Press.

Smith, D. E. (1993). *Texts, facts and femininity: Exploring the relations of ruling.* London: Routledge.

Snyder, I. (Ed.). (1998). *Page to screen: Taking literacy into the electronic era.* London: Routledge.

Snyder, I. (Ed.). (2002). *Silicon literacies: Communication, innovation and education in the electronic age.* London: Routledge

Soja, E. (1996). *Thirdspace: Journeys to Los Angeles and other real-and-imagined places.* Cambridge, MA: Blackwell.

Spender, D. (1980). *Man made language.* London: Routledge and Kegan Paul.

Starfield, S. (1994). Multicultural classes in higher education. *English Quarterly,* 26(3), 16–21.

Starfield, S. (2000). *Making and sharing of meaning: The academic writing of first-year students in the Department of Sociology who speak English as an additional language.* Unpublished Doctoral thesis, University of the Witwatersrand, Johannesburg.

Statistics South Africa. (2001). South African languages statistics and graphs. Retrieved 27 January 2009, from www.cyberserv.co.za/users/~jako/lang/stats.htm

Stein, P. (2004). Representation, rights and resources: Multimodal pedagogies in the language and literacy classroom. In B. Norton & K. Toohey (Eds.), *Critical pedagogies and language learning.* Cambridge: Cambridge University Press.

Stein, P. (2008). *Multimodal pedagogies in diverse classrooms.* London: Routledge.

Street, B. (1984). *Literacy in theory and practice.* Cambridge: Cambridge University Press.

Street, B. (Ed.). (1993). *Cross-cultural approaches to literacy, volume 23.* Cambridge: Cambridge University Press.

Street, B. (1996). Preface. In M. Breir & M. Prinsloo (Eds.), *The social uses of literacy.* Cape Town: Sached Books and John Benjamins.

Stuckey, J. E. (1991). *The violence of literacy.* Portsmouth, NH: Boynton/Cook.

Sumara, D., & Davis, B. (1998). Telling tales of surprise. In W. Pinar (Ed.), *Queer theory in education.* London: Routledge.

Thompson, J. B. (1984). *Studies in the theory of ideology.* Cambridge: Polity Press.

Thompson, J. B. (1990). *Ideology and modern culture.* Oxford: Basil Blackwell.

Thomson, P. (2002). *Schooling the rustbelt kids: Making a difference.* Crows Nest, NSW: Allen and Unwin.

Threadgold, T. (1997). *Feminist poetics: Poiesis, performance, histories.* London: Routledge.

Tollefson, J. (1991). *Planning language, planning inequality: Language policy in community.* London: Longman.

Truth and Reconciliation Commission. (1998). *Truth and Reconciliation Commission of South Africa Report, volume 5.* Cape Town: Juta and Co.

UNESCO. (2000). Retrieved 27 January 2009, from www.uis.unesco.org/en/stats/statistics/literacy2000.htm

United Nations High Commission for Refugees. (1994–1997). Lego posters. Retrieved 1 February 2009, from www.unhcr.org/help/4083de384.html111Lego%20Posters

University of the Witwatersrand. (2003). *Report of the Senate committee on language policy.* Johannesburg: University of the Witwatersrand.

Vasquez, V. (2001). Constructing a curriculum with young children. In B. Comber & A. Simpson (Eds.), *Negotiating critical literacies in classrooms.* Mahwah, NJ: Lawrence Erlbaum and Associates.

Vasquez, V. (2004). *Negotiating critical literacies with young children.* Mahwah, NJ: Lawrence Erlbaum and Associates.

Volosinov, V. N. (1986). *Marxism and the philosophy of language* (L. Matejka & I. Titunik, Trans.). Cambridge, MA: Harvard University Press.

Wallace, C. (2007). *Critical reading in language education.* Houndsmill, UK: Macmillan.

Weber, S. (1999). *Gendered advertising: A critical analysis of the Liqui-fruit Advertising*

Campaigns in 'Y' and 'SL' Magazines. Unpublished Honours long essay, Applied English Language Studies, University of the Witwatersrand, Johannesburg.

Weedon, C. (1987). *Feminist practice and poststructuralist theory.* Oxford: Basil Blackwell.

Welch, T., Witthaus, G. & Rule, P. (1996). *Activities for multilingual classrooms Ditsema Tsa Thuto: Activities Book.* Johannesburg: ELTIC.

Wenger, E. (1998). *Communities of practice.* Cambridge: Cambridge University Press.

Wilshire, D. (1989). The use of myth, image and the female body in revisioning knowledge. In A. M. Jagger & S. R. Borno (Eds.), *Gender/body/knowledge: Feminist reconstructions of being and knowing* (pp. 92–114). New Brunswick: Rutgers University Press.

Wodak, R. (Ed.). (1997). *Gender and discourse.* London: Sage.

Wolf, M. (2007). *Proust and the squid: The story and science of the reading brain.* New York: Harper Collins.

Woodward, B. (2004). *Plan of attack.* New York: Schuster.

Wray, M. and Newitz, A. (Eds.). (1997). *White trash: Race and class in America.* New York: Routledge.

Index

Note: *italic* page numbers denote references to figures/tables.